the
architecture
of death
the neolithic chambered tombs in Wales

George Nash

Logaston Press

LOGASTON PRESS
Little Logaston, Woonton, Almeley,
Herefordshire HR3 6QH
logastonpress.co.uk

First published by Logaston Press 2006
Copyright © George Nash (text, photographs and illustrations)

ISBN 1 904396 33X

Set in Gill Sans Light by Logaston Press
Cover and book design by Eve Perloff
and printed in Great Britain by
Oaklands Book Services,Gloucestershire, England

Cover illustrations
Front cover: The King's Quoit Monument in South-West Wales
Back cover: three illustrations by Sue Twohig of intricate stone carvings discovered at the
Barclodiad monument in Anglesey

For my best friend
Jayne

Preface

There are estimated to be over 40,000 megalithic structures in Europe. The later prehistoric landscapes of the north-western European Atlantic zone, from the Iberian Peninsula to southern Norway, are notable for an outstanding monument assemblage belonging to the oldest architectural tradition in Europe, if not the world (Daniel 1958). The form and distribution of these monuments — some now merely piles of stone — has occupied the imagination of generations of scholars. As a result numerous ideas have been proposed relating to origin, construction methods, use and abandonment. It is now thought that these enigmatic structures — ostensibly a Neolithic phenomenon (New Stone Age 4,000–2,000 BC) — appeared in the landscape, not as a result of random or arbitrary decision-making on the part of Neolithic communities, but in response to a complex set of long-term processes that had influenced the organization of social and ritual space since the Mesolithic (Middle Stone Age 10,000–4,000 BC), or earlier. Indeed, several monuments occupy sites that appear to have been utilised during the Upper Palaeolithic (Old Stone Age 35,000–10,000 BC). As a result of the working out of these processes, spaces became places; chaotic nature was structured, tamed, manipulated, controlled.

One of the most important works produced by a British scholar in this field is Glyn Daniel's seminal volume *The Prehistoric Chambered Tombs of England and Wales* (1950). Many have attempted to repeat or update Daniel's achievement but, arguably, the enthusiasm and integrity have often appeared lacking. Regarding Wales, a number of researchers have, over the past 35 years, discussed the Neolithic in a number of regional studies that embrace ideas initially discussed by Daniel. But many of these studies have been limited by the tendency of researchers to concentrate exclusively on 'their patch' without considering external influences. One should consider that these ideas do in fact transcend modern political boundaries. In some ways this is understandable; confining one's research to an area defined by political boundaries is convenient, facilitating the production of an orderly piece of work — as is the case with this volume. Nevertheless, one can consider the megalithic architecture of Wales to be unique and different from other Neolithic areas of Britain and Europe.

Research for this volume led me to a number of key texts that would establish an overview. Most of these address the problems of regionality, architectural form and influence. One of these key texts is *Megalithic Enquiries in the West of Britain* (Powell *et al.*), which was published in 1969 by Liverpool University Press. In many respects this volume remains unsurpassed. Not only does it deal with monument regionality, but it also establishes an important framework for books such as this. The volume has spawned a number of more specific and detailed regional studies, including Francis Lynch's *Prehistoric Anglesey* (1970, 1991), Christopher Barker's excellent monograph *The Chambered Tombs of South-West Wales* (1992) and volumes by Children and Nash: *The Prehistoric Sites of Monmouthshire* (1996), *The Neolithic Sites of Cardiganshire, Carmarthenshire and Pembrokeshire* (1997) and *The Prehistoric Sites of Breconshire* (2001). More site specific research has been undertaken by Britnell and Savory (1984), Gibson (1999) and Smith and Lynch (1987) respectively, who have investigated the Gwernvale (BRE 7) and Penywyrlod (BRE 14) monuments in Breconshire, the Neolithic enclosure at Hindwell and the Anglesey tombs of Trefignath (ANG 1) and Din Dryfol (ANG 5).

In addition to the above, the Royal Commission for Historical and Ancient Monuments in Wales (RCHAMW) has brought much of the monument evidence together. Its county studies, although sometimes appearing somewhat dated in approach, have provided sound essential empiricist data. The Royal Commission's more recent inventory on Breconshire (1997) has enlightened the study of the only inland Neolithic monument group in Wales. All of these volumes, ancient or modern, have proved an important resource.

Finally, there are a handful of research papers and volumes that have attempted to set these monuments into a theoretical framework, looking at such concepts as importance of location within the landscape or the way

architecture interplays with burial and ritual. Foremost among these is Christopher Tilley's *A Phenomenology of Landscape* (1994) that includes chapters on the Black Mountains and South-West Wales. Other volumes include Richard Bradley's trilogy: *The Significance of Monuments* (1998), *The Archaeology of Natural Places* (2000) and *The Past in Prehistoric Societies* (2002); Mark Edmond's *Ancestral Geographies of the Neolithic* (1999); Julian Thomas's *Rethinking the Neolithic* (1991) and *Understanding the Neolithic* (1999); and Alasdair Whittle's *Problems in Neolithic Archaeology* (1988), *Neolithic Europe: A Survey* (1985), and the more recently published *The archaeology of people: dimensions of neolithic life* (2003). Although some of these books only touch on Wales, they are nonetheless essential reading as they discuss, in particular, why people place monuments in particular places within the landscape. Also well worth considering is Gabriel Cooney's *Landscapes of Neolithic Ireland* (2000). Although this volume does not deal specifically with Wales, it is a fine example of how regional landscape studies should be written.

Over the past 40 years and where possible, radiocarbon dating has been used in order to assess fixed dating in time for a small number of monuments. However, radiocarbon dates are too few to make any valid attempt of the datable chronology (with the exception of sites such as Trefignath (ANG 1) and Gwernvale (BRE 7) (Appendix II). In this book I have used dates calibrated to calendar years and these will be termed BC (see Stuiver 1998 *et al.*). Where this is not possible uncalibrated bc dates are used. In addition, I have also occasionally used BP dates (before present) that have usually been applied to environmental research data. These dates are derived from direct sources and are, in most cases, referenced as such.

Within this book I have followed an established system of classification (also used by Daniel 1950, Powell *et al.* 1969, Lynch 1970, and Barker 1992). This classification system, based on a three or four letter county prefix coding was used in order to prevent possible site duplication. It appears that over the recent past, new sites, of which there are very few, have not followed on this classification system. I have therefore decided to rectify this and where possible continue the system in numerical order.

Note on place names

The author has taken the utmost care to ensure that the correct Welsh spellings are used for sites that appear in this book. However, there may be discrepancies with spellings of certain names. This appears to be an inherent problem, not just with the SMR county lists, but also with the CADW and RCAHMW inventories and the Ordnance Survey.

Rhagair

Fe amcangyfrifir bod dros 40,000 o strwythurau megalithig yn Ewrop. Mae tirweddau cynhanesyddol hwyr rhanbarth ogledd-orllewinol y Môr Iwerydd, o Benrhyn Iberia i dde Norwy yn nodweddiadol am gasgliad hynod o henebion a berthyn i draddodiad pensaernïol hynaf Ewrop, os nad y byd (Daniel 1958). Mae ffurf a dosbarthiad yr henebion hyn — sydd ddim mwy na phentyrrau o gerrig erbyn hyn—wedi mynd â bryd ysgolheigion am genedlaethau. Fel canlyniad, awgrymwyd syniadau di-rif ynghylch eu gwreiddiau, dulliau adeiladu, y defnydd a wneid ohonynt a'r rhesymau dros eu diryddiad. Erbyn hyn, meddylir bod y strwythurau enigmatig hyn —sydd i bob golwg yn ffenomen Neolithig (Yr Oes Garreg Newydd 4,000–2,000 CC) — wedi ymddangos yn y dirwedd nid fel canlyniad penderfyniadau mympwyol a damweiniol ar ran cymunedau Neolithig, ond fel adwaith i set gymhleth o brosesau hirdymor a oedd wedi dylanwadu ar drefniant gofod cymdeithasol a defodol ers y cyfnod Mesolithig (Yr Oes Garreg Ganol 10,000–4,000 CC) neu'n gynharach. Yn wir, mae nifer o henebion yn sefyll ar safleoedd a ymddengys fod wedi cael eu defnyddio yn ystod y cyfnod Uwch-balaeolithig (Yr Oes Garreg Hen 35,000–10,000 CC). Fel canlyniad i'r prosesau hyn, trodd gofodau yn lleoedd; cafodd anrhefn natur ei strwythuro, ei dofi, ei manipiwleiddio, ei rheoli.

Un o'r gweithiau pwysicaf a gynhyrchwyd gan ysgolhaig Prydeinig yn y maes hwn yw cyfrol flaengar Glyn Daniel *The Prehistoric Chambered Tombs of England and Wales*. Mae sawl un wedi ceisio efelychu neu ddiweddaru campwaith Daniel ond, gellid maentumio, heb na'i frwdfrydedd na'i ddidwylledd. Parthed Cymru, mae nifer o ymchwilwyr dros y 35 mlynedd ddiwethaf wedi trafod y Neolithig mewn nifer o astudiaethau rhanbarthol sy'n coleddu'r syniadau a drafodwyd gyntaf gan Daniel. Ond, cyfyngwyd ar lawer o'r astudiaethau hyn gan duedd ar ran yr ymchwilwyr i ganolbwyntio ormod ar eu "milltir sgwâr" eu hunain heb ystyried dylanwadau o'r tu allan. Dylid ystyried nad oes a wnelo'r syniadau hyn mewn gwirionedd â ffiniau gwleidyddol modern. Ar lawer cyfrif, mae hyn yn ddealladwy ddigon; mae cyfyngu maes ymchwil i ardal a ddiffinnir gan ffiniau gwleidyddol yn gyfleus gan hwyluso cynhyrchu darn trefnus o waith—fel yn achos y gyfrol hon. Ond, gellir dadlau bod pensaernïaeth fegalithig Cymru yn unigryw ac yn wahanol i eiddo ardaloedd eraill o Brydain ac Ewrop y cyfnod Neolithig.

Wrth ymchwilio'r gyfrol hon, fe'm harweiniwyd at nifer o destunau allweddol a fyddai'n sefydlu arolwg eang. Un o'r testunau allweddol hyn yw *Megalithic Enquiries in the West of Britain* (Powell *et al.*) a gyhoeddwyd ym 1969 gan Wasg Prifysgol Lerpwl. Ar lawer ystyr erys y gyfrol hon heb ei hail. Nid yn unig yr ymdrinia â natur ranbarthol yr henebion, ond gesyd hefyd fframwaith pwysig ar gyfer llyfrau fel hyn. Mae'r gyfrol wedi esgor ar nifer o astudiaethau rhanbarthol manwl a phenodol, gan gynnwys Prehistoric Anglesey (1970, 1991) Frances Lynch, monograff ardderchog Christopher Barker *The Chambered Tombs of South-West Wales* (1992) a chyfrolau gan Children a Nash: *The Prehistoric Sites of Monmouthshire* (1996), *The Prehistoric Sites of Cardignanshire, Carmarthenshire and Pembrokeshire* (1997) and *The Prehistoric Sites of Breconshire* (2001). Gwnaed rhagor o ymchwil ar safleoedd unigol gan Britnell a Savory (1984), Gibson (1999) and Lynch a Smith (1987) a archwiliodd, yn ôl eu trefn, henebion Gwernvale (BRE 7) a Phenywyrlod (BRE 14) ym Mrycheiniog, y caeadle Neolithig yn Hindwell a beddrodau Trefignedd (ANG 1) a Din Dryfol (ANG 5) ar Fôn.

Yn ogystal â'r rhain, mae'r Gomisiwn Frenhinol ar Henebion yng Nghymru wedi casglu at ei gilydd lawer o'r dystiolaeth am yr henebion hyn. Mae eu hastudiaethau sirol, er o bosibl braidd yn hen ffasiwn eu hymdriniaeth, wedi darparu gwybodaeth empirig ddibynadwy ac anhepgor. Mae astudiaeth ddiweddarach y Gomisiwn ar Frycheiniog (1997) wedi goleuo'r ymdriniaeth â'r unig glwstwr mewndirol o henebion Neolithig yng Nghymru. Mae'r cyfrolau hyn i gyd, yn hynafol neu'n fodern, wedi bod yn ffynonellau pwysig.

Yn olaf, mae dyrnaid o bapurau ymchwil a chyfrolau sydd wedi ceisio gosod yr henebion hyn mewn fframwaith damcaniaethol, gan ymdrin â chysyniadau fel pwysigrwydd eu lleoliad o fewn y dirwedd neu'r modd y mae'r bensaernïaeth yn cyd-chwarae â chladdedigaethau a defodau. Y

ceffyl blaen yn eu plith yw *A Phenomenology of Landscape* (1994) gan Christopher Tilley sy'n cynnwys penodau ar y Mynyddoedd Duon ac ar dde-orllewin Cymru. Mae cyfrolau eraill yn cynnwys trioleg Richard Bradley: *The Significance of Monuments* (1998), *The Archaeology of Natural Places* (2000) and *The Past in Prehistoric Societies* (2002); *Ancestral Geographies of the Neolithic* (1999) gan Mark Edmonds; *Rethinking the Neolithic* (1991) ac *Understanding the Neolithic* (1999) gan Julian Thomas a chyfrolau Alasdair Whittle *Problems in Neolithic Archaeology* (1988), *Neolithic Europe: a Survey* (1985) ac yn fwy diweddar the archaeology of people: dimensions of neolithic life (2003). Er mai dim ond braidd-gyffwrdd â Chymru mae rhai o'r llyfrau hyn, maent serch hynny yn anhepgor gan y trafodir ynddynt yn benodol paham y bu i bobl godi henebion mewn lleoedd arbennig o fewn y dirwedd. Gwerth ei ystyried hefyd yw Landscapes of Neolithic Ireland (2000) gan Gabriel Cooney. Ar nad yw'r gyfrol hon chwaith yn ymdrin yn uniongyrchol â Chymru, mae'n enghraifft ardderchog o sut y dylid ymgymryd ag ysgrifennu astudiaethau tirwedd rhanbarthol.

Dros y 40 mlynedd diwethaf a lle bu'n bosibl, defnyddiwyd dyddiadau radio carbon er mwyn asesu dyddiadau gosodedig nifer fechan o henebion. Serch hynny, mae dyddiadau radio carbon yn rhy brin o lawer i wneud unrhyw ymgais dilys at gronoleg gyflawn (ac eithrio mewn achos safleoedd fel Trefignedd (ANG 1) a Gwernvale (BRE 7) (Atodiad II). Yn y llyfr hwn, yr wyf wedi defnyddio dyddiadau calibredig a ddynodir gan CC (gweler Stuiver *et al.* 1998). Lle nad yw hyn yn bosibl, defnyddir dyddiadau cc heb eu calibreiddio. Yn ogystal, yr wyf hefyd wedi arddel dyddiadau CP (cyn y presennol) sydd fel arfer yn cael eu defnyddio ar gyfer data ymchwil amgylcheddol. Cafwyd y dyddiadau hyn mewn ffynonellau unigol a chyfeirir atynt felly.

O fewn y llyfr hwn yr wyf wedi dilyn system ddosbarthu gydnabyddedig (a ddefnyddiwyd hefyd gan Daniel 1950; Powell *et al.* 1969, Lynch 1970 a Barker 1992). Defnyddiwyd y system ddosbarthu hon, wedi'i seilio ar fyrfoddau sirol gyda thair neu bedair llythyren, er mwyn osgoi'r posibilrwydd o ddyblu henebion. Dros y blynyddoedd diwethaf hyn, mae'n ymddangos na ddilynwyd y system hon ar gyfer henebion newydd a ddarganfuwyd yn ddiweddar. Penderfynais felly gywiro hyn o wall gan barhau, lle mae'n bosibl, gyda'r system mewn trefn rifiadol.

NODYN AR ENWAU LLEOEDD

Cymerodd yr awdur gryn ofal i sicrhau cywirdeb yr enwau Cymraeg a ymddengys yn y llyfr hwn. Serch hynny, fe all fod anghysonderau a gwahaniaethau gyda sillafiadau enwau arbennig. Mae hyn y broblem gynhenid, mae'n debyg, nid yn unig gyda rhestrau sirol yr SMRau ond hefyd gyda rhestrau Cadw a'r Gomisiwn Frenhinol a chydag Arolwg yr Ordnans.

Acknowledgements

This volume has, like its author, gone through a number of metamorphoses. I had the idea of publishing something large-scale in 1998. However, with one thing or another the text was not started properly until early 2004. Before this, I had the pleasure of dragging my children around all 100 Neolithic cromlech sites (and more), I am sure they are scarred for life.

The photography used in this book is testament to the lengths I have been to get the imagery right and hope that each photograph will speak a thousand words. I hope that the book will be used to visit these most interesting of prehistoric monuments, come rain or shine.

This volume could not have been written without the support from my fellow colleagues and friends and I would like to thank the following people who helped with the production of this book. Firstly, sincere thanks to Richard Jones (Cambria Archaeology), Jeff Spencer (Clwyd-Powys Archaeological Trust), Sue Hughes (Glamorgan-Gwent Archaeological Trust), Kate Geary and Nina Steele (Gwynedd Archaeological Trust).

I would also like to thank the members either deceased or living of the Cambrian Archaeological Association. It is their inquisitive and tenacious minds that provided much inspiration to this book.

Thanks also to Christopher Barker, Peter Dorling, Ian Kinnes, Frances Lynch, Tim Malim, Sian Rees and Terry Williams who took their valuable time to read through and comment on the various chapters. Special thanks to Frank Olding who translated the preface into Welsh and to Frances Lynch whose wisdom, foresight and patience taught me a thing or two about the monuments in North Wales and Anglesey.

Thanks also to my dear friends Abby George, Adam Stanford, John Swann, Laurie Waite and Thomas Wellicome who read through the various sections of the text and made invaluable comments. Thanks to Andy Johnson and Ron Shoesmith at Logaston Press who made this long awaited project possible and turned it into such a handsome book. Also thanks to my old friend, George Children, who was initially involved in the project.

Finally, I would like to thank all my loyal friends who gave support through difficult times.

Contents

Construction in progress at the Lligwy monument in Anglesey (illustration by Brian Byron)

North Wales Group

Anglesey Group

Lleyn Peninsula Group

Harlech Group

South-West Wales Group

Gower Peninsula Group

South-East Wales Group

Black Mountains Group

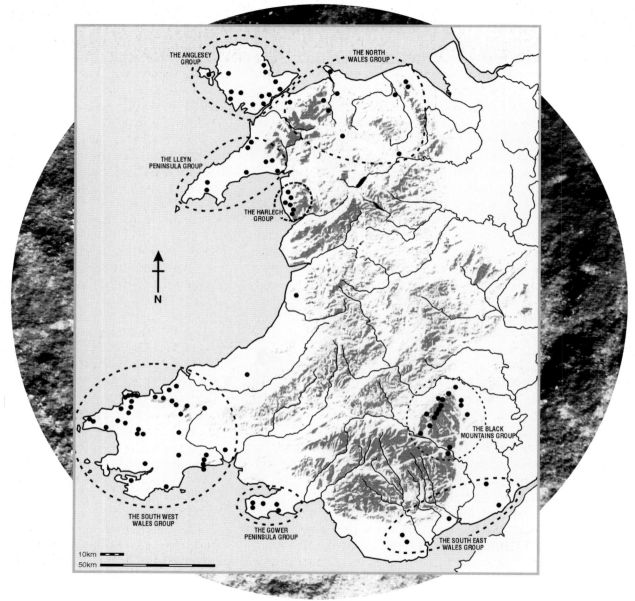

Neolithic Monuments in Wales

What is Neolithic? The term Neolithic, first conceived by William Lubbock in 1872, saw technology and economy as the primary mechanisms that controlled and manipulated society. Secondary to this was the ritual and symbolic act of burial of the dead and the evidence that accompanied it. Prehistorians have tended to suggest that the Neolithic is a period that reflects death, whilst seeing the preceding Mesolithic (10,000–4,000 BC) as a period that reflects economy. The evidence in Wales and in other Neolithic core areas of Western Britain for this act of burial can be seen through a series of monuments that are generically referred to as stone burial chambered tombs. These monuments, usually remaining as no more than a confused pile of stones, conjure an evocative picture of how people in this distant time prepared and buried their dead. However, in complete contrast, the archaeological evidence for *Neolithic* economy and society is limited to a handful of settlement sites, some of which are little more than lithic scatters. The burial evidence and limited settlement, plus the associated material culture forms what is termed as the 'Neolithic Package'. Associated with this package are farming and the production and use of pottery.

It was originally thought, prior to the application of radiocarbon dating, that the duration of the Neolithic spanned around 400 years (Piggott 1954, 379–381). At this time the period was divided into two phases: Primary and Secondary Neolithic. The Primary phase represented the colonization by settlers from the Continent whilst the secondary phase included the possible integration with the indigenous Mesolithic hunter/gatherer/fisher communities. The Primary phase, it was believed, also saw the migration from the Continent of tomb builders, and through a diffusionary process the idea of building mausoleums for the dead was then spread to many areas of Britain. Subsequently, Savory (and others) has divided the Neolithic into three stages spanning a considerably greater length of time: Early Neolithic (4,500–3,750 BC), Middle Neolithic (3,750–3,250) and Late Neolithic (3,250–2,000) (Savory 1980, 207). The earlier and later dates of the Neolithic would have transcended into the Mesolithic and Early Bronze Age (EBA)[1] periods respectively. In addition, the new date for the Early Neolithic is represented not by the introduction of burial monuments but by domestication, and in particular, woodland clearance as witnessed through pollen analysis and sedimentological analysis. Monument building is then seen to gain momentum during the early part of the Middle Neolithic, arguably following a period of socio-political crisis (Ashbee 1978, Burgess 1980).

Farming, for which the woodland was cleared, can be seen as merely an economic system whereby the knowledge of when and what to harvest, and the management of domesticated animals comes into practice. Indeed, this is the primary mechanism that supposedly divides the hunter-gatherers of the Mesolithic from the agriculturists of the Neolithic. The reliance on an annual harvest could have been considered risky and it is probable that a more complex economic system was in place. I have previously suggested that the Mesolithic/Neolithic transition was no overnight affair and happened at different times between regions (Nash 1998). A transition from an economy based on hunting, fishing and gathering to one of limited agriculture, in the form of allotment-style cultivation along with animal husbandry probably took over 1,000 years (between 4,500 and 3,500 BC). Anthropologist Barbara Bender suggests 'food production was a question of technique; agriculture a question of commitment, in this case, a long-term commitment' (1987, 204). The mechanisms of change, evident through the material culture, although dominating the archaeological record do not fully reflect Neolithic society, and what I would term a mixed economy existed where hunting and gathering were as important to society as farming.

In the coastal areas there would have been a greater emphasis on estuarine and marine foods. Here, large marine mammals such as seal, porpoise and whale would have been important food resources. Freshwater fish and estuarine shellfish, according to Jarman *et al* (1982), would have also provided an important source of protein. Certainly, limpet shells have been found within the floor debris in hut platforms at the Clegyr Boia settlement (Williams 1953, 24–29) whilst salmon bone was found at Coygan Camp (Wainwright 1967, 190), both in Pembrokeshire and both Neolithic in date. Within a burial context, limpet, mussel shells and fish bones have also been found at Barclodiad-y-Gawres (ANG 4) and Lligwy (ANG 14) in Anglesey (Powell and Daniel 1956, 16–17 and Lynch 1970, 53), suggesting that people using these monuments had an affinity with the sea. It is important to stress that 75% of Neolithic monuments in Wales lie within 2km of the coast, suggesting a widespread ritual association with the sea.

The Neolithic in Britain, in particular in western Britain, is now generally agreed to span some 2,000 years, between 4,000 and 2,000 BC. But the idea that the Neolithic neatly occupies a distinct chunk of time is, at best, naive, relying — implicitly or explicitly — on the idea of invasion, conquest and colonization. It is surely unrealistic to assume that brand new forms of social organization, economic exploitation and symbolic behaviour appeared in Britain overnight, as it were, sometime around 4,000 BC, and that this lifestyle disappeared just as abruptly in 2,000 BC, to be replaced immediately by another. Researchers have tended to compartmentalize prehistory; one period and its distinct and dominant material culture ends and another begins. To come closer to the truth, I must regard the onset of the Neolithic as a gradual process — what one might refer to as Neolithicisation — rather than as a specific, revolutionary event. Over time, gradual social, political, economic and symbolic change influenced the behaviour of mobile hunting and gathering societies and their relationship with the landscape. Many textbooks proposed two distinct worlds — the Mesolithic and the Neolithic — and ne'er the twain shall meet. Mesolithic and Neolithic cultures are seen as mutually exclusive: where one existed, the other could not flourish. It was said they represented radically different economies; one extensive in its harvesting of natural resources, the other exploiting land intensively in order to increase its productivity. The adoption of a Neolithic cultural package, therefore, meant the sudden and irreversible extinction of the Mesolithic way of life. Such rigidity has been a convenient fiction. As this book shall show, these worlds did not collide; they merged, coalescing gradually, perhaps imperceptibly, over time. A theme of this book is the interplay between the economy and ritual of the Old World and that of the New. Arguably, there was a degree of co-existence. The same process of assimilation and integration of material culture is true of the Neolithic/Bronze Age transition (between 2,500 and 2,000 BC). It is suggested, therefore, that any invasion is likely to have been one of ideas rather than conquering tribal groups, although one cannot ignore the possibility of migration and the introduction and utilisation of continental food stuffs and livestock, as proposed by Case (1969).

Traditionally, the Mesolithic of Wales, and indeed western Britain, spans roughly 6,000 years from 10,000 BC to 4,000 BC (Wymer 1977). These transition dates vary according to author and conveniently mark either environmental or material culture change. At around 10,000 BC there was a progressive warming of the climate in Western Europe. Prior to this, between 40,000 and 15,000 BC, the Devensian Ice Sheet had scoured the landscape. Over the next 5,000 years there had been several cold-snaps but generally the climate was gradually warming. At about the time of the Late Upper Palaeolithic/Mesolithic transition, the hunter/fisher/gatherer tool kit becomes more specialised, mainly due to the varied and prolific amount of quarry that was being hunted and the wide range of resources present. Again this change does not occur at once, there is a lengthy transition from the Late Upper Palaeolithic to the Early Mesolithic that probably spans at least 2,000 years.

The changes in lithic industries from broad blades to shaped blades and microliths occurs with the change from coniferous to broad-leaved woodland. Obviously, with this gradual change in vegetation there was a need to rethink resource strategies. The wildwood, or 'climax woodland' as it is referred to, began to colonize the valleys and intermediate slopes of Wales from around 8,500 BC. This change can be seen as a sweep from south to north and includes tree species such as oak, elm, hazel and alder. With the emergence of climax woodland, a new set of forest dwellers began to emerge, including roe and red deer, wild cattle and pig.

There is sporadic settlement evidence in Wales during this period and Caseldine (1990) has identified up to 19 sites that indicate anthropogenic activity. In the southern part of Breconshire, for example, at Nant Helen and Coed Taf, quantities of datable charcoal and tree pollen have been found which suggest the encroachment of early Holocene (post-glacial) forests, along with possible pre-Neolithic peoples following a slash-and-burn woodland clearance strategy. It has been suggested by Huntley (1990) that by 10,000 BC birch, willow, juniper and, in some areas, pine had started to migrate northwards to northern Britain. These species were subsequently replaced by alder, elm and lime. The so-called 'Climatic Optimum' that commenced around 8,000 BC was marked by the arrival of oak and hazel when average summer temperatures were around 18–20 degrees centigrade. Jacobi (1980, 105) charts this part of the Holocene into three broad stages. The first stage is a warming phase that lasts for up to 3,500 years until 6,500 BC when ash and lime began to colonize the wooded valleys and encroached up to altitudes of 450m. At around the same time, the land bridge across the Bristol Channel begins to close. This is followed by an optimum phase, which lasts for a similar duration until 3,000 BC. The final stage is a cooling phase that continues into the historic period. This climatic process was ongoing throughout North-West Europe.

The possible henge at Bryn Celli Ddu showing the first phase of the monument (illustration by Brian Byron)

Case suggests that the first farmers came to southern Britain during the early fourth millennium in boats laden with cattle, sheep and grain (Case 1969). When in Britain, it is suggested that these colonists began to clear small areas of woodland and created allotment-style gardens. However, according to pollen evidence some of these areas were abandoned and forest regeneration ensued. Subsequently, the same areas were again cleared. This process, referred to as *landnam* would have incorporated slash-and-burn clearing. The burning of shrubs and undergrowth would have provided nutrients to the soils, but would have also encouraged woodland fauna to graze cleared areas thus providing ideal opportunities for hunting and foraging. This process of woodland clearance can also suggest that Late Mesolithic communities rather than early farmers were utilising the woodlands.

Gradually, on the deeper more fertile soils permanent clearances provided the basis for long-term settlements, thus establishing sedentism. According to Evans (1975) mixed agricultural regimes were in practice whereby wheat (emmer variety) and barley were grown. Archaeological evidence shows that the fields prior to cultivation were prepared using ploughs, and crops would have been harvested using wooden hoes, spades and flint reaping knives. Grain would have been stored in clay-lined storage pits like those found at the Late Neolithic/Early Bronze Age site of Four Crosses, near Llandysilio, Powys (Warrilow 1986, 60).

Supporting the theory that hunting and gathering remained equally important, some storage pits within a crop-marked enclosure at Bryn Derwen, Llandysul contained wild foods such as hazelnuts (Gibson 1990, 13). According to Smith (1974) the evidence points more to a pastoral rather than an agricultural society, with less evidence within the archaeological record of cereals than for cattle and, in particular, pig. At the same time forest and woodland regeneration occurs – the ideal habitat for the domestication and husbandry of pigs.

Architecture and Death

In Wales, as in southern Britain, the Neolithic is most visibly and, in some cases, spectacularly represented by stone and earthen burial monuments. It is most likely that chambered monuments were used by and for social elites (Atkinson 1968), but there has been much debate about when and what type of monument was constructed first.

The group of Neolithic monuments included in this book lie within Wales and along or just across its border and is a diverse set of structures

Carreg Coetan (PEM 3), an example of a Portal Dolmen

occupying eight core areas together with a number of isolated monuments.

The eight core areas are referred to as the: North Wales Group; Anglesey Group; Lleyn Peninsula Group; Harlech Group; South-West Wales Group; Gower Peninsula Group; South-East Wales Group and the Black Mountains Group (Daniel 1950; Powell *et al.* 1969). Within each of these core areas a number of smaller sub-groups are evident, based upon architectural similarity, geographical proximity and similarities in landscape setting. For example, five such local monument building traditions have been identified within the Black Mountains Group. Here, it is similarities in geography and topography, rather than architecture, which are emphasized. Within the Black Mountains area, and also in others, architectural style varies considerably from monument to monument.

In essence, there are five major types of monument architecture, some appearing to remain in fashion well into the Early Bronze Age. The Portal Dolmen classification is probably the earliest type, followed by the Cotswold-Severn tradition. The Passage Grave tradition, followed by the Gallery Grave tradition and the small, but ritually significant Earth-fast monuments appear to date from Middle/Late Neolithic to the Early Bronze Age. These five groups are further sub-divided into regional variations, again based on architectural idiosyncratic traits (Daniel 1950, Lynch *et al*, 2000, Powell *et al.* 1969).

The Portal Dolmen tradition is found mainly within North-West Wales: on the Lleyn Peninsula, encircling Snowdonia and along the western coastline south of the Lleyn. Portal Dolmens are, however, also found within the Nevern Valley in south-west Wales and on the Gower Peninsula. Interestingly, they are not found in Anglesey (Lynch 2000a, 70), although, the earliest phase at Trefignath (ANG 1) may in fact be a Portal Dolmen. Architecturally, Portal Dolmens usually consist of a squarish chamber that is enclosed by a series of large upright stones (or orthostats) which support a large sloping capstone. Classic Portal Dolmens include Gwern Einon (MER 1), in North Wales and Carreg Coetan (PEM 3), in south-west Wales. Both these and other Portal Dolmens are set within a small, round or elongated cairn mound that seldom survives. They are usually located on the lower intermediate slopes, within a coastal location. Included within this tradition are monuments that possess rectangular chambers (ibid., 70), but there are other monuments that possess rectangular chambers that are not Portal Dolmens.

The monuments of the Cotswold-Severn tradition are found mainly in south Wales and the Black Mountains area. The blueprint for this group of monuments appears to be indigenous and derives from the earthen long mound tradition of southern England, a tradition that spread far and wide and that appears to have been in use for a long time. There are, according to Powell et al. (1969) and Lynch (2000a, 66) also a number of monuments that possess Cotswold-Severn characteristics which are located in North Wales, such as Capel Garmon (DEN 3). The architecture is uniquely distinct and complex, usually consisting of a series of lateral chambers, each of which are approached by a short passage. These are then incorporated into a long mound, nearly always trapezoidal in plan. At one end of the cairn mound is a fore-court area partly enclosed by horns, which is constructed of drystone walling and supporting cairn. Based on systematic archaeological excavation, especially within the forecourt areas of Gwernvale (BRE 7) and Penywyrlod (BRE 14), there is evidence of ritual activity, and at Gwernvale the remains of a series of post-holes belonging to a possible wooden mortuary platform. In the forecourt area of some tombs of the Cotswold-Severn classification, notably within the Black Mountains Group, are what are termed 'false or dummy portals', a stone setting which creates symmetry within the forecourt area and gives the impression that a passage and chamber arrangement lie immediately behind them. Paradoxically, other monuments such as Parc-le-Breos-Cwm (GLA 4) and Tinkinswood (GLA 9) possess entrances which lead to the passage and chambers via the forecourt area. Dating for this group of monuments is difficult in that recent radiocarbon dating on disarticulated human bone, a burial trait associated with the Cotswold-Severn Group of monuments, produced a dating range between 3,700 and 3,000 BC at Parc-le-Breos-Cwm (Whittle and Wysocki 1998). This range is unusually early for dates normally ascribed to this monument style. The style's demise is represented by the infiltration of Early Bronze Age burials, grave goods and the deliberate blocking of the entrances to the passage and chambers, as seen as Gwernvale (Britnell and Savory 1984, 78–79, fig 23) and elsewhere throughout Europe.

There are two definite passage graves on Anglesey – Barclodiad-y-Gawres (ANG 4) and Bryn Celli Ddu (ANG 7), both of which are regarded as Late Neolithic in date (Lynch 2000a, 73). Interestingly, Bryn Celli Ddu, excavated by Hemp between 1925 and 1929, revealed an earlier henge monument underneath, delineated by the kerb setting of the passage grave (Hemp 1930). The passage grave classification, consisting of a small entrance, long passage and chamber arrangement

Capel Garmon (DEN 3) has Cotswold-Severn characteristics

Bryn Celli Ddu (ANG 7) is one of two Passage Graves in Wales

**Bedd yr Afanc (PEM 27) in the South-West Wales Group:
an example of a Gallery Grave**

**Devil's Quoit (PEM 25), a possible example of an Earth-fast
monument which may have been free standing**

set within a large circular cairn mound, has its origins in southern and western Europe. It is clear that the people who built and used the Anglesey monuments were in contact with other Irish Sea Province farming groups, such as those in the Boyne Valley of central and eastern Ireland, for both groups possess complex megalithic rock-art. The destroyed Calderstones monument in Liverpool with its unique set of carvings is also classified as a passage grave. In addition Lynch (1976, 79) has recognised through excavation, a 2m long passage at Carreg Samson (PEM 18) in south-west Wales. However, this and other monuments scattered throughout Wales are probably hybrids, as they bear little resemblance to the passage graves found in the rest of Europe.

The Gallery Grave tradition, possibly originating in southern Europe, but reaching Wales via southern Ireland is represented by probably two monuments: Bedd yr Afanc (PEM 27) and Heston Brake (MON 3). Gallery graves are constructed of two rows of parallel uprights that support roofing slabs to form an elongated gallery that lacks any chambers; and which would have been covered by a cairn or earthen mound. They are considered a Late Neolithic tradition. I regard the Heston Brake monument, which is enclosed at the western end, as a suspect gallery grave. However, the Bedd yr Afanc

monument, located within the bog of a classic U-shaped valley, is similar in plan to gallery graves found in Western Europe, in particular in Ireland and Northern France.

The Earth-fast tradition is the latest Neolithic architectural phase occurring in Wales and probably extends into the Early Bronze Age. Based on limited antiquarian excavations, there is evidence of Bronze Age artifacts being found in cremated bone deposits within the chambers. Earth-fast monuments are usually constructed of one or two uprights that support a capstone, part of which is embedded in the ground. This type of monument is sited within view of the coast and is found exclusively in Pembrokeshire. However, one should be cautious concerning the earth-fast element. A number of monuments such as the King's Quoit at Manorbier (PEM 26) or Devil's Quoit at Angle (PEM 25) clearly show evidence of collapsed and/or missing uprights suggesting that they are not earth-fast, but free-standing.

There are at least two areas of Wales occupied during the Neolithic, however, which do not have stone burial monuments; the Walton Basin and Welshpool have, unusually, a probable late Neolithic circular palisade enclosure and several cursus monuments (Gibson 1999). These monuments along with other henge-types found within the Central Marches area repre-

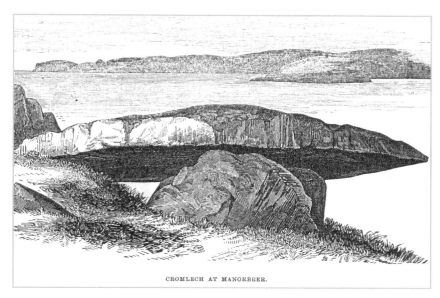

King's Quoit (PEM 26), another example of an earth-fast monument which my have been free-standing

sent a different type of Neolithic society in which the living and the monument interact. In the case of the henge within the Walton Basin, which incidentally is the largest of its kind in Europe, its function may have also included the corralling of livestock.

Pottery is also found within some monuments. Recognized wares found within the Welsh Neolithic include Abingdon, Ebbsfleet and Peterborough wares (Abingdon wares being the earliest). Each of these wares are noted for their distinct shapes and designs, in particular the impressed cord and stamped comb coarse pottery belonging to the Peterborough ware assemblage (Peterson 2003). These pottery types are not just restricted to Wales, but are found all over Britain.

Diversity, Regionalism and Architectural Form

Why such diversity? One answer could be that, within each group, different architectural techniques are being employed at different times, a suggestion that could be reinforced by carbon-dating were it not for several potential problems. Firstly, very few Neolithic burial places have been properly exca-

vated in Wales over the last 50 years and earlier excavations were usually undertaken without the necessary scientific rigour. Consequently there is little datable material available. The other problem is that radiocarbon dating only fixes a monument's use at one particular point in time and, as stated earlier, one must consider the burial place prior to it becoming Neolithicised.

Within the core areas of Neolithic Wales and elsewhere, there are a number of architectural traditions that to their builders and users were considered the correct way of doing things. Builders were establishing their 'mark' on the monument, creating a unique architectural identity, but at the same time allying themselves to a regional and identifiable tradition. For example, during the Late Neolithic in Anglesey, a ritually induced necessity dictated that the place of burial must be round and contain a passage and a large chamber. At the same time, in south-west Wales, there was a need to create a small, confined burial place using a capstone propped up by a single upright (or orthostat), usually with no covering mound. This is merely a generalization, however, for Anglesey and south-west Wales contain a number of monuments which are architecturally diverse and located in different landscapes. Thus within these core areas there are sub-groups that possess their own unique architecture and material culture, and adopt their own attitude to landscape position. The term 'Neolithicisation' must therefore embrace a number of traditions that are regionally influenced over time and space, what one could term 'variations on a theme'.

Burial practice also differs. For example, in south-west Wales, earth-fast monuments have a small chamber excavated beneath the capstone that was usually found to accommodate cremated human remains. It is clear that the burial practice evident in these monuments is very different from the method found, for example, at Parc-le-Breos-Cwm (GLA 4) on the Gower coast or at Ty Isaf (BRE 5) in the Black Mountains, of interring disarticulated skeletal remains. This variation in burial practice can also either be explained in terms of regional preference or as a product of time. Britnell (1984, 5) suggests that skeletal remains from monuments within the Black Mountains Group were deposited in an incomplete state, suggesting either excarnation or disarticulation practices (or both). One can suggest that identical practices were occurring within similar monuments elsewhere in western Britain. If one looks at modern material culture and the changes, say, in rites within English communal burial since the 15th century, one is able to see that change is both subtle but at the same time, significant.[2] If we are able to witness ongoing change within the space of 600 years, then we can perhaps accept that similar changes in Neolithic burial practice would be likely to occur over a period of 2,000 years or more.

Multi-phased Building Activity

Monument building in Wales and elsewhere cannot be regarded as a single event. The archaeological record suggests that nearly all the burial monuments in Wales possess more than one building phase; even hybrid monuments recognized by Corcoran (1969) have some form of secondary phasing. Their long use, maybe over many hundreds of years, could not have escaped the numerous architectural influences and trends that moved around the Neolithic landscape. For example, the Black Mountains monument of Ty Isaf (BRE 5) has at least two phases of building activity. Grimes (1939a) suggests that Phase 1 consisted of a circular mound with a single passage and chamber, which was followed by Phase 2, a trapezoidal-shaped mound added to the northern section of the circular mound. It appears that during the middle Neolithic, c.3,000 BC, trapezoidal mounds became popular and this is shown with the hybrid trapezoidal monuments that are found throughout Wales. At Heston Brake (MON 3), there is, according to Daniel (1950, 212), a passage that was added to an existing chamber.

Probably the most spectacular addition to any monument is the cairn and eastern chamber to Dyffryn Ardudwy (MER 3). According to Powell (1973) the first chamber, which was enclosed by a semicircular cairn, was later incorporated into a trapezoidal mound built of cairn. At the eastern end of the monument a rectangular chamber was constructed within a forecourt area and, as with other monuments of this date and form, two horns were added either side of the new chamber.

It is not just through additions to the architecture that one can see changes in society, but also through the limited material culture that is present in these monuments. In some cases one can witness different types of burial activity occurring within the same chamber. Due to adverse soil conditions along with Medieval and Post-Medieval disturbance, evidence is somewhat limited, but there are a number of monuments, in particular on

Multi-phased activity at Dyffryn Ardudwy (MER 3)

Anglesey, which clearly indicate multi-period activity. At Lligwy (ANG 14), near Penrhos-Lligwy, excavations in 1908 revealed the remains of 15–30 individuals of all ages (Baines 1908). Also present were an array of animal bone, mussel shell and pottery fragments. Interestingly, the pottery dated from the Neolithic and Bronze Age, a dating span of around 1,300 years. Similarly at the Ty Isaf monument (BRE 5) there is evidence of different types of burial activity, including crushed disarticulated bone from the western chamber, articulate skeletons from the eastern chamber and passage, along with associated Neolithic and Bronze Age grave goods (see later). It is clear from the burial evidence that this monument was in use for at least 1,500 years. The difference in time between the construction of the circular mound and its incorporation into a larger trapezoidal mound may only be a few years. Dating of the burials is, therefore, based partly on what was going on elsewhere in Britain and western Europe at that time.[3]

A Monument for all Periods

One of the most celebrated excavations of the modern era is that undertaken at Gwernvale (BRE 7), near Talgarth, in 1977–1978 (Britnell 1984), which revealed a period of use spanning some 10,000 years. Beneath the actual fabric of the monument were a number of lithics dating as far back as the Late Upper Palaeolithic period, c.10,000 BC. Overlying this material was diagnostic flint of the Mesolithic period. Incorporated into what can now be described as a multi-phase monument was recent evidence of the chambers being used as a sheep shelter. Similarly, the nearby monument of Ty Illtyd (BRE 6) has evidence of a hermit known as St Illtyd using the chamber as a hermitage during the Medieval period; a series of Christian symbols are faintly scratched on several of the uprights that support the capstone. More subtle evidence of multi-phase use can be seen within the Nevern Sub-group of monuments in south-west Wales. Here the five monuments that surround the Nevern Valley are embedded within a number of landscapes, both prehistoric and historic.

On the western side of the valley, on the capstone of Trellyffant (PEM 2) are up to 35 cup-marks which probably date from the Bronze Age. On the eastern side of the valley at Pentre Ifan (PEM 5), running along the edge of the mound on its eastern side are a series of ritual pits which, according to Grimes (1948, 3–23), appear to pre-date the mound. On two uprights within the forecourt area Lynch (1972) has argued that rock art exists which I believe may date from the Bronze Age. Similarly, at Carreg Coetan (PEM 3), in the village of Newport, diagnostic Mesolithic flint lies close to the robbed out mound. Similar acts of multi-phased activity are present on monuments in North Wales and in Anglesey. The questions must be asked: why are these monuments multi-phased and why are such ritual monuments situated close to domestic and utilitarian sites from other periods?

Within modern times and especially in Wales one sees additions to ritual buildings. More importantly some of these, although recognized as ritual buildings, change their meaning over time. For example, one will see in Wales changes of meaning and status to chapels. These buildings, which were part of popular religious movements during the 17th, 18th and 19th centuries, have been invariably changed both in form and meaning; many now having a domestic use. There is, of course, a period of transition when the initial meaning of the building ceases, and it falls into decay. The grave-yard becomes unattended. The meaning of the building becomes forgotten, albeit vaguely recognized as a place of worship. This is seen through the style, the architecture of the building and where it stands within the community. After a period of transition, the modern planning procedure will invariably allow the building to be transformed. However, due to its ritual importance, its age and architectural style, its main fabric will be protected. After planning permission is granted, the building, which is now a shell — its internal form and freestanding furniture removed, is transformed into a space with a different use. Despite this transformation the original meaning, i.e., the chapel, stays the same. This simplistic approach to style and change in architecture and its meaning can be applied to the multi-phase activity of chambered monuments. Nowadays, we are in a fortunate position, through the access to detailed historical records and the Listed Buildings Register, to know when, why and how buildings such as chapels changed their identity (but not their form). In the case of chambered monuments, the when, the why and the how are near impossible to assess. We do know that change did take place at some point in time; but the why is pure speculation.

Living in the Promised Land

Today, the places of the dead are extremely visible, yet the living have left few traces. The archaeological record in Wales contains around 150 free-standing monuments of Neolithic date; 100 of these are discussed within this volume. Perhaps another 200–300 monuments have been either lost or destroyed, only some of which have been documented. Associated with these monuments are numerous find spots and lithic scatters. Other monuments that date to the Neolithic and found in Wales include henges, pit alignments and a possible causewayed enclosure. Henges appear to be found sporadically throughout Wales, sometimes incorporated into later monuments such as Bryn Celli Ddu (ANG 4). However, large-scale formal settlement is less evident; only a handful of sites have been discovered and fully investigated. (Whether one wishes to include large flint scatters as evidence of settlement is open to debate.) Two multi-phase sites in south-west Wales, Clegyr Boia (see plan page 24) and Coygan Camp, have revealed evidence of Neolithic, as well as Bronze Age and Iron Age activity. A further site is located just outside Wales in Herefordshire on Dorstone Hill, close to Arthur's Stone in an area known as the Golden Valley. The importance of this site is down to two factors: its size and the quantity of the diagnostic lithic assemblage found.

This latter site was discovered by field-walkers on Dorstone Hill and is equidistant between Arthur's Stone (HFR 1) and Cross Lodge Long Barrow (HFR 4). Excavated by Christopher Houlder and Roger Pye between 1965 and 1970, this extensive settlement (NGR SO 326 423) covers approximately 18 acres (Children and Nash 1994). The settlement was enclosed on the west side by a crude stone wall, on top of which was a wooden 'stockade' fence. Also present were storage pits (possibly used for grain), occupation floors and undisturbed 'buried soils', ideal for dating. Within these soils were discovered over 4,000 pieces of flint (including many arrowheads), pottery, and more than 50 polished stone axe fragments. The stone and flint used to create these prestige items were, in part, imported from as far away as south Wales and the Cotswolds. The contact/exchange of axes, for example, between all three areas, highlights the importance and prestige of farming groups within the Golden Valley.

The size of the Dorstone settlement suggests that a large population, probably in excess of 250 people, occupied the upland areas of the Golden Valley during the Neolithic. This settlement utilised the slopes, ridges and tops of the eastern uplands — from Merbach Hill in the north-east to Canns Hill in the south. By settling on the eastern slopes, the community would have lived within full view of the Golden Valley and, more importantly, of the symbolically significant Black Mountains. Below, the fertile woodland of the valley floor would have been slowly cleared for allotment-style farming.

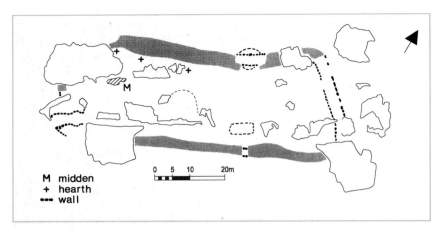

M midden
+ hearth
... wall

0 5 10   20m

Plan of Clegyr Boia in South-West Wales

More land would have been brought into production as the population grew. Remaining pockets of woodland scattered throughout the valley would have contained red deer and wild boar, additional resources that could have been exploited by Neolithic people in the same way as their Mesolithic hunter ancestors.

The two settlements in south-west Wales, in particular Clegyr Boia, are difficult to research in as much as the soils are very acidic and shallow. Much of the stratigraphy of Clegyr Boia was extremely ephemeral, in part due to subsequent disturbance. The settlement is set within later rectangular ramparts measuring 100m x 25m, and possibly of Iron Age date. Outside the settlement area, a large number of Mesolithic flint scatters suggest continuous occupation of the peninsula for well over 4,000 years.

The Clegyr Boia settlement consists of three possible Neolithic house structures, a fire pit and a midden. One of the houses was oval, the other rectangular. The excavation revealed a possible third hut, located centrally within the rampart area (Baring-Gould 1902). This rectangular structure, measuring 7m x 3m in plan, comprised two rows of posts which may have supported a timber roof (Williams 1953, 24–29). An 'unused pit' investigated inside this structure was compared by the excavator to similar pits discovered under the Pentre Ifan monument (PEM 5).

The oval hut yielded evidence of extensive burning. Barker (1992) has suggested that this, coupled with the deposition of pottery, indicates possible ritual abandonment. I would argue that the settlement and the two nearby monuments of Carn Llidi (PEM 21–22) and Coetan Arthur (PEM 3)

are contemporary, and that the former may have died out naturally towards the end of the Neolithic. Pottery from the oval hut appears to be identical with examples found in the rectangular structure and in the midden to the west. Three different Neolithic pottery styles have been identified in all, and have been compared to wares found in Cornwall, southern Ireland and the Wessex region suggesting that a possible exchange network linked these areas. Barker (1992) proposes a Middle Neolithic (3,200–2,700 bc) date for the pottery from Clegyr Boia.

A series of hearths to the west of the oval hut yielded a flint arrowhead and a partly polished stone axe of gritty volcanic tuff. Limpet shells, pottery and oak and birch charcoal was recovered from the midden. Cattle bone was found in both huts. The bone, together with the shells, suggests that the people of Clegyr Boia thrived on a mixed economy of hunting gathering and fishing with an element of domesticated herding. The settlement may have supported only two or three small family units at any one time.

The second settlement identified in south-west Wales is located on Coygan Hill and dates from the Early Neolithic, around 3,750 BC (3,050±95 years bc). An earlier phase of Mesolithic occupation has also been suggested (Wainwright 1967). Located close to the sea and the mouths of the Afon Tywi (Towy) and Taf, Coygan Camp revealed a number of datable organic remains, including charred hazelnut shells and animal bone recovered from a small fire pit (Taylor 1980). The shells and the bone, which date to 5,000±95 BP, suggest hunting and gathering remained an important component of daily Neolithic life.

Approximately 3km to the north of the Clegyr Boia settlement are two tombs that belong to the St David's Sub-group of monuments. These are earth-fast in form and small enough to be constructed and managed by just a small family unit. To the east of both monuments is a series of prehistoric field systems that are arguably of a later date. Nevertheless, apart from the rearing of cattle and fishing of seasonal marine fauna, including mammals such as porpoise and seal, communities on the St David's Peninsula may have relied upon the produce from small gardens, although no pollen record has been undertaken to suggest this.

The choice of different economic resources would have established a safety net against the slowly deteriorating climate that commences from the mid to late Neolithic onwards. Peter Fowler has suggested that the coastal areas of south-west Wales and North Wales were ideal for agriculture, these areas benefiting from the warm currents of the Gulf Stream. He postulates further that there were up to 365 potential crop-growing days per year on Anglesey, St David's Head and the Gower coast, 300 days along the Lleyn Peninsula, the Menai Straits and the Gwent Levels, as opposed to just 240 days within central Wales, where the Black Mountains Group is located (Fowler 1983, 24).

To utilise time constructively, tomb building may have been undertaken during the winter months. Alternatively, it may have been the initial task undertaken by the first farmers in order to establish control and social-political identity within the locality, as well as creating a ritual and symbolic focus.

Megalithic Art: The Act of Ritual and Symbolism

In Britain, megalithic art usually dating from the Neolithic is rare and is mainly associated with the passage grave tradition. Savory (1980, 222) suggests that megalithic art has its origins in Iberia. According to Joussaume (1985, 73) megalithic art was either engraved or painted, however evidence for the latter has long since disappeared. In western England and Wales there are three passage grave sites which possess complex carved designs, two of them in Anglesey: Barclodiad-y-Gawres (ANG 4) and Bryn Celli Ddu (ANG 7). If one is to ignore current political boundaries, one could include within this group the third site of the Calderstones in Liverpool (LANCS 1, NGR SJ 405 875); all three have similar carved designs. There are a number of other sites that contain cupmarks, both single and multiple, e.g. on the capstones of Trellyfant (PEM 2) and Bachwen (CRN 7). This phenomenon, however, is regarded as a later tradition probably dating to the Early Bronze Age. Also from the same period is a cup-and-ring carving (see page 27).

When Barclodiad-y-Gawres was excavated in 1952–1953, five uprights with complex carved decoration were recorded. In the excavation report chamber and incorporated into an ante-chamber is Stone 19, which has a single clockwise spiral in its centre.

Finally, Stone 22, probably the most complex of the megalithic art within this monument, lies at the junction of the passage and chamber. This stone, measuring 1.47m in height, contains three sets of designs. At the top of the stone is an anticlockwise spiral, part of which is missing. Immediately below this are five complete horizontal zigzag lines and three part zigzag lines. Forming part of the lower zigzag are two chevrons, one below the other. Either side of the face of this upright and continuing the lower set of part zigzag lines is a multi-lined curvilinear pattern that continues to the base of the upright. This particular design has certain similarities with the nearby Pattern Stone at Bryn Celli Ddu.

A selection of Neolithic flint artefacts from around the Black Mountains, including a blade, three leaf-shaped arrowheads and a scraper (from Brecknock Museum)

Flint blades and points from Tenby Museum

Megalithic art in the form of a spiral from Calderstones, Liverpool

Carved footprint from Calderstones, Liverpool

Bryn Celli Ddu was excavated by F.D. Lucas in 1865 and later by W.J. Hemp in 1930. It was the latter excavation that revealed an ornately carved stone referred to as the Pattern Stone. Uniquely, this stone was carved on both faces and on the top, the designs on both faces appearing to be inter-linked. Measuring 1.5m in height by 1.64m in width, the stone was found during excavation overlying a central pit. It is not known if it, along with an undecorated stone, belonged to the passage grave or an earlier henge monument. Interestingly the pit is centrally located within both monuments. Shee-Twohig (1981, 230) suggests that the Pattern Stone may have once stood at the centre of the henge monument or it may have been a dedica-tion stone for some form of ritual during construction of the passage grave. The decoration, which only covers two-thirds of the stone, in my view belongs to a stone that would have stood upright. On one of the faces is a double serpentiform (snake-like design) pattern that has the end terminating into an anticlockwise spiral. One section of this pattern is similar to the lower section of patterns on Stone 22 in Barclodiad-y-Gawres. In my view there appears to be very little symmetry to the patterning on this face. However, the pattern does appear to be emerging from the top of the stone and spreading outwards. Likewise, on the reverse the lines appear to be running down the stone. On this face the patterns are similar in form yet more confused. In this plethora of design is a single cupmark.

The Calderstones (LANC 1) in Calderstone Park, Liverpool are believed to be part of a large passage grave and possess similar designs which are arranged in a more complex way than those designs found in Anglesey (Forde-Johnston 1956, 73). All six stones are decorated and include clockwise and anticlockwise spirals, merging spirals, concentric circles and lozenges. There are also eight carved footprint designs on three of the stones and a Maltese-type cross (Shee-Twohig 1981, fig. 265). These designs, however, may be later additions to the megalithic art. The foot print designs, rare in Britain, are also found on the capstone of the Pool Farm, Somerset, cist burial. Incidentally, the capstone is now housed in Bristol City Museum.

The question arises as to why only three monuments in this part of Britain possess this form of complex megalithic art? I have stated earlier that the idea of constructing chambered tombs is based on a transmission of ideas: we came, we saw, we copied. Both Daniel (1950) and Powell et al. (1969) have discussed extensively the architectural links between certain monuments, for example the replication of the Cotswold-Severn type of monument within Wales. It is clear that certain architectural traits such as the introduction of horns and false portals must have originated from somewhere and these fashionable traits were transmitted to other monument builders. Likewise, there must have been a point in time during the Middle Neolithic that megalithic art became important. The distribution of such an art form is concentrated in nine areas of western Europe: Portugal, northern Spain, central/west France, the Paris Basin, Brittany, the Channel Islands, Orkney, Ireland and North Wales (Shee-Twohig 1981, 12). Each of these areas has a unique set of artistic designs, all of which are carved onto megalithic monuments.

The megalithic art recorded throughout southern Ireland, although more complex than the North Wales material, does have similar traits. The

Considered rare in Wales, a cup-and-ring carving discovered in 2005 at the Garn Turne Monument (PEM 11)

Fourknocks site in County Meath has identical spirals on several stones to those found at Barclodiad-y-Gawres. Similarly, spirals are found at Loughcrew and at Newgrange in County Meath. The distribution of megalithic art in Ireland is confined to the east, within the central valleys such as that of the Boyne, and within Northern Ireland.

An even larger concentration of sites with megalithic art is found in Brittany, the most ornate of these being the passage grave of Gavrinis, located in the Gulf of Morbihan. This passage grave, now located on an island, has all its passage and chamber uprights carved with complex abstract imagery. It was probably at Gavrinis, along with other Breton megalithic sites, that a north-west European megalithic art tradition was born, due to the concentration of the number of sites and the complexity of the art. According to Burl (1985, 14) megalithic art in Brittany commenced around 4,600 BC. Lynch (1969a) claims that Bryn Celli Ddu is one of the latest megalithic burial monuments in Anglesey despite replicating the architecture of some of the Breton passage graves. If this is the case, Irish megalithic art probably commenced after contact with the Breton groups. The concept of decorating a burial monument in this way finally reached Anglesey, possibly sometime after 2,800 BC.

The Prestige of the Axe

Generally speaking, grave good assemblages from Welsh chambered tombs are poor (Savory 1980, 220). There is a handful of sites, however, where there has been a wealth of finds including polished stone and flint axes. It has been regarded that these items have ritual and symbolic associations, and that they would have accompanied the deceased to the next world. Axes, although limited in number, have been found within the chambers at the destroyed Ffynnondruidion monument (PEM 28) in Pembrokeshire, where accounts state that five flint axes (celts) were found in the early 19th century (Fenton 1811, 24). Axes have also been found at Bryn yr Hen Bobl, Angelsey (ANG 8), Din Dryfol (ANG 5), Ty Isaf (BRE 5) and Ty Newydd (ANG 3).

Despite limited funerary deposition, the majority of axes that have been found are usually classified as un-provenance stray finds. However, one cannot assume that these finds are the result of accidental loss. Their functionality has been widely discussed and it would appear that they are more than just utilitarian items. Axes found within non-funerary settings in each of the Neolithic core areas of Wales originate from a variety of unique geological source areas, sometimes outside Wales. The time and effort, either in trading with other Neolithic groups or in embarking on long-haul expeditions to axe-source areas, collecting rough-outs and then shaping and polishing them suggests these are special items. It would appear, therefore, these items possessed a number of uses for the living as well as the dead.

Stray finds may form part of a votive offering, suggesting a ritual-symbolic use. Axes in a burial context were probably gender-encoded, representing maleness. They are usually associated with other prestige items such as leaf-shaped arrowheads, diagnostic flint tools, flint debitage and pottery. There were probably many other items associated with burial that have not survived the archaeological record.

Apart from burial and possible votive deposition, polished flint and stone axes offer a unique insight to axe production, trade and exchange mechanisms. Axes found within Wales originate from a number of areas of Britain, and their trade would have formed part of the mechanism which ensured contact with other Neolithic groups. It also provided the impetus for Neolithic people to travel many hundreds of kilometres in order to successfully trade other goods. Contact and exchange would have also provided the impetus and knowledge to replicate new forms of monument design as well as new ideas of ritual, especially in the treatment of the dead.

According to a number of researchers, in particular Grimes (1951, 23), axe shapes conform to four basic types: a) axes with pointed butts; b) axes with broad thin butts; c) elongated forms; and d) double-edged axes with square ends. These axe types do not correspond to certain dates within the Neolithic, and it would appear that several types were in use at the same time and may represent two different regional trends. Prior to experiments undertaken by Danish archaeologist Ivenson in 1946, polished jadeite flint and stone axes were considered functional tools, in particular used for cutting down trees. However, after several blows, these axes were shown to splinter or shatter on impact. Similar results could be expected for axes made in Britain.

The axe factory at Langdale, Cumbria

In Wales, it is not just a question of the distribution of axes, but also their production, axes forming part of the national petrological group numbering 1–24 (I–XXIV). Research in particular by Houlder (1988, 133–136) has outlined the location of axe factories in Wales, of which there are six. Three of these are located in south-west Wales (Groups VIII, XIII and XXIII); one on the Lleyn Peninsula (Group XXI), one west of the Great Orme at Penmaenmawr (Group VII) and one in central Wales close to the source of the River Severn (Group XII). These groups, according to Darvill (1989), are divided into Early Neolithic and Late Neolithic stone sources. It would appear that axes from these areas are widely distributed throughout Wales and England, probably the result of social exchange and interaction between neighbouring and more distant groups, but the extent of distribution falls away with distance from the source. For example, 70% of all Group VII axe finds are within a 70km radius of the axe factory, with only 5% found outside central and north Wales suggesting periodic or limited contact/exchange between local and regional Neolithic groups. Likewise, a similar graduated distribution is witnessed with Group VIII, located in Pembrokeshire, with 40–50% found within a 30km radius of the Preseli Mountains and only as a

Polished flint axe from Breconshire
Brecknock Museum (acc. no. 168)

small percentage found within the Cotswold-Severn Group of tombs in Gloucestershire. One should also note that axes which have been quarried and polished outside Wales are also found in Wales, notably south-west Wales, in particular axes from the factories of Cumbria (Groups VI, XI and XV, see page 28) and Cornwall (Groups I and III). For example, an axe found at the Ffynnondruidion monument (PEM 28), made from either gabbro or quartz diorite (both coarse-grained igneous rocks), probably originated from the Isle of Man or Cornwall. This suggests that power and prestige were to be gained by acquiring axes from production centres outside the locality. However, not all axes come from known 'axe factories'. Clough and Cummins (1988, 246–255) list a total of 89 polished stone and flint axes found within Pembrokeshire and a further 41 and 45 in Cardiganshire and Carmarthenshire respectively, of which only approximately 40% are from specific axe manufacturing areas, (the majority of which lie within the Preseli Mountains).

It is only since the emergence of experimental archaeology that polished stone axes have been regarded as prestige items, and it is now clear that, since the early Neolithic, stone from the Preseli Mountains was viewed as a prestige raw material. It should also be noted that the famous bluestones

A collection of polished stone axes
from South-West Wales (Tenby Museum)

(blue-grey dolerite) which form the inner circle at Stonehenge derive from three outcrops at Carn Meini, within the heart of the Preselis, close to the axe factories. This alone would have attracted interest from social elites outside south-west Wales.

Tilley (1993) argues that axes were an extremely important symbol for the ritual and the burying of the dead. Within southern Scandinavia, polished stone and flint axes form an integral part of the burial package, but there appear to be a number of complex issues surrounding the deposition of axes within burial monuments. I would suggest that axes had an aesthetic value and were regarded as objects of desire which more than probably commanded status, especially within a burial context. However, twice as many axes have been found in non-burial contexts.

Three individual quarries have been discovered within the Preseli Mountains. Clough and Cummins (1988) and others have recognized one of these Preseli axe factories — Group VIII — as an early Neolithic stone source. This source, located on the southern flank of the mountains, is of igneous tuff and the quarry dates between 3,000–2,500 BC. The stone from the other two groups, XIII and XXIII, is spotted dolerite and was used to manufacture axes after 2,500 BC. Pitts (1980, 8) has suggested that igneous tuff has a predominant flaking characteristic, while dolerites have a pecking quality. Both stones would have served different uses: the tuffs for axes and the dolerites for making later (Neolithic and Early Bronze Age) perforated implements. Within the area, both types are well represented. Outside, in particular within the Cotswold-Severn region, axes from the Preselis frequently occur although only a small percentage of the total output. Communication would have provided the impetus to establish valuable trading partners that would involve the exporting of other commodities in and out of each area. It could even be that axes from the three local quarries were so valuable or rare that an exchange imbalance between local axes and other goods was in operation.

The axe factories in north Wales are located between 180–350m AOD on the outcrops and scree slopes of Penmaenmawr Mountain and are referred to as the Graig Lwyd axe factory group.[5] The site covers an extensive area, the limits of which have yet to be determined. Excavations undertaken in 1920 revealed the method of extracting stone and, more importantly, the process of manufacture. According to Savory (1980, 223) axes from Penmaenmawr date from the Mid-to-Late Neolithic and dominated the local market in north Wales. Apart from north Wales, axes from this factory have been found in Paviland Cave on the Gower, Merthyr Mawr and Kenfig (both near Bridgend in south Wales). Outside Wales, Graig Lwyd axes have been found at Avebury, Cairn Papple, Woodhenge and Upware (Castleden 1992, 391; Grimes 1951, 23). A fragment of a Graig Lwyd macehead was also found within the causewayed enclosure at Windmill Hill.

Rough-outs, probably taken away from their geological source to be shaped into the finished axe, would invariably be ovate or oblong and according to Grimes 'flat and tabular or spindle-like' (1951, 23). According to Houlder (1988, 134) up until 1989 there were only 27 rough-out finds sourced from Wales. It is therefore more probable that most axes were either being polished at their geological source and/or that the success rate for polishing outside the source area was high, with little accidental fracturing or wastage.

Other finds identified by Houlder include battle axes, axe hammers and mace-heads. However, these account for a small percentage of the total number of stone tools found and sourced within Wales and these too can be associated with high status people. Also found within the 1920 excavation at Penmaenmawr was a stone plaque, which had been decorated with hatched chevron symbols. This measured 13cm across and may have been a talisman. Similar finds have been found at other mine and quarry sites such as Grimes Graves in Norfolk and Harrow Hill in Sussex.

Over the recent past, many of the potential stone extraction sites on Penmaenmawr Mountain have been largely destroyed by modern quarrying or, according to Castleden, buried beneath quarry waste (1992, 391). The stone used for Neolithic axe manufacture was augite granophyre, also known as Penmaenmawr granite, largely taken from the scree slopes. According to Grimes (1951, 21), this rock is extremely tough and difficult to utilise which is certainly reflected in the large number of broken axes that have appeared on the site. Unlike most Neolithic axe factory sites in Britain, Graig Lwyd does not continue in use beyond the Neolithic.

The Population of Neolithic Wales

Most preceding Mesolithic occupation sites lie close to the sea, and also close to or beneath Neolithic sites, in particular burial monuments. These sites vary in size from small lithic scatters, for example, around Freshwater East, to the large exposed settlement on Nab Head (both in Pembrokeshire). The Nab Head site comprises early (Nab Head I) and late Mesolithic (Nab Head II) assemblages, and includes evidence of a number of (dwelling) structures and datable features, including a shallow pit that was filled with burnt soil and charcoal which was radiocarbon dated to 7360±90 BP (OxA-860). On the same site a possible hearth has also been found, dated to 6210±90 BP (OxA-861) (David 1990, 210–212). Despite this site, evidence for Mesolithic settlement overall is rather fragmentary. It is probable that small bands of hunter/gatherers exploited small territories and that settlement was temporary, consisting of make-shift encampments.

However, in order to gain a clearer picture of settlement, one must look outside Wales, for example, to southern Scandinavia, where preservation of settlements fares much better. The large habitation sites at Sveardborg (excavated by Friss Johansen 1919), Klampenborg (excavated by Westerby 1927), Åamosen (excavated by Mathiassen 1943) and Vedbaek (excavated by Mathiassen 1946), have revealed a mixed economy whereby marine and terrestrial resources are being utilised. During the early part of the Late Mesolithic, known as the Kongemose phase (5,500–4,300 BC), the area around Åamosen (bog), Zealand, would have been densely populated and possibly marks a hiatus for inland habitation. The main food resources would have been red deer, fish, shellfish and woodland fruits and berries. The density of occupation of such areas has prompted researchers such as Peter Rowley-Conwy (1981) to suggest that the population of such settlements would support between 45 and 250 individuals. I am not suggesting that such numbers were present on sites in Wales, but that the complexity of society and land division may have been comparable. Because of the absence of major settlement, with the exceptions of Clegyr Boia and Coygan Hill in south-west Wales and Dorstone just across the Welsh border in Herefordshire, the evidence we have for the Neolithic is more difficult to assess. It has been suggested that early Neolithic settlement within the core areas of Wales is similar to that of the late Mesolithic settlement distribution. More or less the same resources were available.

Population density may also be roughly assessed alongside the distribution of flint. Contained within each of the eight core areas are a large number of flint sites. These vary in size and diagnostic tool type, with some sites having evidence of multi-phased activity suggesting long periods of use. In the case of Gwernvale (BRE 7), it is not only Mesolithic flint that is present but also earlier Upper Palaeolithic flint.

In addition to flint distribution, pollen evidence suggests that many of the fertile valleys within these core areas were densely wooded (Caseldine 1990, 43–47). For example, at Mynydd Troed (BRE 10) within the Black Mountains there is pollen evidence within a buried soil suggesting the area was a mixture of heathland and open woodland (Crampton and Webley 1966). Similarly, at Dyffryn Ardudwy (MER 3), the pollen evidence portrays a landscape covered in broad-leaf woodland (Dimbleby 1973). Such habitats would have provided the resources to enable the establishment of a settlement.

It is probable that as populations became more sedentary and increased in number due to the wide availability of seasonal resources during the Climatic Optimum (10,000–6,000 BP), and that over time settlement moved inland to occupy the fertile valleys of the main tributaries around coastal Wales. It is clear that the distribution of chambered tombs in, say, the hinterlands of the Black Mountains show not only ritual use of the landscape but also a landscape in which settlement — social and economic space — is equally important.

Frances Lynch (2000a, 46–47) has listed up to 96 megalithic tombs in Wales, along with numerous polished stone axe finds. The axe finds are usually confined to the Neolithic core areas and this distribution of both tombs and axes suggests that the Welsh population was indeed concentrated. I would argue that, based on the four regional Sites and Monuments Records (SMRs) for Wales, the issue of population density is far more complex in that axes in particular are usually found in clusters, perhaps representing a more densely populated area. However, this phenomenon may in part reflect areas that have benefited from concentrated field walking surveys. In addition to the 100 monuments covered in this book (of which a few are just across the border in England), as has already been suggested it is likely that Wales once had a further 200 to 300 megalithic tombs, many of which have been destroyed. The limited number of henge monuments and Late Neolithic/Early Bronze Age stone circles should also be taken into consideration, adding to this complexity. Even so, assuming a minimum of 300 chambered monuments, one must consider there would have been at least 300 settlement sites. If one envisages that several settlements accompanied a single monument, then the number of settlements obviously rises higher still. Settlements would have varied in size and prosperity, and this is reflected in the construction of some of Wales' larger monuments, such as Bryn Celli Ddu (ANG 7), Gop Cairn (FLT 1) and Tinkinswood (GLA 9). The monuments themselves are a testament to the success of the settlements.

Startin and Bradley (1981, 289–296) have estimated that a tomb such as Ty Isaf (BRE 5), which I would term a medium sized monument, could take between 7,000 and 16,000 hours of labour to construct. This would depend on the hardness of the stone or bedrock quarried and the distance the materials had to be moved to the site. Another factor was the availability of a workforce. Startin and Bradley suggest that the construction of an average monument would require ten people to work an eight-hour day, seven days a week for three to seven months. This simplistic formula does not take into account additions to the monument or the idea that a monument was treated as an organic structure in that it was constructed over a long period of time. Either way it is important to stress that the monument belonged to a community. I would argue that inter-group co-operation may have been the only way of constructing monuments such as Arthur's Stone (HRF 1), Tinkinswood (GLA 9) and Garn Turne (PEM 11), all of which have massive capstones, and in the case of Garn Turne a capstone that weighs an estimated 60 tons (Children and Nash 1997, 91). I would also suggest that smaller monuments would have received the same inter-group co-operation, especially if one considers Colin Renfrew's hypothesis of core-periphery distribution. This suggests that monuments are either placed within the centre of territories or along their boundaries. Monuments, therefore, may have acted as territorial markers. As vast amounts of labour and time would have been required in order to build a tomb such as Tinkinswood (GLA 9) or Garn Turne (PEM 11) if these were at the edge of a territory, complex social and political organisation would have been essential and may have involved co-operation between neighbouring groups.

On St David's Head, south-west Wales, the Clegyr Boia settlement boasts just two houses, each house probably home to between 10 and 15 individuals who would have constructed small earth-fast monuments such as Coetan Arthur (PEM 3) and Carn Llidi (PEM 21 and 22), both located on St David's Head and both utlising local stone. The size and construction methods used for these two monuments would have been ample for a unit of this size. However, one must beg the question of how many individuals would have been needed to construct, and more importantly place the capstones, on Pentre Ifan (PEM 5) and nearby Carreg Samson (PEM 18). Monuments of this size throughout Wales would have required complex planning prior to and during their construction.

Assuming, therefore, that there were 300 monuments in existence and that perhaps 150 were being constructed and in use at any one time during a 2,000 year period, and that an average settlement of the style of Clegyr Boia consisting of 20–30 individuals would have constructed one tomb; it can be deduced that the adult population of Neolithic Wales was around 4,000–5,000 people. This rough estimate also assumes that collective co-operation between neighbouring groups is present for larger tomb building as well as more mundane chores in Neolithic society.

Unfortunately human remains found within a number of the tombs provide no great help in substantiating or otherwise this suggested population figure. For one thing, the usually acidic soil means that relatively few bones have survived. Even so, archaeologists have been able to determine the gender and age group that have been interred in monuments such as Ty Isaf (BRE 5) and Parc le Breos Cwm (GLA 4). According to its excavator, Sir John Lubbock, Parc le Breos Cwm monument contained up to 24 skeletons 'much broken and in no regular arrangement' which were found within the chambers. One then has to consider whether these remains are just those of the elites over a long period of time, or do they represent a communal grave for the group? If an elite is using this monument as a repository over a long period, would radiocarbon dating have detected a chronological sequence? Assuming that the average life expectancy was up to 40 years of age, with a high infant mortality rate,[6] then the 24 skeletons probably represent the elite. Likewise at Ty Isaf, up to 33 individuals were found within the western chamber, two more in the eastern chamber and further remains in the passage. Again, are we looking at corporate monumentality or communal burial? Unfortunately, the problem in Wales is made more difficult with the inconsistency of burial material from each of the monuments. For example, within the earth-fast group of monuments in south-west Wales, the preferred burial practice appears to be cremation and in some cases, in particular Morfa Bychan A, there is a stratified sequence that includes a few fragments of charred bone (Ward 1918, 69–70) and little else. Thus it is difficult to calculate the potential population from the evidence of human remains within these monument types.

As for the people themselves, Lynch has suggested that they were 'of small stature' ranging from 1.5 to 1.64m in height who lived an active life, thus developing 'well marked muscle channels and flattened shin bones' (2000b). Furthermore, from the limited number of skulls recovered from a burial context, they are described as having an elongated skull (dolichocephalic). These pronounced features are only derived from a limited number of burials and in essence I would suggest that these people are no different from ourselves. I would further suggest that the short life expectancy was partially due to climatic conditions and they would have suffered the usual ailments such as rheumatoid arthritis and osteoarthritis.

Concerning diet, Neolithic communities would have utilised both domestic and wild resources. Although not present in a Welsh context, there is evidence for Paget's disease and Rickets elsewhere in Neolithic Europe that may be the result of poor diet. One cannot also rule out that within a 2,000-year period some form of natural catastrophic epidemic event may have affected the population (*ibid.*, 175–185). For example, bovine tuberculosis can spread to humans through the drinking of infected milk or the eating of infected meat and attacks the most vulnerable in society, notably children (Roberts and Manchester 1995, 134). According to Sherratt (1981) the milking of domestic cattle occurs in southern Europe from the fifth millennium. Tuberculosis and other diseases recorded in the Neolithic such as infantile paralysis (poliomyelitis) could have tipped the balance in small Neolithic communities. That this type of event may have occurred during the Neolithic/Bronze Age transition is indicated by a change in monument building from corporate monumentality to single status burials.

Monuments and their Recent Past

In 1993, I can remember walking around Falköping, a provincial town in central Sweden that boasts of having over 35 megalithic chambered monuments within its bounds. Many of these monuments, referred to as *gongriffen* (or passage graves), had been incorporated into garden bedding whilst several have been used as ornamental features within public spaces. In certain places the sites, which are constructed of local sandstone and are in various states of preservation, dominate the locality. In the recent past, there appears to have been a desire to include these monuments within the townscape. Despite their heritage value it is clear that the original meaning of these monuments is not fully understood; to many, they are merely stones that have been symmetrically constructed by ancient people; they are divorced, alien from the modern world. Likewise, there are a number of monuments in Wales that have been incorporated into modern landscapes such as gardens and parklands, for example The Hanging Stone (PEM 24). There are others which have provided shelter to cattle, sheep, even families and hermits; monuments of the dead have therefore become dwellings for the living. Monuments such as Plas Newydd (ANG 9) have been incorporated into a recent historical setting, their formal arrangement of either stones or a mound drawn into a recently constructed artificial landscape. Arguably this artificiality exhibits and complements the artificiality of the monument, itself an (ancient) social construct.

Many Neolithic and Early Bronze Age monuments continue to exist as striking features within the landscape. Others are more unobtrusive, either because they were deliberately hidden, accessible only to those possessing the necessary ritual knowledge, or because the physical traces of their exis-

A monument in the park: Kyrkerör, Falköping, Vastergötland, Central Sweden

tence have been eroded over the millennia and are now barely discernible (often having been incorporated into stone and turf boundaries). A few monuments survive only in the pages of antiquarian journals or as folklore; for example a couple of sentences and a picturesque engraving by Theophilus Jones, made in 1809, are all that remain of the Black Mountains monument of Croesllechau (BRE 11).[7] A plan published in Lhwyd's *Parochalia* (1699) informs us that there was once a burial chamber, probably a passage grave, at Llanymynech Hill, Montgomeryshire. Likewise, an antiquarian sketch of unknown date, probably 19th century, depicts the original chambered monument at Llanfechell, Anglesey (ANG 15), today just 'a heap of fallen stone' (Lynch 1970, 43). Following their abandonment or partial destruction many monuments remained largely intact until the 17th century and it is only during the last 300 years that destruction has occurred on a significant scale. There are a number of reasons for this. One is the increasingly common practice of plundering monuments for building stone. The antiquarian accounts of Arthur's Stone in Herefordshire (HRF 1) suggest cairn robbing accounted for the partial destruction of the monument during the 18th century (*cf.* Crawford 1925). Superstition no doubt also played a role, but the evidence for this is rather sparse.

Concurrent with these instances of destruction, however, was the rise of scholarly and artistic interest in the Neolithic tombs of Wales, coinciding with William Stukely's studies of the Wessex megaliths. Stukely (1687–1765) produced a large number of panoramic illustrations during the early to mid-18th century that reveal the condition of the monuments and, in the case of Stonehenge, the agricultural regime. In some cases a methodology for the surveying of monuments is also provided. For Stukely and other artists, of course, romance and mysticism must also have played a role. The spread of antiquarianism can be accounted for in part by the fact that Neolithic chambered tombs and the monuments of the Bronze Age, particularly those of stone, offered the artist an ideal focus for any landscape composition, in some cases embellished by the liberal use of artistic licence.

The artistic movement in Wales focuses on a number of sites that have both a dramatic architecture and a dramatic backdrop. The Bachwen monument (CRN 7) (see page 35), painted in watercolour by Moses Griffith shows the portal dolmen with a series of outliers and recumbent stone centrally placed, with a backdrop of a field boundary and mountains beyond. The once recumbent stone and outliers are no longer present. To the right of the monument is an ancient bard paying homage to the monument, probably inferring druidical links.

Antiquarian drawing of Bachwen
(*Archaeologia Cambrensis*)

Richard Tongue, a painter from Bath, painted the most famous of all Welsh megalithic scenes, that of Pentre Ifan (PEM 5) (see page 35) in 1830. Like all painters of this period Tongue was concerned with what was going on around the megalith. As a result the subsequent researcher is shown the remains of a chamber outline within the centre of the monument. The backdrop appears to show a very rugged Mynydd Carningli. To the right of the picture is a peasant-like figure sitting on one of the outliers. This figure gives some idea of scale as well as a romantic feel to the painting.

Staying with the theme of 19th-century landscape painting and the dramatic changes to monuments since then, there is Pryce Carter Edwards' sepia drawing of the Gwernvale monument (BRE 7) painted in 1832. To the left of the monument is a track that is now the A40 trunk road between Talgarth and Crickhowell. The monument overlooks what can be regarded as a figment of the artist's imagination — the backdrop shows a dramatic mountainscape with what appears to be a lake between the monument and the intermediate slopes of the mountains. The actual view from this position is very much less dramatic. The drawing shows the monument consisting of a series of uprights with a supporting capstone. Nowadays, the chamber uprights still exist, but the capstone has long since gone. It could be the case that the capstone was considered to be part of the romantic image of the past and it is probable that Gwernvale no longer possessed any of its chamber or passage capstones when Edwards made his drawing.

Within the eight core areas of Wales 17th-, 18th- and 19th-century antiquarians have published a number of important volumes that give some insight as to how these monuments appeared. Some antiquarians have merely described what they have seen; others have gone somewhat further and excavated the monument. Most of the descriptive accounts occur during the mid- to late 18th century when Thomas Pennant undertook his *Tours in Wales*, published in 1783. His accounts are regarded as descriptively useful but are limited to monuments in north Wales. David Thomas's list of monuments in the *Cambrian Register*, published in 1799, provides a list of sites and shows the number that have been destroyed between the late 18th century and the publication of *Megalithic Enquiries* (1969).

The Reverend John Skinner's *Ten days' Tour through the Isle of Anglesea*, published in 1802, is an important account that describes a number of monuments, some of which have been completely destroyed whilst others have collapsed. It is probable that Skinner was in part influenced by earlier antiquarians such as Thomas Pennant and David Thomas. Accompanying Skinner's descriptions are a series of sketches and references to folklore. The sketches show each monument as a curiosity rather than a site of historical and archaeological interest. Yet Skinner also provides the best account of Bryn Celli Ddu (ANG 7) following the near destruction in 1780 of the western cairn, and the discovery of the chamber and passage of the eastern cairn during the mid-18th century.

With the birth of archaeology as a scientific discipline during the mid-19th century, journals such as *Archaeologia Cambrensis* started to reproduce

Arthur's Stone (HRF 1)   **Bachwen (CRN 7)**   **Pentre Ifan (PEM 5)**

engravings that concentrated purely on the monument. These engravings have proved to be invaluable when assessing the potential for excavation. For example, the mid-19th-century engraving of Bryn Celli Ddu shows the site to be in a ruinous state. Present is the central chamber with supporting capstone and a confused arrangement of stone, probably representing the remains of a passage. On top of the capstone there is what appears to be a mixed earthen cairn deposit that is probably the remains of the covering mound. The engraver has skillfully placed a shepherd figure close to the passage entrance in order to give some idea of scale. A similar noteworthy engraving is Henry Longueville's depiction of Ty Illtyd (BRE 6) in 1887. Again, the archaeologist is given some idea of the state of preservation of the site, a state that seems not to have changed since the late 19th century. Over a period of 50 years *Archaeologia Cambrensis* produced up to 40 illustrations showing the condition of Neolithic monuments throughout Wales. Accompanying these illustrations were in some cases quite detailed descriptions of both the monument architecture and, in cases where excavation was taking place, detailed accounts of the stratigraphy, in particular within the chamber areas. Some of these illustrations appear in this book.

I intimated earlier that Neolithic sites possess a history both before and after that of the monument itself. It has been stated, for example, that the chambers at Gwernvale (BRE 5) were used as sheep pens during the 18th and 19th centuries. Arthur's Stone (HRF1) and Penywyrlod (BRE 14) were used as quarries. In some cases the monument has been incorporated into later boundaries. One can therefore suggest that although the site has a physical presence, its meaning and status has changed. There is, however, a resurgence in Wales concerning the symbolic status of Neolithic burial monuments. Many will be aware that over the past 100 years stone circles have been erected that symbolise Welsh culture and identity through the annual gathering of the Eisteddfod. The revival of the Eisteddfod occurred in the late 18th century through the efforts of Edward Williams. Williams, also called Iolo Morgannwg, was obsessed with creating a mythical past for the Welsh. One aspect of this was the Gorsedd of the Bards that was first performed on Primrose Hill in London in 1792. Part of the ceremony included the throwing down of a circle of pebbles that symbolised a miniature stone circle in which Williams and his brethren could act out their rites. In 1819 Williams went to the Eisteddfod in Carmarthen with the same pebbles and created another stone circle within the grounds of the Ivy Bush Hotel. At this time the symbolism had little to do with chambered monuments and Druids. During the mid- to late 19th century, the Gorsedd of the Bards became firmly associated with the Eisteddfod, and every year a stone circle is constructed to commemorate the festival. Associated with the idea of ancient ancestry, in particular the lunar and solar cycles, many of the rites

Feasting and death in the façade at Pentre Ifan (illustration by Elle McQueen)

associated with the Eisteddfod are now performed around the Neolithic monuments. Interestingly, this concern with Welsh identity and religion has added to the history of such monuments.

Although one can appreciate the illustrations of both the antiquarian and the 19th-century archaeologist, one cannot detract from the systematic approaches of excavation and recording which first made its entrance during the late 19th and early 20th centuries through the recording methods of people such as E.N. Baynes, O.G.S. Crawford, W.J. Hemp and General Pitt-Rivers, to name but a few. One should also mention Sir Mortimer Wheeler who was Director of the National Museum of Wales and did much to professionalise archaeology during the early part of the 20th century.

Although systematic recording techniques were in place, many Neolithic sites were still excavated in an unsympathetic manner. For example, the Morfa Bychan monuments in Carmarthenshire (CAR 2–5) were each excavated (in 1910) within a couple of days. Similarly, the chambers of the Ffostyll North and South (BRE 3 and 4) monuments were 'dug' in 1921 in the space of two days in order to retrieve artifacts and record the chambers (but nothing else). The excavator was not interested in the stratigraphic sequence of the chamber deposits. As a result, the position of the entrances to the chambers is not fully understood. Despite this, there were a number of sites that were excavated throughout the 20th century that did receive a sympathetic approach.

Antiquarian drawing of Coetan Arthur,
(Archaeologia Cambrensis)

According to the inventories listed by Powell *et al.* (1969), Daniel (1950) and Grimes (1951) the majority of excavations and non-intrusive investigations took place between 1910 and 1975. In 1921, for example, W.E.T. Morgan and George Marshall, members of the Woolhope Naturalists' Field Club, excavated Pen-y-wyrlod (BRE 1)[8] to reveal a circular/oval mound some 11m in diameter. Within the centre of the mound was a simple rectangular terminal chamber that contained the remains of a number of individuals.

Close by, at Ty Isaf, W.F. Grimes excavated a 30m long trapezoidal cairn. The systematic excavation revealed a false portal, three chambers and associated passages along with two phases of monumentality. Within the chambers up to 33 individuals along with cremated bone and an array of artifacts were discovered. One of the most notable excavations was that of Pipton Long Cairn (BRE 8), excavated by H.N. Savory in 1949. Accompanying the report were a series of plans that gave an insight to the chamber architecture and the stratigraphy, in particular the location of artifacts and human remains within the chamber area.

This approach is all-important in understanding how burial practice may have been performed during the Neolithic. Accompanying the increasingly systematic approaches to excavation was the use of photography. Like its predecessors the engraving and the painting, photography gave an insight into the methodologies used in excavation. More importantly, the use of photography was able to curb fanciful speculation.

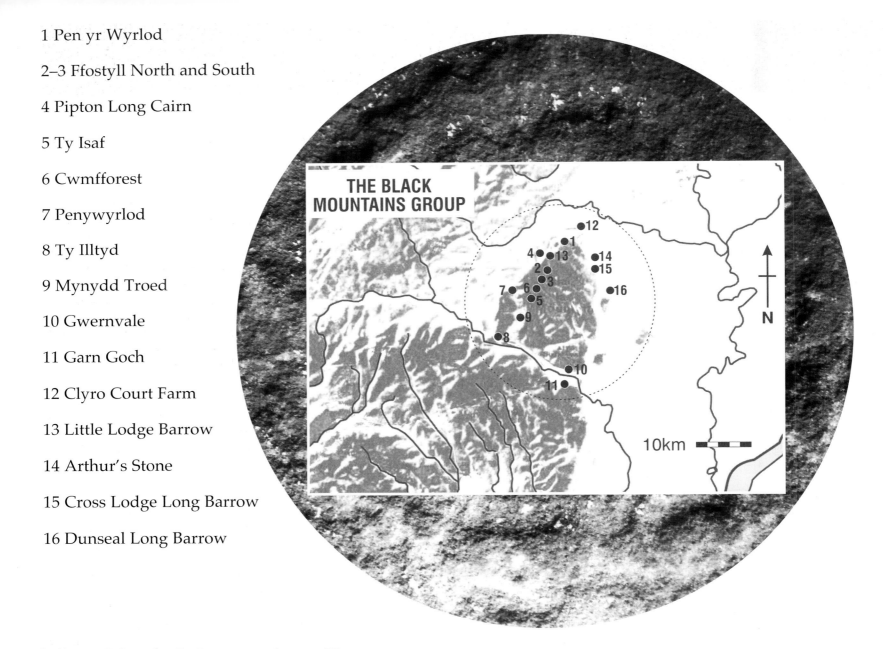

1 Pen yr Wyrlod

2–3 Ffostyll North and South

4 Pipton Long Cairn

5 Ty Isaf

6 Cwmfforest

7 Penywyrlod

8 Ty Illtyd

9 Mynydd Troed

10 Gwernvale

11 Garn Goch

12 Clyro Court Farm

13 Little Lodge Barrow

14 Arthur's Stone

15 Cross Lodge Long Barrow

16 Dunseal Long Barrow

THE BLACK MOUNTAINS GROUP

10km

N

The Black Mountains Group

Chapter Two: The Black Mountains Group

This group of monuments lies within the fertile hinterlands of the Black Mountains, a large, basal sandstone massif of some 35sq km which forms a boundary between the undulating valleys and lowland pastures of the Welsh Marches and the uplands of central Wales. The Black Mountains and the Brecon Beacons, both formed by Geological (Cenozoic) uplifting some 40 million years ago, form the mountain zone of Breconshire and are located mainly in the south and east of the county. The Black Mountains rise to over 600m and gently dip towards the south-south-east.

The solid geology consists mainly of Old Red Sandstone (fine marls, mudstones, siltstones and occasional sandstone conglomerates) formed 370 million years ago during the Devonian period, when much of the area was covered by a warm, brackish sea. The sandstone beds are up to 950m thick and the rocks have produced very little fossil evidence. To the south of the county, along the border with Monmouthshire, is an extensive outcrop of limestone and millstone grit dating from the Carboniferous period (280–345 million years ago).

The shaping of the landscape during the last ice age (referred to as the Late Devensian Glaciation) completes the geomorphological story. The rapid retreat of the Welsh Ice Cap left large accumulations of till (boulder clay deposits) and re-shaped the valley profiles, creating numerous fluvio-glacial landforms (such as eskers, kames, melt-water channels, moraines and ice-dammed lakes). Llangorse Lake and the classic U-shaped Cwm Sorgwm Valley, near Talgarth, are products of the glacial retreat around 14,500 BP. It is around these rich fertile valleys that encase the Black Mountains that one starts to witness the utilization of the landscape by people of the Neolithic, Webley (1959) suggesting that the freely drained base rich soils were a major factor in determining settlement.

According to the dating of lithics found at Gwernvale, this utilization of the landscape in fact commences during the Upper Palaeolithic. This continuous use of landscape is important inasmuch as the Neolithic cannot be considered in isolation. What we are probably witnessing is a gradual social, political and economic use of the valleys. During the Late Mesolithic and prior to monuments being constructed, the landscape would have been inhabited with small mobile hunter-gatherer groups that arguably would have seasonally 'farmed' the land (Children and Nash 2001, 14). The knowledge of when to harvest wild berries, fruits and nuts as well as hunting certain animals at certain times of the year would have been essential.

Monument building, which forms an integral part of the Neolithic package, would have derived from one of two ideologies; either there was a migration of people (supported by Case 1969; Stanford 1990; Savory 1980) or a migration of ideas. Migration of ideas would have involved contact and exchange networks with hunter-gatherers who imported, either directly or again indirectly, ideas from the Continent and Ireland. If the former is true, Britnell (1984, 3) has suggested that competition between Late Mesolithic hunter-gatherers and incoming migrating agriculturists may have created severe demand for land. I would suggest, however, that an invasion of ideas is the more likely course in that the eastern and central European agricultural revolution was very much ideologically fuelled by already well-established territorialised hunter-gatherer groups.

This group of monuments is the only inland group of chambered tombs in Wales and comprises 18 visible structures, five of which stand in neighbouring Herefordshire.[9] Four of the monuments provide the most detailed evidence of burial deposition within this group: Gwernvale (BRE 7) excavated by Britnell (Britnell 1984), Penywyrlod (BRE 14) excavated by Savory (Savory 1984), Pipton (BRE 8) excavated by Savory (Savory 1956) and Ty Isaf (BRE 5) excavated by Grimes (Grimes 1939). Human bone, usually found within the chamber and passage areas, is disarticulated and dervies from both sexes and all age groups. Heaps of human bone found in one of the chambers at Pipton Long Cairn have been interpreted as foundation deposits, possibly representing a symbolic offering following the construction of the monument. These bone heaps may have originally been placed within a wooden box made from pieces of timber tied together with twine (Atkinson 1961). I would also suggest that they represent secondary deposits which may have originated from other tombs. Overlying the bone heaps within each of the four monuments is evidence of deliberate in-filling of the chambers with soil; similar deposition has been found in the chambers at West Kennet Long Barrow (WILTS 4) (Piggott 1962, 68).

The first coherent account of this group was made by Crawford in 1925 and was later refined by Grimes in 1936. Early sources suggest there were once as many as 21 monuments around the rivers Dore, Rhiangoll, Usk and Wye (Crawford 1925, Daniel 1950, Powell *et al.* 1969, Nash 2000, Olding 2000). The majority of these monuments belong to the Cotswold-Severn tomb tradition (a term first coined by Daniel in 1937) and were either influenced by or influenced other tomb builders in regions to the east and south probably through contact/exchange links.

This monument group possesses a number of diagnostic architectural traits dating to the 3rd millennium BC that appear to have their origins in western France (Savory 1980, 222). Such traits include terminal and side chambers, passages leading to these chambers, a forecourt area and a false entrance (also referred to as a false portal); they are also built within an elongated or trapezoidal mound frequently enclosed by drystone walling.

The Black Mountains monuments exhibit a number of characteristics that are found outside the area to the south and east, embracing what is termed the Cotswold-Severn tradition (Britnell 1984, Children and Nash 1994, Olding 2000 and Nash 2000). However, Britnell argues that there is still no consensus as to how elements within the architecture, such as the forecourts, were used (1984, 7). Dating of the monuments is problematic in that only two have been radiocarbon dated: human bone for Penywyrlod (BRE 14) has been dated to around 3,020 bc, whilst radiocarbon dates from Gwernvale suggest that the monument was in use for up to 600 years; construction commencing around 3,100 bc with the last formal use of the monument at around 2,500 bc.

The group extends in an arc around the northern, western and south-western hinterlands of the Black Mountains. It is possible that further monuments to the south and south-east may exist and thus completely encircle the Black Mountains. Monuments appear to be locally oriented, either with the neighbouring valley or towards prominent features of the immediate landscape (Tilley 1994) and usually occupy the intermediate slopes facing the mountains. Beyond, there appears to be little or no Neolithic activity (Children and Nash 1994, 17).

A small number of the tombs are found on high upland ridges and plateaus, close to and in full view of the mountains, such as Ffostyll North and South (BRE 3 and 4) and Ty Isaf (BRE 5). To the north and east, the Wye and Dore provide a focus for eight monuments, including one,

Parkwood (HRF 2), that is now lost. Despite the significance of the Black Mountains to most monuments in the group, farther west are two monuments that appear to ignore their influence. Instead, both have commanding views over the Brecon Beacons and the lowland pastures of Llyn Llangors and Afon Honddu. Mynydd Troed (BRE 10) is one of the least impressive mounds, yet it is set in one of the most dramatic of all Black Mountains landscapes. Lying between the mountains of Mynydd Troed and Mynydd Llangors, the monument faces south-east towards Cwm Sorgwm and Pen Allt-mawr. It also has views to the west, towards Llyn Llangors. The area around the mound may have marked the transition from open scrub to woodland (Grimes 1932; 1936a), and if so, the mound would have been concealed from view, in spite of standing well over 254m AOD. However, clearing a swathe of vegetation from around the monument may have enhanced visibility. The oval mound is oriented north-east/south-west and encloses a simple terminal chamber and at least one other, but recent historical disturbance makes reconstruction near impossible. However, Mynydd Troed does resemble other monuments within the group, notably Ty Illtyd, Ffostyll North and Penywyrlod.

Outside the main group, but possibly associated territorially with Mynydd Troed, is the isolated Ty Illtyd (BRE 6). Positioned on a west-facing ridge approximately 6.6km due west of Mynydd Troed, Ty Illtyd incorporates a visual setting that includes the eastern portion of the Brecon Beacons. Both chamber and capstone are aligned towards Pen-y-Fan, the highest point in the Beacons. The monument is of a single capstone overlying a rectangular chamber delineated by eight uprights, and is set into a raised oval earth mound. The mound and chamber are oriented north/south with a small rectangular forecourt or ante-chamber at the northern end that has been interpreted as a second chamber (Corcoran 1969).

The southern and western monuments are not so concentrated together and follow a different pattern of construction. Here we may be witnessing a temporary development in monument design, indicating the importance of particular areas at different times. Several of these monuments appear to have been in use for long periods: Ty Isaf, near Talgarth, reveals evidence of multi-phase building, whilst Gwernvale, Crickhowell, shows that the site was periodically in use for up 6,500 years before the construction of the monument.

Only two tombs, Gwernvale and Carn Goch (BRE 12), near Crickhowell, stand close to the flood plain of the lower Usk Valley. Both are set on low ridges: Carn Goch takes Table Mountain (3km to the north-east) as its focus, while Gwernvale is aligned to the River Usk. Of the four passages at Gwernvale, three point towards the Usk and to local spurs and escarpments. The south-eastern passage is also slightly angled. A large doorway stone suggests visual access to the chamber was restricted, while the angled doorway hints at secret ritual-symbolic activity (see later). Similar passage plans are found at Arthur's Stone (HRF 1) and Pipton Long Cairn.

Finds from these monuments can be considered limited, which may be partly due to antiquarian plundering. The majority of finds originate from the four monuments that have received sympathetic excavation: Gwernvale, Penywyrlod, Pipton and Ty Isaf. A small but significant assemblage of finds including human remains has also come from Little Lodge Barrow (BRE 2). Only one flint was found in chamber I at Pipton whilst in chamber I at Ty Isaf two polished flint axes, a bone pin and pottery fragments were found and in chamber II there were six pottery vessels. Again, small assemblages were found in the chambers at Penywyrlod including part of a leaf-shaped arrowhead, a flint knife and a few sherds of pottery. The pottery from each of the monuments is classified according to Smith (1974, 108) as Abingdon ware, dating to the Early Neolithic. Interestingly, and in chronological sequence later Neolithic Ebbsfleet and Peterborough wares were associated with the blocking (abandonment) deposits at Gwernvale (Savory 1984, 6).

The Neolithic in Herefordshire is divided into two small but definite pockets: the largest in the Golden Valley that has the monuments and which forms part of the Black Mountains Group, and the Goodrich/Doward area that has no burial monuments. Both areas have yielded the majority of Neolithic finds in Herefordshire, including at least 30 polished stone and flint axes. Apart from Neolithic monuments and finds, earlier Mesolithic activity in the Golden Valley indicates the importance of this ancestral location over many generations (e.g. Gavin Robinson 1934). Such familiarity with the landscape would have involved social, economic and ritual knowledge, creating a sense of belonging and an identity.

There has been no recent excavation of any Herefordshire tomb, so very little bone, pottery or flint has been examined in context. This is unfortunate as the distribution of artifacts and the spatial arrangement of human and animal bone can reveal much about the symbolism surrounding burial. Farther west, at Ty Isaf (BRE 5), near Talgarth, the crushed bones of at least 17 individuals together with Neolithic pottery, a polished stone axe and a selection of flint arrowheads were arranged so as to suggest the deliberate

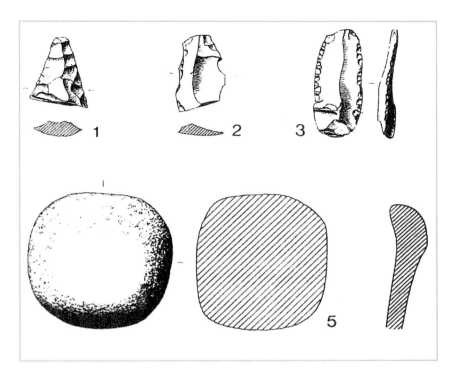

Artefacts from Penywyrlod include:
1–3 Lithics, 4–5 Stone tools, 6 Bone flute and 7 Pottery items
(Britnell and Savory 1984)

deposition of bodies with artifacts. Similar ways of burying the dead are practiced all over the world today. Even in Victorian Britain the dead were interred with small items of jewellery, having been prepared and dressed for their final journey.

Apart from the more obvious remains such as Arthur's Stone and Cross Lodge Long Barrow (HRF 4), other smaller, damaged monuments exist along the northern and eastern portions of the Golden Valley: Parkwood Chambered Cairn (HRF 2), Bach Long Barrow (HRF 5) and Dunseal Long Barrow (HRF 6). A number of standing stones within close vicinity of these monuments may be contemporary.

As with many other areas of high Neolithic activity, Herefordshire has revealed very little evidence of settlement. However, one notable example was discovered by field-walkers on Dorstone Hill, equidistant between

Arthur's Stone and Cross Lodge Long Barrow. Excavated by Christopher Houlder and Roger Pye between 1965 and 1970, this extensive settlement (NGR SO 326 423) covers approximately 18 acres. It was enclosed on the west side by a crude stone wall, on top of which was a wooden stockade fence. Storage pits were present (possibly used for grain), occupation floors and undisturbed 'buried soils', ideal for dating. Many finds were unearthed from within this ancient soil, including over 4,000 pieces of flint including arrowheads, pottery, and more than 50 polished stone axe fragments.

The stone and flint used to create these prestige items were, in part, imported from South Wales and the Cotswolds. The contact/exchange of axes and other commodities between these three areas highlights the importance and prestige of farming groups within the Golden Valley.

The size of the Dorstone settlement suggests that a large population, probably in excess of 250 people, occupied the upland areas of the Golden Valley during the Neolithic, utilising the slopes, ridges and tops of the eastern uplands from Merbach Hill in the north-east to Canns Hill in the south. By settling on the eastern hills, the community would have lived within full view of the Golden Valley and, more importantly, of the symbolically significant Black Mountains. Below, the fertile woodland of the valley floor would have been slowly cleared for allotment-style farming. More land would have been brought into production as the population grew. Remaining pockets of woodland scattered throughout the valley would have harboured red deer and wild boar, additional resources that could have been exploited by the Neolithic people in the same way as their Mesolithic hunter ancestors.

Pen yr Wyrlod, Llanigon

The Pen yr Wyrlod monument (BRE 1; SO 2248 3986) is located on a north-west facing slope, some 250m AOD. According to the RCAHMW (1997, 60) the monument is sited on the edge of farmland which was probably enclosed during the late 18th century; a field bank cuts across the north-western side of the mound and until 1991 was covered with trees. It is more than probable that the material from this field bank once derived from the mound. The site has been further damaged by a road that runs from the village of Llanigon and by local quarrying. Further re-shaping of the monument has been caused by excavation, in particular investigations by the Woolhope Club in 1921–1922 under the direction of the Reverend W.E.T. Morgan and George Marshall (1921). The excavation methodology has been heavily criticized.

The remains of this denuded monument comprise four sandstone uprights, measuring approximately 2m by 1m (the chamber uprights standing 1m above the existing ground level)[10] and traces of an elongated, pear-shaped mound, approximately 18.5m long and 9.6m wide. Presently, the uprights splay outwards suggesting that they would have supported a heavy capstone, certainly in 1898 a reference is made to the site being a Druidical Altar suggesting that a capstone was present (Morgan 1898, 40). It has been suggested that many if not all of the *in situ* uprights were reset during the excavation and this may have caused subsequent resettling and splaying outwards (RCAHMW 1997, 60).

During the 1921–1922 excavation, the mound was found to consist of large flat stones that were irregularly placed on top of one another (Morgan and Marshall 1921). Smaller stones were used as infill. This arrangement suggests that sections of drystone walling were in place, a style of architecture present on other Black Mountain sites.

The excavation of the terminal chamber revealed a black earth deposit that contained several human bones. More human bone was found at the base of the chamber, along with two black coarse potsherds.[11] The chamber base itself was constructed of irregular paving slabs. The bones can be considered the remains of a primary inhumation. Very few artifacts were found, but among them were fragments of 'rough pottery and a few flint flakes'. Vulliamy, and later, Gwynne investigated spoil heaps left by the excavators and found flint, traces of Beaker pottery, a Roman brass coin with the head of Crispus (dated AD 317–326),[12] and many blue glass beads and tubes believed to be from an early (possibly 6th-century) Anglo-Saxon or Romano-British burial. Sir Arthur Keith, responsible for the osteology of the 1921–1922 excavation, claimed that the bone and teeth represented up to 20 individuals including children of various ages, men and women.[13]

Pen yr Wyrlod looking north

However, the provenance of the bone material was difficult to determine due to poor excavation conditions. According to excavation records, a charcoal deposit was found to the south-east of the eastern chamber measuring up to 5cm in thickness.

A plan published by Vulliamy in 1922 suggests that the eastern chamber was an enclosed structure and access to it was via the top of the mound. However, the plan in Grimes (1936b, 275) argues that the remains of a passage may exist several metres to the north. Grimes's plan also shows the mound to be pear-shaped rather than oval.

At the north-western end of the mound there are traces of a small-chambered structure, consisting of three uprights, which would have supported a small roofing slab. Both Vulliamy and Grimes place a fourth stone in different places; either to the north or east of this small chamber respectively.

It has been suggested that the shape of the mound may be the result of multi-phased building activity, with the eastern section of the mound along with the chamber once forming a circular mound (Corcorcan 1969). If this were the case, Pen yr Wyrlod would have been in use over a long period

Pen yr Wyrlod looking south

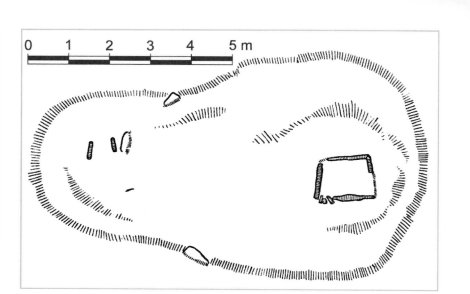

Plan of Pen yr Wyrlod (after Grimes 1936b)

of time, serving over many generations. However, the poor drawing record plus the disturbance made by the field bank, road and excavation makes any idea of such multi-phasing difficult to promote. I would suggest that Pen yr Wyrlod was constructed as a single-phased monument; mainly based on the idea that so many architectural traits found within this monument are present within other single-phased monuments.

Its position within the landscape suggests a symbolic strategic importance, in that the orientation of the mound (south-west/north-east) follows the orientation of the Wye Valley. The tomb also stands on a high, truncated spur with views across the valleys of the Wye and Llynfi, but it is not intervisible with the Neolithic monument at Clyro Court Farm (3.5km), nor Little Lodge Barrow (4.7km) and Pipton Long Barrow (7km). It would appear that Pen yr Wyrlod was sited in order to control the hinterlands to the west. Ironically, one only has to walk a few paces north in order to achieve intervisibility with Clyro Court Farm, its closest neighbour.

Ffostyll North (BRE 3; SO 1791 3495) and South (BRE 4; SO 1789 3489)
stand about 70m apart in a field some 200m north of Ffostyll Farm. The two
barrows are around 312m AOD. The mounds have been widely reported
since the mid-19th century when, in 1842, Reverend T. Price observed that:

> ... the most notable grave mounds I saw in Wales are in the parish of
> Llanelieu, Brecknockshire, on the land of the farm called Ffos-t-yll. The
> biggest of these mounds is 45 yards [41m] long, 20 yards [18m] wide
> and about two yards [1.8m] high; and they showed that they were full
> of cistvaens [cists or small chambers] of the same size — one of which
> was lately broken for the sake of the stones. There are still enough left
> to show its size its workmanship. It was 10 feet long, five feet wide and
> eight feet deep, formed of great stones one at each end and two at
> each side and covered with corresponding stones.

Both monuments, along with others within the group, were subjected to
poor excavation especially during the early part of the 20th century. Indeed,
O.G.S. Crawford unsuccessfully attempted to impose statutory protection
for both monuments in order to prevent any further damage to the mounds
following Vulliamy's excavation of 1921–1923. However, evidence of earlier
destruction of these monuments dates back to the late 19th century when
it was reported by the owner of Ffostyll Farm that the southern mound had
been quarried for road ballast around 1875. As a result of the quarrying,
human bone had allegedly been found and the height of the mound greatly
reduced.

The monuments are directionally opposed: Ffostyll North (BRE 3) is
oriented roughly east/west, while Ffostyll South has a north/south orientation. The latter, the smallest and best preserved of the pair, has a single 3m
gallery-type chamber at the north-eastern end. Here, ten uprights support
two dislodged capstones. According to Vulliamy, who investigated the
mounds in three very brief seasons between 1921–1923, both had been
disturbed (1923). He remarks:

> At first glance the southern one appeared to have suffered a more
> searching devastation. Here, we have found that a vast amount of stone
> had been moved from the southern end, and there was considerable
> disturbance which I expected to contain the principal cist. Furthermore,

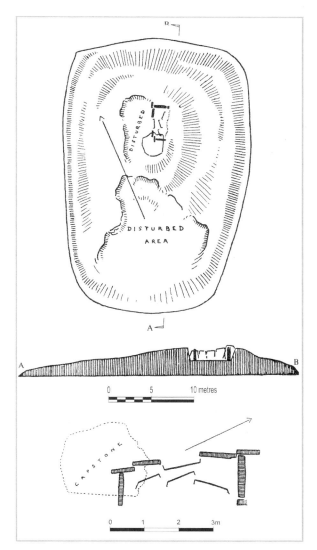

Plan and cross section Ffostyll South (Vulliamy 1929)

Ffostyll South looking west

a large covering stone lay tilted on the face of the mound. On examination, I came to the conclusion that neither of these disturbances had touched the burial chamber, which, though its form was not clear, was traceable in the centre of the highest part of the barrow. From information supplied by Mr Gwillym the tenant of the farm, I learned that the stone had been removed from the lower southern-end of the barrow about forty-five years ago [c.1875], to supply material for road-making; and at that time quantities of human bone had come to light.

Ffostyll South

According to the RCAHMW (1997, 41), the Ffostyll South monument measures 36m in length by 23m in width and is oriented north-north-east/south-south-west. However, it should be noted that at the southern terminal end there is an extensive rubble spread that distorts the actual shape of the mound. The rubble may be the result of spoil generated by the Vulliamy excavation.[14]

This monument was excavated on 20th September 1921, the excavation lasting just four days! An entire 'cist', measuring 3.35m long by 1.2m wide with displaced roofing slab (measuring 2.4m x 2.1m), was uncovered. According to excavation records, the eastern section of the chamber had collapsed inwards revealing a series of individual slabs with a maximum height of 2m. Revealed within the chamber were at least two deposits. Located at the base of the chamber was a layer of burnt human bone, and a limited assemblage of domestic animal bone including those of a cat, and some bones which could not be properly identified. Overlying this was a further burnt charcoal deposit that contained mainly the remains of domesticated animals such as goat, ox and pig. According to Vulliamy (1923):

> The bones were in the utmost confusion; only in a few instances were they in anatomical relation to each other, and by far the greater number were split and broken. Some of the bones were wedged between the surrounding stones. The remains included 70 fragments of cranium and lower jaw (mandible), 36 metacarpals, metatarsals and phalanges, six vertebrae, 30 detached teeth, 135 fragments of long bone and 240 unidentified fragments, including non-human remains. Subsequent osteological analysis revealed some interesting characteristics: there was a man of about forty years old, whose head was very narrow, relatively high, and rather small. There was an old woman who must have had a face cast in a small, almost delicate mould. There was another man with a prominent ridge over his

eyes; and there were children. In no instance was there a complete skeleton. All the individuals were short, the adult males being about 5 feet 4 inches in height. (1923, 162).

It was concluded that the bone material represented at least nine individuals.[15] Sir Arthur Keith, of the Royal College of Surgeons, commented on the pathology of the bones, suggesting that the material was typical 'of an ancient date' (it must be remembered that radiocarbon dating was not available during the 1920s). No traces of pottery were discovered, but three pieces of flint were found in the cist.

Vulliamy also excavated the chamber at the northern end revealing more cremated remains, including those of an adult and very young child, as well as pig or goat. Fragments of crude, black pottery (later interpreted as the remains of a round-bottomed bowl of Neolithic A type) and 17 pieces of flint and chert were also recovered, all of which had been burnt (1923, 320–324). Vulliamy noted a surprisingly low number of vertebrae within the skeletal assemblage. Indeed, a large percentage of bone material was absent, suggesting Ffostyll South (and North) may have been a final ancestral resting place. This monument may have had a similar purpose, therefore, as that of the Neolithic monument at Quanterness, on Orkney, where ancestral bones were moved around the landscape from tomb to tomb, before eventually coming to rest in the largest monument within a specified group (Renfrew 1979). Interestingly, the Ffostyll monuments are indeed the largest, most visible and, arguably, the most central to monument activity within the Black Mountains group.

Ffostyll North

The larger northern mound is considered multi-phase and possibly trapezoidal in plan (Corcoran 1969). The mound, which has been damaged by excavation and livestock, incorporates three chambers. A destroyed eastern chamber consists of five upright stones of local sandstone, with no surviving capstone. Two further chambers are located centrally and at the south-western end. Unfortunately, none of the chambers has evidence of a passage. The main chamber contained human remains and those of horse,

Ffostyll North

dog, ox and pig. These were found over the chamber floor in undisturbed deposits, some of them retaining their correct anatomical relationship. Flint flakes and pottery fragments were also recovered. Vulliamy (1923, 163) describes the human remains thus:

> One of the men had been the possessor of massive thigh-bones, and a remarkably heavy but well-modeled jaw. The neck-bones of a woman showed that she had suffered from rheumatism. Two of the burials were those of children, six and eleven years of age.

The northern mound is positioned slightly higher up-slope than Ffostyll South so may be considered the dominant monument and perhaps the earlier. Although directionally opposed, this pair of monuments may be considered to encompass a complete landscape with extensive views to the east, west and south.

The remains of Pipton Long Cairn (BRE 8; SO 1604 3727) consisting of a single upright and disturbed cairn material, stand at around 145m AOD in the corner of an east-facing field and overlook the north-western extent of the Black Mountains. The monument, one of four known hybrid Cotswold-Severn monuments within this group, stands between the River Wye and its tributary the Afon Llynfi. The site was excavated by H.N. Savory in 1956.

The topography of the area is similar to the surroundings of other nearby tombs. Ffostyll North and South, Little Lodge Barrow and Pipton all appear to acknowledge corresponding features within the landscape — the spurs of Y Das and Hay Bluff. This small group of monuments also shares intervisibility. The monuments of Penywyrlod, Ffostyll North (BRE 3) and South (BRE 4), and Little Lodge Barrow (BRE 2) can be clearly seen from Pipton. The cluster may, therefore, constitute a territory.

The mound, once covered with trees and thought to be originally oval in shape (Grimes 1936b, 269), measures 37m in length and 22m in width.[16] The mound was delineated by a drystone revetment wall (first published in 1925 and later excavated by H.N. Savory). In fact trapezoidal in shape, the mound has two horns and a 'dummy' or false portal at the northern end. These features are also found at Penywyrlod (BRE 14), Ty Isaf (BRE 5) and Gwernvale (BRE 7). There is evidence to suggest the monument may have been constructed in a number of phases; a circular structure at the end of the monument may predate the main mound. This feature is recognized as an internal revetment wall that may have been of structural use in supporting the inner cairn, whilst the outer revetment wall was merely cosmetic. Both revetment walls, a feature also found at Gwernvale, Penywyrlod and Ty Isaf, would have been constructed as a single phase. The mound is oriented roughly north/south and overlooks the River Wye.

There are a number of similarities with other monuments within the Black Mountains Group. For example, Arthur's Stone (HRF 1) has an identical T-shaped northern chamber and passage arrangement. The west-facing passage, centrally placed within the cairn fabric, is angled in two places, with two door-stones, thereby inhibiting visual access. The passage entrance, which is on the north side, has a small sill formed by a series of upright slabs

and is narrower than the central, deeper sections. Headroom within the main chamber (also referred to as 'the gallery') was, like Arthur's Stone, around 1.3m. The chamber is divided into two. A north transept, measuring 3.5m x 1m, is further sub-divided by a door-stone halfway along its length. The smaller south transept, measuring 1m x 0.8m, was blocked by a single (door-stone) slab. A second chamber (Chamber II), measures internally 1.9m x 1m, faces south-west and has no passage. However, an earlier phase of construction has been recognized (Savory 1956). The second chamber may be a closed cist, entered from above, suggesting that a passage would not be necessary. The outer cairn may originally have attained a height of nearly 2m (RCAHMW 1998, 49).

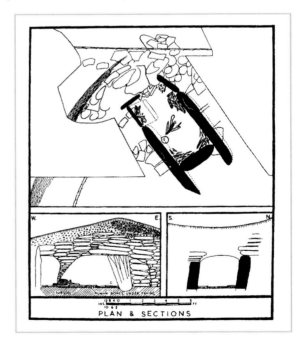

Pipton Long cairn: plan and sections of the chamber area (after Savory 1956)

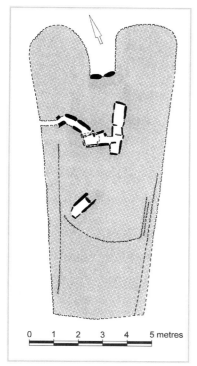

Plan of Pipton Long Cairn

Pipton Long Cairn looking east towards the Black Mountains

The plan suggests a similarity with the multi-phase construction at Ty Isaf. At the terminal end of the mound on the south-western side, are two canted slabs which may be an earlier architectural feature. Prior to construction, the ground was carefully prepared. On the southern side, earth was scooped away to create a level surface. Charcoal, sandstone chips and a piece of unidentifiable Neolithic pottery was found within this context. Whilst the sandstone fragments may be associated with the building process, the charcoal could be the remains of ritual activity associated with the preparation of the ground. Savory also noted a number of low upright stones that appear to have had no structural significance and which may be interpreted as marker stones delineating this section of the monument (Savory 1956). Like other monuments within the group, the chambers were surrounded by a cairn of angular sandstone blocks and flags. Water-rolled blocks and pebbles would have been brought up from the nearby Afon Llynfi. The mound is supported by a series of revetment walls that may represent different construction phases. The inner revetment appears to be more crudely constructed than the outer wall, which, in places, rises to 24 courses and a height of 0.75m. A need to amplify monumentality in order to create something more visually impressive (see also the plan of Ty Isaf) could be in evidence here, as elsewhere within the Cotswold-Severn region. Alternatively, the reason could be structural rather than aesthetic (Children and Nash 2001).

In Chamber I and the passage, an incomplete assemblage of disarticulated human bone was found beneath the floor slabs of the south transept, representing possibly four individuals. Human, as well as animal bone and a flint flake were found in the passage area. Human bone was also discovered beneath the floor of Chamber II and seven bone heaps representing possibly seven individuals were placed against the side wall of the chamber. Covering the bone was a layer of earth, which may have been introduced as part of an interment ritual. The bone may have come from elsewhere (Savory 1956); and if so Pipton was either the final abode of the dead or an interim resting place.

One of the more carefully excavated tombs in Wales, Ty Isaf (BRE 5; SO 1819 2906) stands on a small east-facing ridge in a field above a farm at around 211m AOD. The monument was excavated in 1938 by W.F. Grimes and is regarded as a Cotswold-Severn type monument (1939a). Typically, it has a complex series of chambers and passages set within a trapezoidal mound (oriented north/south), a false portal or doorway, extended horns and a deeply recessed forecourt area. Although the excavation plan is complex, today the remains comprise a few protruding uprights and traces of an elongated mound (30m x 18m). However, the monument's landscape setting may be regarded as an important element of its overall meaning.

The monument, sited on a small knoll and close to two small streams is set in one of the most dramatic landscapes within the Black Mountains Group. The land rises steeply to the east and west; Mynydd Troed to the west reaches 609m AOD and Waun Fach to the east rises to 811m AOD. To the north and within view is a circular knoll on which an Iron Age hill enclosure stands. According to Grimes (1936b, 263), located between the hill enclosure and Ty Isaf is the remains of primeval woodland.[17] It is within this woodland that the badly damaged Cwmfforest monument stands (BRE 9). Grimes postulates, correctly in my view, that (damp oak) woodland would have extended over the site of Ty Iasf and that extensive clearance would have been necessary in order to construct this monument (ibid., 264).

The plan reveals that Ty Isaf is a multi-phase monument, with at least three phases of construction and use. The earliest phase consists of a small round cairn, about 12m in diameter, at the southern end of the mound. Within the cairn, a passage runs south-east and the chamber is oriented south-west/north-east. The cairn has been seen as an addition to the larger mound (Corcoran 1969), but it is probably the earliest structure (Castleden 1992). The larger northern mound, which contains two chambers (with passages), and a curious false portal (or doorway) at the northern end, between two horns, probably represents the second phase of construction. The mound itself has a double drystone revetment wall. The monument is very similar in terms of plan and orientation to Pipton Long Barrow (BRE 8), another hybrid tomb in this group. The lateral passages open out towards

Mynydd Troed, to the west, and Waun Fach, to the east, whilst 100m or so to the west the Afon Rhiangoll flows southwards. These landscape features may be symbolic components of the overall plan.

Ty Isaf has revealed much information about the treatment of the dead during the Neolithic. The crushed bones of 17 of the 33 individuals recovered from the tomb were found in the western chamber,[18] accompanied by leaf-shaped arrowheads, a flint axe and undecorated Neolithic pottery, while the eastern chamber contained a possible complete skeleton and at least six Western (Neolithic) bowls. A light grey, asymmetrical lozenge-shaped, partially polished and ground axe was also found (Grimes 1939b, 130–132). Savory (1980, 219) suggests that bones form this and other Cotswold-Severn monuments may represent a re-burial phase, either orig-

Ty Isaf looking south-east

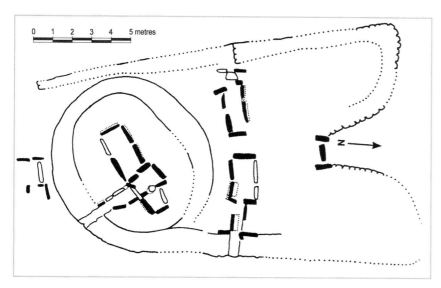

Plan of Ty Isaf (after Grimes 1939a)

inating from other chambers within the monument or from other monuments. The crushed bones appeared to be deliberately placed in small piles against the sides of the chamber, as well as in niches between the chamber walls and the uprights. In contrast, the remains of two articulated skeletons were recovered from the passage area of lateral chamber II on the eastern side of the mound. A sandstone pendant with an hour-glass-type perforation (25mm in diameter) and more pottery were found near the entrance of this chamber. Pottery was also recovered from the old land surface against a section of the eastern wall. The chamber and passage of the southern circular cairn (chamber III) contained the remains of five individuals with the articulated remains of a further four individuals inside the passage. The burials in the passage may have been the last to be interred.

A small isolated and heavily disturbed chamber (chamber IV) at the southern end, representing the final construction phase, contained a middle Bronze Age cremation urn and a series of burnt wooden boxes. The successive phases of building and the varied manner in which the dead were interred suggest Ty Isaf remained in use for hundreds of years; certainly throughout the latter part of the Neolithic and the Early Bronze Age.

This monument, (BRE 9; SO 1833 2944) is sited around 300m north of Ty Isaf (BRE 5), close to the Afon Rhiangoll. Discovered in 1924, only some drystone walling and a large capstone are visible today (Grimes 1939a). Crawford, who visited the site with Mortimer Wheeler (1925, 54–55), complained that the monument was very difficult to find and its precise location had to be pointed out by the owner of Ty Isaf Farm. At that time, it was hidden in 'a dense thicket of brambles and young saplings' (ibid., 54). Crawford claimed that the chamber, said to be exposed at the south-eastern end of the mound, was built of drystone walling, with the capstone set over the chamber; both centrally placed within a small mound oriented south-east/north-west. The south-eastern end of the mound is narrower and Crawford felt it may have formed an entrance passage to the chamber, an observation that has subsequently been reinforced (Corcoran 1969). A steep ditch or gully lies parallel to the mound and within it are a number of cairn stones that probably formed part of the outer covering of the monument.

Cwmfforest and Ty Isaf share a dramatic valley/pass landscape and are also similar architecturally (Castleden 1992). Therefore, they may have been in use at the same time, but like Ffostyll North and South (BRE 3 and 4), performing different social and symbolic roles within their communities.

The recently published RCAHMW volume suggests the Cwmfforest monument is in fact the remains of a corn-drying kiln that is constructed of a 'rectangular kiln chamber and low, slab-roofed flue passage facing into the river gorge below' (1997, 65). However, conversations with local landowners cannot recall the structure having been used as a corn drying kiln. Furthermore, it should be noted that with the altitude of this monument at 274m AOD and local land use devoted mainly to sheep grazing, it is unlikely that any corn was dried in the immediate area.

Penywyrlod, Talgarth

Standing 253m AOD on the crest of a ridge above the Afon Llynfi valley, the monument (BRE 14; SO 1505 3156) is clearly valley aligned, although the orientation is directly towards Mynydd Troed. Also worth noting is that the monument is intervisible with three other nearby tombs: Ffostyll North and South (BRE 3 and 4) and Pipton Long Cairn (BRE 8). All are similar architecturally and appear to share an affinity in terms of landscape topography and valley alignment.

Not to be confused with Pen yr Wyrlod (BRE 1), Llanigon, this monument stands on a small rise overlooking Mynydd Troed. Partly hidden by tree cover, Penywyrlod was discovered during quarrying when human remains were reported to the National Museum of Wales on 27th June 1972. It was excavated later that year by H.N. Savory. The mound, one of the largest in the Black Mountains Group, is considered a laterally-chambered hybrid-type of the later Cotswold-Severn design; in other words, constructed as a single phase monument (Savory 1984). The mound is oriented roughly north/south, whilst three chambers (referred to as Chambers NE I, NE II and NE III) with associated passages open out towards the Black Mountains. The western side of the monument that opens out towards the Brecon Beacons was not excavated. Previous comments by Children and Nash (2001, 66) have incorrectly stated that no chamber activity existed on this side of the mound. However, there is evidence of a large chamber located immediately west of Chamber NE I that would have opened out towards the Brecon Beacons.[19] Further chambers on the western side of the mound may exist which symmetrically oppose chambers of the eastern side.

Quarrying had nearly destroyed one chamber (NE I), exposed another (NE II) and revealed a false portal and central chamber lying beyond the main axis. Quarrying had also revealed sections of the original outline of the mound, which incorporated substantial revetment walling at the north-eastern end and south-eastern forecourt area. Exposed within this excavation trench was a probable lintel stone that was found lying in the central area of the forecourt. This stone probably once lay on top of three portal stones that form a false portal, located between the horns. Also recovered were small fragments of human skull, some of which were burnt, that may represent some form of excarnation activity. A temporary timber mortuary structure, similar to that found from post-hole evidence within the forecourt area at Gwernvale, may have been utilised (Britnell 1984, 6).

Excavation trenches at both ends of the axis suggest the mound measured 52m x 22.5m. A total of five trenches, mainly along the north-east side of the mound, were excavated and exposed three side-chambers, the inner remains of a western (main) chamber and the revetment wall of the north-eastern horn. The unexcavated western chamber, which probably opens out to the west, comprises two uprights (still visible) and is in-filled with earth and sandstone. I would suggest that this is not a 'main' chamber but a side chamber similar to NE I or NE II. Savory's excavation report suggests these were tilted inwards in order to support a large capstone(s) (1984). This structure was covered by a sandstone rubble block and slab cairn that consisted of two building phases, and sections of the revetment wall that delineates the cairn survive up to 0.3m in height. Savory (1984) suggests that these revetment walls would have not exceed 0.5m. However, the revetment walls around the forecourt area are considerably higher, measuring up to 1.5m in height.

The north-eastern chamber (NE I) had been almost totally destroyed, only the plan of the western section of the chamber appeared to show any form. The chamber formed two separate compartments measuring 2m x 1.2m and 1.6m x 1m. The latter was entered from a short passage between two revetment walls. Fallen uprights indicated that a second chamber (NE II) which measured 2.85m x 1m x 1.3m was located 9m north-west of chamber NE I. A slab sealed the chamber, giving the impression of a false entrance, a feature commonly found within the Cotswold-Severn region. The two chamber compartments of NE II were comprised of 10 uprights and the whole was entered by a short passage opening out to the west. The third excavated chamber (NE III) lay at the end and revealed an entrance with revetment walls that supported a capstone.

The human remains from chamber NE I are considered to represent a dedicatory deposit. Disarticulated human bone, possibly representing more than six individuals, was recovered from chamber NE II where long bones

Penywyrlod looking south towards Mynydd Troed. The visible cairn is exposed due to quarrying

were piled against the base of the side-walls. This structure may be the remains of an ossuary deposit (RCAHMW 1997, 40). In chamber NE III, the fragmented remains of seven individuals were found. A further two partial skeletons were found in various deposits within the entrance blocking. Within the entrance area of chamber NE III, a further possible ossuary deposit was discovered. A flint knife, a bone flute and many animal bones were also found within this chamber. In addition, several fragments of Abingdon ware were recovered from within the same chamber area, beneath the entrance.

The incomplete bone flute found within the entrance of chamber NE III is regarded as one of Britain's oldest musical instruments, radiocarbon dated to 3020±80 bc. The bone from which it is made comes from an ovicaprid (sheep) metapodial, measures 74mm in length and has three punched holes.

Savory concludes that chambers NE I and NE II were utilised and sealed when the monument was first constructed. Further bone deposits found within a small cist located underneath the north-eastern horn may represent foundation activity whereby human remains rather than building stone legitimises the place as a site for burial.

Ty Illtyd (also known as Ty Illtud and Maen Iltyd) (BRE 6; SO 0984 2638) stands opposite Manest Court Farm, approximately 215m AOD, on a west-facing ridge. Although classified within the Black Mountains Group, it stands apart and appears to take the Brecon Beacons as its focus, overlooking the flood plain of the Usk and the eastern extent of the Brecon Beacons. Both chamber and capstone are aligned towards Pen-y-Fan, the highest point of the Beacons. John Aubrey first investigated the site in the 17th century and was followed by Edward Lhwyd, who described the monument as having three uprights and a capstone, with clear graffiti on both side stones leading to the chamber. He also noticed that the chamber stood within a circular structure/mound.

The monument itself comprises a single capstone overlying a rectangular chamber delineated by eight uprights which are set into a raised, oval, earthen mound measuring 23m (north/south) × 15.7m (east/west). The mound slopes away to the south and west and the chamber, measuring 1m × 2m, is oriented north/south, with a small rectangular forecourt or ante-chamber at the northern end, which may be a second chamber (Corcoran 1969). Rather than repeat an apparently endless set of dimensions (RCAHMW 1997), it is perhaps sufficient to draw attention to an engraving by Henry Longueville Jones (1867) which clearly shows the uprights and capstone. The two outer uprights depicted may represent the inner sections of two horns.

Five uprights are inscribed with what appear to be medieval graffiti, including a harp (five-stringed lyre) and the dates 1312 (in Roman numerals) and 1510. A side-chamber upright bears at least eight crosses and what are presumed to be personal initials. Another has at least 60 carvings, mostly lozenges, diamonds and crosses. Longueville Jones (*Archaeologia Cambrensis* 1867, 347–355) considered them to be the work of 'shepherd boys'. O.G.S. Crawford (1925, 156) and the Abbé Breuil (in RCAHMW 1997, fig.16) have argued that some of the graffiti is prehistoric and possibly contemporary with the use of the tomb. On the other hand, the graffiti are similar to masons' marks contemporary with the robbing of the monument for building stone (RCAHMW). However, Grinsell (1981, 131–139) thought the tomb had been re-used by St Illtyd as a hermit's cell and that the symbols are there-fore medieval in date. The marks, as illustrated, are now thought not to be prehistoric for there are no direct parallels with prehistoric art elsewhere. However, this is no 'idle graffiti'. If the crosses are Christian, they may signify a refuge against religious persecution, similar to incised art I have found in caves around the Cathar region of South-West France.

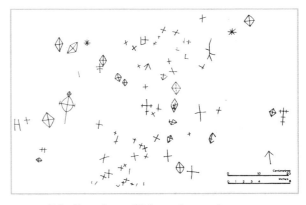

Medieval graffiti on the orthostats
(RCAHMW 1997, *Archaeologia Cambrensis* 1981)

Ty Illtyd: an engraving by Henry Longueville
(from *Archaeologia Cambrensis*)

Ty Illtyd, looking west towards the Brecon Beacons

Mynydd Troed, Talgarth

Mynydd Troed (BRE 10; SO 1615 2843), one of the less impressive monuments within the Black Mountains group, stands 350m AOD at the foot of Mynydd Troed, and is the highest within the group. The site was discovered by O.G.S. Crawford in 1921 and sketched by Grimes in 1926. The sketch shows three possible uprights and three exposed stone faces within the centre of the mound as well as extensive disturbance within the southern section. In 1966 Crampton and Webley excavated a series of sections that were cut in the mound's western and eastern sides in order to locate any walling and to take environmental samples (Caseldine 1990, 49–54). The excavation duly identified 22 courses of drystone perimeter wall approximately 0.43m high and 11m long (Crawford 1925), which had collapsed on the western side but was protected by 'a canted pile of slabs' on the eastern side (ibid., 35). The wall was similar to that recorded at Gwernvale (BRE 7). The excavation also produced cherty flint flakes and a range of Neolithic pottery similar to types found at Ty Isaf.

Three definite hollows within the mound structure may represent chambers, the tops of a number of upright stones being visible in two of the hollows. Past interpretation suggests the stone alignments within the mound core represent a terminal chamber, although they may be the remains of a western passage that led to a central chamber. Had it not been for extensive recent disturbance, especially within the northern section, investigations may have revealed further passage and chamber alignments and an overall plan to rival nearby Ty Isaf (BRE 5) in complexity. It is precisely because the monument is so poorly preserved that very little has been said about it, but it does have architectural similarities with nearby Pen yr Wyrlod, Ffostyll North (BRE 3) and Ty Illtyd (BRE 6). Looking beyond the confines of the monument, however, more can be said, as Mynydd Troed is set within an impressive landscape. The monument stands between Mynydd Troed and Mynydd Llangorse, facing south-east towards Cwm Sorgwm and Pen Allt-mawr. Views westwards take in Llangorse lake and the surrounding hinterlands. Ty Illtyd (BRE 6) and Mynydd Troed (BRE 10) are equidistant, suggesting the monuments may be linked territorially.

The area around the mound marks the boundary between open scrub and woodland (Grimes 1936b, 265). In spite of the monument standing

Mynydd Troed looking south-east.
Mynydd Troed (the mountain) lies to the east

around 350m AOD, such a location would have inhibited visual access. If Mynydd Troed was constructed in order to be seen, as it probably was, a large area of scrub and woodland must have been cleared by the users of the monument in order to expose the mound to the surrounding landscape.

Gwernvale (BRE 7; SO 2110 1920), a hybrid Cotswold-Severn monument, has been excavated many times, on the most recent occasion by William Britnell in 1978 (Britnell 1979, 132–134; Britnell 1984, 42–154). Prior to this excavation, it was thought that very little of the monument had survived, for since early Post-Medieval times a main arterial route between the Marches and central and south-east Wales had cut into the northern section of the mound, destroying cairn revetment walling and the northern horn.

Gwernvale aroused some early interest from Theophilus Jones, who, in 1804, remarked:

> This cromlech, one end of which adjoined the Brecon turnpike road on the south side, was immediately opposite Gwernvale, about half-a-mile from Crickhowell: it consisted as usual of a huge tablet of unhewn stone mounted upon five supporters pitched edgewise in the ground, the super incumbent stone or cover inclining to the south and open in the front to the north; it was placed on a high mound, long overrun with brushwood and brambles, and formerly there seem to have been stones placed edgewise also round what is now almost a semicircle; whether before the turnpike road was made they extended it so as to describe an irregular circle I know not; but I am inclined to think that the appearance of the spot was materially altered by the intersection of the highway; and that upon that occasion the workmen ... anticipated our attempt to make discoveries under the cromlech; in that case the object, though far different from ours, was probably equally unsuccessful ... The experiment in 1804 proved nothing either way (as to the sepulchral or other object of the cromlech).

A quite different account, from the unpublished diary of Sir Richard Colt Hoare, states:

> Saturday May 26th 1803. This morning was devoted to opening a cromlech or kistvaen adjoining the turnpike road near Crickhowell and opposite the house of Mr Everest with some difficulty the upper stone measuring ten feet in length, being removed, we dug to the base of the surrounding upright stones, which had supported the recumbent one, but found no signs of an internment or relics; but a few pieces of charcoal seemed to indicate cremation. The history of the cromlech has not as yet been sufficiently ascertained, and it remains a doubt whether it

was designed for an altar or sepulchre. The kistvaen or stone chest was clearly designed for an interment.

O.G.S. Crawford (1925, 60) noticed the chamber was being used as 'a receptacle for old pails, bottles and jam jars'.

Gwernvale and nearby Carn Goch (BRE 12) are valley monuments which stand on river terrace gravels and sand respectively (Grimes 1936b, 265). The site, standing at around 69m AOD was occupied, albeit periodically, for at least 6,500 years prior to the construction of the long cairn during the Neolithic. The discovery underneath the southern section of the cairn and within the forecourt area of Late Upper Palaeolithic flint suggests the site was long utilised as an encampment. The encampment may have been sited along an ancestral migratory route used seasonally by megafauna such as elk, horse and reindeer. Small hunter-gatherer groups may have used the site and its immediate area to make tools and utilise the carcasses

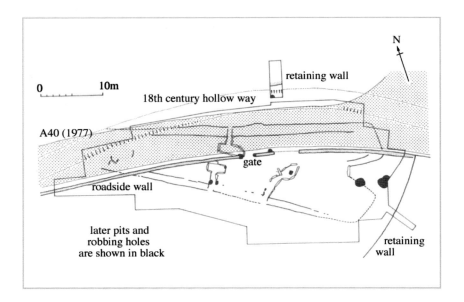

Plan of Gwernvale (after Britnell 1984)

of hunted animals, similar to sites like the Meindorf and Stellmoor stations in northern Germany where significant reindeer carcass utilisation is evident (Grønnow 1987). Diagnostic tools included backed blades. Early and Late Mesolithic flint was also found within the same areas of the site suggesting a spatial continuity between periods. This specialised tool kit, used for different hunting needs, included finished and unfinished microliths, microburins, notched and truncated flakes and awls (Healey and Green 1984, 113–132).

Forty-five meters in length and standing on a low west-facing terrace, the mound was once thought to be circular in form (Fenton 1804, Crawford 1925). At the eastern end are two horns and a false portal. Two lateral chambers at the southern end of the mound are both clearly visible, the largest chamber comprising six large uprights. A passage opens towards two dominant topographic features: the River Usk and Mynydd Llangatwg in the south-west. A third chamber has been badly damaged and a small single chamber on the northern side has also been noted.

Very few human remains were found during the 1978 excavation; it is believed many were removed during the 1804 excavation. Nevertheless, human bone was found in all four chambers, and skull fragments within timber-revetted bedding trenches formed when the mound was constructed that extended beneath the northern section of the monument. The monument itself is built over an earlier Neolithic settlement, four pits, associated pottery and the remains of two rectangular buildings have been found. Evidence of intensive early farming activity has been dated to 3,900 BC (Burnham 1995, 15). Two rows of three post-holes, probably forming a six post-hole structure, were found within the forecourt area, beneath the northern horn. These post-holes were located within two clear timber bedding trenches and may represent an early Neolithic shrine or, more probably, a mortuary house or platform. The platform may have

Lateral Chamber at Gwernvale looking north-west

been used to expose the dead (excarnation) prior to internment, and similar structures have been found within and underneath the forecourt areas at Fussell's Lodge[20] and Wayland's Smithy (Berkshire 1). But It has also been suggested that it represents domestic activity (Britnell 1984, 6).

The elongated mound, which has a double revetment wall, is oriented east/west. Traces of a possible ancient cement were noted between the uprights and walling during the 1977–1978 excavation (Britnell 1979, 132–134). Following the excavation, the A40 road was widened and the work involved has extensively damaged the southern section of Gwernvale, including patricularly the destruction of the southern horn.

Garn Goch (BRE 12; SO 2123 1771) (also referred to as Carn Goch) is possibly the remains of a hybrid Cotswold-Severn tomb. The monument stands on a small sandy rise, 84m AOD, overlooking the River Usk and towards surrounding mountains to the north and east. It measures 17.4m across and 1.6m high, is oval-shaped, with its northern end oriented towards Table Mountain, a prominent truncated spur at the southern extent of the Black Mountains. The mound has recently been disturbed by tree roots and further damaged by 'vandalism'. Grimes (1936b, 265) suggests that this site, along with Gwernvale (BRE 7), was constructed within an open landscape, sited on riverine gravels and sands.

Garn Goch was discovered accidentally in 1847 by workmen clearing stones from Llangattock Park. According to an anonymous account (Anon 1854, 148) the mound contained a 'cist' or 'cromlech' supported by four 'rude uprights' under a covering stone. Inside were human remains, some of which had 'crumbled to dust' (extracts from *Gentleman's Magazine* 1847, part 2, 526). A humerus, maxilla (with a row of teeth) and part of a skull were, however, found intact. It appears that the bones lay within a

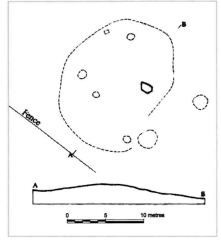

Garn Goch plan and cross-section

centrally placed chamber measuring 2.6m x 1.22m x 0.7m. Accompanying the bones was a 'quantity of fresh-looking charcoal'. The bones and six coins that came from the cairn were sent to Lord Northampton, but have since been lost. It is believed that the coins dated to the reign of Constantine I (AD 307–337). On the north side, where the chamber was discovered, a large capstone, measuring 1.6m x 1.5m, is also present. Loose stones, probably from the cairn, lie on top of the mound.

The form of the monument is difficult to establish. Crawford, visiting in 1924 with Mortimer Wheeler, suggested it was a long cairn and 'typical of other Brecknockshire examples'. Grimes (1936b) also suggested that Garn Goch was a long cairn, possibly similar in form to nearby Gwernvale. The mound is certainly oval and therefore typical of other megalithic structures in the region. Furthermore, large stones 'placed' on top of the mound delineate a simple rectangular chambered structure. Finally, many of the landscape traits attributed to monuments in this region, such as topographic orientation, also apply to Garn Goch. Daniel (1950), however, argues that it is no more than a cist or round mound of Bronze Age date.

Garn Goch looking south

Clyro Court Farm Long Barrow (RAD 1; SO 2123 4313) is located 20m south-west of the farm buildings, on a ridge facing south-east, standing 90m AOD. The visible remains are restricted to a low mound and a few uprights, recognized as a barrow in 1973 by W.E. Griffiths, although the site has been referred to as Carnaf (or cairn) for at least 200 years. According to the RCAHMW (1997, 63) the area around the site has been disturbed and there is evidence at the northern end of the mound of stone dumping which has invariably changed the shape of the mound. At the north-western end of the mound is the remains of a low field bank, possibly medieval in date.

The locally quarried sandstone uprights within the centre of the mound delineate either a small chamber and passage or two chambers. This area measures roughly 4.4m by 2.5m and is marked by up to 12 uprights. These uprights are arranged into two chamber wall sections; the southern alignment forming a right-angled corner of a chamber, whilst the northern alignment is more difficult to discern. The two largest uprights appear to form the walls of either a chamber or, more likely, a passage that is oriented roughly north. The mound, measuring around 33m in length by 17m in width has a maximum height of 1.1m (*ibid.*, 63). The tomb has outstanding views across the Wye Valley, incorporating the north-western extent of the Black Mountains. In addition, Mynydd Troed, an isolated peak, can also be seen, approximately 15km south-south-west.

The mound is valley-oriented, being aligned south-west/north-east. Another long barrow several hundred metres to the south-east (SO 2159 5377), is now believed to be destroyed. In spite of their proximity, each tomb may have functioned in quite different ways from the other, similar to, say, Arthur's Stone (HRF 1) and Cross Lodge Long Barrow (HRF 4) at Dorstone. In neither case can any pattern of intervisibility be identified. The Clyro Court Farm monument is positioned in such a way that Pen yr Wyrlod (BRE 1) (3.5km) and Little Lodge Barrow (BRE 2) (4.6km) are completely hidden. At the same time, however, the monument is positioned in full view of the south-western flanks of the Wye Valley and would have possessed intervisibility with the Bach chambered monument (HRE 5), located some 6.5km to the east.[21] Extensive lithic scatters dating between the Mesolithic and Bronze Age have been found in the vicinity of the monument. Also recently discovered by the landowner were two Neolithic axes, one flint, the other polished stone, the latter probably deriving from the Penmaenmawr axe factory in North Wales.

Clyro Court Farm Long Barrow, looking west

Little Lodge Barrow (BRE 2, SO 1822 3806) stands some 340m west of Little Lodge Farm, within an old orchard. The monument, which possibly would have been intervisible with Pipton Long Cairn (BRE 8), some 2.3km due west, stands 137m AOD on a west-facing slope. The mound, which rises to a height of 1.8m, is constructed over a small platform, 56m x 22m (17m at the southern end), above a tributary of the River Wye.[22] Over the recent past the eastern side of the mound has suffered plough damage and stone has been robbed for use elsewhere. According to Grimes, this monument had been heavily denuded by quarrying, the result of which has almost completely obliterated part of the cairn (Grimes 1936b, 270). In addition, parts of the mound and chambers have been severely disturbed by hawthorn roots.

Excavated in 1929 by C.E. Vulliamy, the monument contained unburnt human bone and charcoal flecks, and the remains of red deer,[23] sheep and cattle.[24] The human bone was thought to represent five adult males, an elderly female and perhaps three children. However, a re-evaluation suggests four adults and one youth (all male).[25] A single red deer molar, apparently notched, was also re-examined. These remains were all found in a chamber complex just south of the centre of the mound.

The mound is oriented roughly north/south, with two, or perhaps three chambers present: a simple chamber at the southern end, the remains of a lateral chamber opening out to the west, and a possible third chamber indicated by a single upright at the northern end. The southern chamber consists of 12 uprights. This confused area of the site was recorded on a plan by Vulliamy, but in no great detail. It would appear that a passage exists on the south-western side of the mound, suggesting that the chambers are side-transepted types. Interestingly, if this is the case all the ritual activity of the monument faces up slope towards the prominent spur of Hay Bluff, for similar landscape affinities are recorded elsewhere within the group.

The mound appears to be typical of the Cotswold-Severn classification, with a possible horned forecourt to the northern section. The chambers may have been entered from passages on the western side of the mound, suggesting a false portal or entrance at the northern end, similar in architectural detail to Pipton Long Cairn (BRE 8). Both chamber and passage would have had extensive views across the Wye Valley. Vulliamy's hurried excavation failed to establish a clear architectural form as he was probably interested only in the contents of the chambers, however the external architectural detail may survive on the western side of the mound, which is protected by a hedge. In and around the site are a number of large stones which may represent the remains of further chambers, especially within the northern section of the monument.

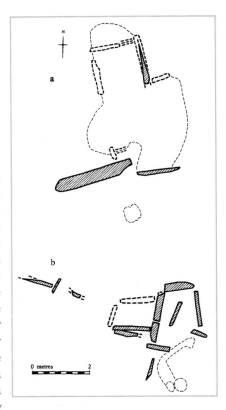

**Little Lodge Barrow.
detail of central chamber area
(adapted from RCAHM [W])**

Little Lodge Barrow looking east

Arthur's Stone, Dorstone

This impressive barrow (HRF 1; SO 3180 4313) is one of the most notable of all prehistoric monuments along the Welsh border. However, it is also a monument that has received only superficial investigation and discussion and has never been excavated (Watkins 1928; Daniel 1950; Darvill 1982; Grimes 1936b; Hemp 1935; HWCC 1981; Stanford 1990; Children and Nash 1994; Nash 1997, 2000; Olding 2000; Sant 2000). Fortunately, antiquarian interest has been restricted to site visits.

This monument, once referred to as Artil's Stone, is first described by Nathaniel Salmon in his *A New Survey of England* (1728–1729). Comments by Salmon suggest the monument had changed little in appearance over the past 200 years. The northern edge of Arthur's Stone Lane (which runs along the spine of Arthur's Stone ridge from Merbach Hill to Dorstone Hill and past the monument) forms part of the parish boundary between Dorstone and Bredwardine. The monument was probably also used to delineate part of this recognized boundary.

Set within an oval mound (approximately 26m x 17m), the monument has nine upright stones forming a polygonal chamber, an unorthodox right-angled passage and an enormous capstone, estimated to weigh more than 25 tonnes (Corcoran 1969, 23). Hemp (1935, 288) describes the chamber as kite-shaped, approximating the form of the capstone. The chamber is regarded by Daniel (1950, 74) as being laterally sited. Several metres south of the capstone and chamber is a large upright sandstone slab which, allegedly, has as many as twelve large shallow cupmarks on the inner face, probably dating from the Bronze Age (Crawford 1925, 147; Daniel 1950, 118). Also present and extremely visible on the upper part of the stone are a series of graffiti with clear dates, one of 1912. It is believed that this stone represents part of an ante-chamber (Daniel 1950). Lying between the chamber and the sandstone upright is a single stone which Crawford (1925, 47) suggests is recumbent. It is likely that this stone, along with the cupmarked upright, formed part of a southern axis chamber entered by a separate passage on the south and west side of the mound (Children and Nash 1994).

The Old Red Sandstone capstone (measuring approximately 5.8m x 3m) is split into three pieces (as a result of weathering processes) and is oriented north-east/south-west with the south-western end pointing towards the southern section of the Golden Valley. A large section of the capstone has also split horizontally, with an enormous fragment collapsing into the central chamber.

The chamber has, at its western end, a false portal stone (partly blocking the doorway to the main chamber) and an inner passage that is oriented north. However, the passage changes direction to the north-west, pointing towards the impressive Hay Bluff and the northern extent of the Black Mountains (Children and Nash 1994, 26; Tilley 1994, 140). Crawford (1925, 147) has suggested that the chambers of Arthur's Stone and Gwernvale (near Crickhowell) are similar, although the former is much larger. The unorthodox redirection of the passage and the orientation of the capstone suggest that Arthur's Stone may have been positioned deliberately so as to completely encompass the visual aspect of the Black Mountains. The tomb also incorporates views from both the southern and northern extents of the Golden Valley (Nash 1997, 20). Many other tombs within the Wye, Lynfi and Usk valleys (in Powys) appear to be similarly positioned (Children and Nash 1994; Olding 2000).

Members of the Woolhope Naturalists' Field Club, visiting the site in July 1872, remarked that a series of stones laid out in a circular fashion surrounded the monument. These may represent the outer kerbing, or what 18th- and 19th-century antiquarians termed a peristalith, enclosing the mound. However, there was no sign of any kerbing by 1928 (Watkins 1928, 150). An alternative view, and one that I support, suggests Arthur's Stone may have been trapezoidal in form, or at least elongated, and that the monument extended across the lane, with the present passage on the side of the monument.[26] The actual forecourt area (with false portal) would have been located in the south-east and is represented by the upright which is recognized as being an ante-chamber. Within fields to the east of the lane is a large selection of stones that cannot be considered as naturally occurring rock-outcropping, and it is possible that these stones, along with smaller stone debris, comprise one end of the monument. The destruction of this part of the monument must have occurred prior to the early 18th century, with one piece of stone reputedly being taken for use as an altar in the

Arthur's Stone terminal chamber looking north-east

church at Peterchurch; accounts by Nathaniel Salmon suggest Arthur's Stone was as it is today, although later witnesses remark that the site was being robbed of its stone for building (*cf.* Crawford 1925). Furthermore, discernible monuments such as Arthur's Stone, with its folklore and local superstition, would have suffered destruction especially during the 16th and 17th centuries.

The monument is one of the most northerly chambered tombs of the Cotswold-Severn Group and is one of five tombs that dominate the Neolithic landscape of the northern reaches of the Golden Valley (Children and Nash 1994; Darvill 1982; Nash 1997). Other monuments within the group lie further south and west, and occupy the hinterlands of the western reaches of the Black Mountains.

Located between nearby Cross Lodge Long Barrow (HRF 4) and Arthur's Stone is the Dorstone Hill settlement (SO 326423) that was excavated between 1965 and 1972 by C. Houlder and R. Pye. This rare example of a Neolithic settlement yielded 4,000 pieces of flint, including more than 30 arrowhead fragments and 60 polished stone axe fragments (HWCC 1981; Children and Nash 1994, 17). Another possible settlement site may be present on nearby Cefn Hill at Abbey Farm, Craswall (Gavin-Robinson 1934).

Arthur's Stone and other chambered monuments in the area appear to be part of a continuous human presence since at least the Late Mesolithic (6,000–3,500 BC). Diagnostic lithics, in particular microliths, have been found beneath and around Arthur's Stone (Brown 1963, 76–91; Children and Nash 1994, 25; Gavin-Robinson 1934; Tilley 1994, 118). So, even during the Neolithic, Arthur's Stone would have possessed a history and, more importantly, an affinity with its ancestors. It should also be highlighted that diagnostic lithics dating to the Bronze Age have also been found along the west-facing slopes of Arthur's Stone ridge, including several barbed and tanged arrowheads (Brown 1963, 80). The continuous use of Neolithic sites is not uncommon, for example, Gwernvale, Crickhowell where Upper Palaeolithic and Mesolithic flint assemblages have been found beneath the southern section of the forecourt area (Healey and Green 1984, 129–130). Similarly, along the western reaches of Merbach Hill and to the south along Arthur's Stone ridge to Vowchurch Common, a large number of lithic scatters have been found which date to the Late Mesolithic (Brown 1963; Gavin-Robinson 1934). These sites may represent only a fraction of the total number of hunter/fisher/gatherer sites that once existed in this area.

Arthur's Stone shares a landscape affinity with many other Neolithic monuments, both within the Black Mountains Group and elsewhere. The monument stands on the western ridge of Merbach Hill and has clear, uninterrupted views across the northern, western and southern extents of the Golden Valley, across Cefn Hill and to the eastern slopes of the Black Mountains — from Hay-on-Wye to Pandy, a total distance of about 40 km. To the east of the site, views are restricted to the nearby eastern ridge of Merbach Hill, some 300m away. Interestingly, there is no further archaeological evidence for Neolithic activity, in the form of earlier lithic scatters or monuments, further east (Children and Nash 1994). This would suggest that such activity is confined to the area within sight of the Black Mountains. A similar distribution of lithics and monuments is found along the lower Usk and Wye valleys.

The relationship between Arthur's Stone and the immediate landscape, together with the spatial organization of the tomb, suggests that its builders clearly understood how certain parts of the monument should be constructed and sited. Standing at around 274m AOD, views from outside the small forecourt area into the entrance and outer passage are uninterrupted. However, views into the inner passage and chamber are restricted due to the right-angled bend half way along the passage. Likewise, restricted visuality is in operation when viewing the outer passage and entrance from the chamber. It is as if a conscious attempt is being made to separate human space, the realm of order and control, from the outside world. The transition between the two is achieved precisely at that point, equidistant between chamber and entrance, where the passage abruptly changes direction. It is here that culture meets nature. However, this is only part of the meaning behind the monument's construction. The redirection of the passage and the orientation of the capstone suggest Arthur's Stone may have played a key role in the socio-symbolic process of territory formation. The monument was probably constructed as to visually encompass the entire length of the Black Mountains. In this way, the mountains were incorporated into the social and symbolic identity of the Neolithic settlers, helping to create a sense of belonging. Other tombs in the Wye and Usk valleys interact with the landscape in the same way.

Like many other chambered burial monuments of this date, Arthur's Stone is not on the highest point within the immediate landscape but slightly away from Merbach Hill's summit (Nash 1997, 20). It could be argued that there is a clear attempt to control the surrounding landscape from the monument. However, the monument cannot be seen from any part of the Golden Valley. I would suggest that a form of restricted visual access was in operation, increasing in extent as one moved into the tomb with its bend in the passage. It's possible that Neolithic communities could have been stratified on at least three levels. Those occupying the first, lower level would have had no visual access to the monument. The second tier may have been allowed visual access, but only to the outside, while the third level were able to access the inside of the monument to bury the dead and perform ritual activities, probably associated with death, fertility and political and social consolidation. This could have been further complicated by the way in which the monument is constructed.

Social complexity can be especially seen with the passage arrangement. Of the twelve Old Red Sandstone slabs recently recorded by the author (and previously by Grimes 1936a), eight large stones construct the walls of the passage. and one can be interpreted as a doorstone, similar to door-stones found at Parc-le-Breos-Cwm on the Gower Coast (GLA 4) and Ty Isaf, near Talgarth (BRE 5). The upright stones would have supported a series of small capstones, thus enclosing the passage. What has been noticed within this arrangement is that the passage appears to be constructed in order to restrict visual access. The door-stone blocks visual access from the entrance/forecourt to the chamber and vice-versa. Further restricted visual access is also present with the way in which the passage stones are arranged. Between the entrance and the chamber, each of the stones appears to gain height. As well as witnessing a gradual rise within the passage roofing, the uprights appear to widen as one moves through the passage. A similar architectural trait occurs with the passage grave tradition in Wales, Ireland, central southern Sweden and Denmark (Children and Nash 1997; Tilley 1993). It could be the case that the passage acts as a boundary between life (outside the monument) and death (inside the chamber) creating a liminal space or a rite of passage — similar to the spatial divisions inside a Christian church.

I have suggested in previous research (1997) that Arthur's Stone, along with other monuments within the Black Mountains Group, utilises both organic and inorganic architecture in its construction; monuments that have

Arthur's Stone: the entrance and passage looking south

chamber and passage stones (inorganic) which were also once covered by a mound (organic). Recently, the siting of monuments has been interpreted fundamentally as a form of statementing the landscape: turning a space into a place (Bradley 1993; 1998). Both ritual and socio-political knowledge make this place special. In part, this is fair comment. However, I would stress that Arthur's Stone with its covering mound was hidden away; organic and incognito with its surroundings. Certainly, an artist's reconstruction of this monument at the site would suggest this.[27] Even so, it would still have been a territorial marker, noted and referred to by the heads of society.

This monument, also known as Great Llanavon Farm (HRF 4; SO 3235 4178), is classified as a long mound (Powell *et al.* 1969) and stands at around 180m AOD on a west-facing slope, approximately 300m from Llanafon Farm. Three large ash trees mark its location. The northern section of the mound has been damaged by ploughing and some of the stones littering the field may once have formed part of the tomb structure, perhaps its kerbing. Possibly much larger during the Neolithic, the elongated oval mound, approximately 18m × 10m × 2.5m, is locally oriented (north-west/south-east) to the Golden Valley. Like Arthur's Stone (HRF 1), the monument also appears to visually encompass the Black Mountains. To the south-west of Cross Lodge Long Barrow is the River Dore which flows south-south-east.

Either side of the monument along the west-facing ridge are extensive Neolithic lithic scatters. On Vowchurch Common, some 4.5km to the south-east, up to eight separate lithic scatters have been found which date to between the Mesolithic and Bronze Age. Along the same ridge to the north-west, a total of seven Mesolithic and Neolithic lithic scatters are present. Further later prehistoric lithic scatters are found to the west of the monument on Cefn Hill.[28]

During the Neolithic, Cross Lodge Long Barrow would have been visible from the valley floor and also from the large settlement of Dorstone Hill (SO 3260 4230), approximately 1km to the north. This Neolithic settlement, which lies on a spur between Cross Lodge Long Barrow and Arthur's Stone, was discovered in the early 1960s. The positioning of settlement and monuments appears to be deliberate. The settlement, moreover, represents a link between socio-economic activity and the realm of ritual and symbolism.

Arthur's Stone and Cross Lodge Long Barrow differ architecturally, suggesting that one pre-dates the other. Arthur's Stone is probably the earlier of the two as a small Mesolithic flint assemblage has been found there suggesting the site was already in use at the beginning of the Neolithic. The different architectural styles may, however, indicate different meanings; Cross Lodge Long Barrow is aligned with the valley, whereas Arthur's Stone may represent a valley-end territorial marker. More time and effort would have been needed to erect Arthur's Stone, judging by the size and weight of the uprights and capstone. Obviously, construction time would depend on the availability of suitable sandstone and the labour needed to transport these blocks across the landscape.

Cross Lodge Long Barrow looking east

Dunseal (HRF 6; SO 3913 3382) — intact and unexcavated — stands on a narrow ridge in the corner of a small field at around 175m AOD. Outstanding views open out over the lower part of the Golden Valley and Black Mountains to the west. To the south and west of this monument is the River Dore which flows in a south-south-east direction. Within the vicinity of the monument are a number of Neolithic and Bronze Age lithic scatters; and approximately 4km to the north-north-west is an intense series of lithic scatters that date between the Mesolithic and Neolithic. Interestingly, and in common with other monuments within the area, very little Neolithic activity is found to the east of the monument; all monuments and lithic scatters are concentrated on the west-facing slopes.

This monument and nearby Parkwood chambered tomb (SO 356 334) (now destroyed) mark the southern extent of Neolithic activity in the Golden Valley and the south-eastern extent of the Black Mountains Group.[29] The first farmers appear to have used this and other monuments within the group to define a territory, controlling the landscape and, in the process, establishing an identity (e.g. Renfrew 1976). In this case, the landscape includes the lower southern sections of the Dore, Ecscley and Olchon Valleys (forming the hinterlands of the Black Mountains) and the Grey Valley to the south-east.

The date of construction of the site remains a mystery. The few surface finds (from ploughing) suggest a Neolithic and/or Early Bronze Age date. The oval mound measures approximately 27m x 14m x 2m and may once have been circular, suggesting a Bronze Age date. However, its location, high on a west-facing ridge with panoramic views, especially to the south and west, suggests strongly that Dunseal is a Neolithic long barrow.

The Dunseal Long Barrow monument is unexcavated

17 Parc-le-Breos-Cwm

18 Maen Ceti

19 Sweyne's Howes North

20 Sweyne's Howes South

21 Penmaen Burrows

The Gower Peninsula Group

Chapter Three: The Gower Peninsula Group

This group, referred to by T.G.E. Powell (1969, 17) as the south-eastern Wales Coastal Group, consists of up to seven monuments, five of which are discussed below. Two monuments that are not on the Gower Peninsula but included within Powell's inventory are Tinkinswood (GLA 9) and Maes-y-Felin (GLA 10); both are included in the next chapter on the South East Wales Group. Omitted from this inventory is the chambered long cairn at Nicholaston (GLA 11) (SS 5075 8881) and the uncertain long mound at Upper Killay (GLA 12) (SS 5848 9227). Monument distribution is concentrated in three areas: Rhossili Down, the central upland area of Cefn Bryn and the southern coastal area of Penmaen. Unlike the core areas of the Black Mountains Group and South-West Wales there are no geographical sub-groups recognized.

All monuments from this area possess very different architecture, varying from the classic hybrid Cotswold-Severn Parc-le-Breos-Cwm (GLA 4) to the large capstoned dolmen of Maen Ceti (Arthur's Stone) (GLA 3). The landscape setting for each monument is also very different. Maen Ceti dominates Cefn Bryn and, unlike many other monuments on the Gower, has extensive views. Sites such as Parc-le-Breos-Cwm and the Nicholaston monument are hidden away within secluded valleys, whilst the Pen-Mean Burrows monument (GLA 5) was until recently hidden within a dune system overlooking Pennard Pill.

Judging by the different architecture of the monuments on the Gower it is more than probable that they were constructed and used at different points in time during the Neolithic. However, the Maen Ceti and Sweyne's Howes monuments (GLA 1) and (GLA 2) and possibly the Penmaen Burrows monument may have been in use at the same time. Each has a series of uprights supporting a large capstone to form a chamber. The Parc-le-Breos-Cwm monument and possibly Nicholaston are contemporary in construction and use; the now shapeless mound of the Nicholaston monument revealed a central chamber that may be of a similar hybrid shape and construction to the Parc-le-Breos-Cwm monument. If this is the case, both date from the middle to late Neolithic.

The majority of the Neolithic sites on the Gower coast have within their view a large number of Late Neolithic/Early Bronze Age and Bronze Age monuments, including standing stones, ring-cairns and circles (RCAHMW 1976, 43–120). The cairns, ring-cairns and circles lie on the ridges of these upland areas.

To the east of the Gower Coast and located in an undulating landscape are the truly megalithic monuments of Tinkinswood and Maes-y-Felin. Theystand less than a kilometre apart and represent Cotswold-Severn monuments, each possessing simple terminal chambers which are set within long mounds. Excavation has shown that the Tinkinswood monument has a distinct trapezoidal mound, similar to that of Parc-le-Breos-Cwm. It should be noted that other monuments located on the Gower Coast also possess terminal mounds which may have once been trapezoidal in plan, such as the two Sweyne's Howes monuments.

Parc-le-Breos-Cwm (also known as the Giant's Grave) (GLA 4; SS 5372 8983) is one of only a handful of tombs in Wales that have been excavated by antiquarians in the 19th century, subsequently by archaeologists in the 20th century and then restored. The monument, standing at around 31m AOD is located on the floor of a hidden, narrow, dry limestone valley with no visual access to the sea that is approximately 2km to the south. The drystone walling that forms the skin of the monument visually dominates both the valley floor and the surrounding limestone hillside. The landscape potential though is limited, with visual access from the south only. Similarly, Ty Isaf (BRE 5), another Cotswold-Severn hybrid, is set within a small isolated valley and also appears to be deliberately hidden. A series of freshwater springs are located a few metres south of the monument that flow into Pennard Pill. Approximately 1.8km to the south-south-west is the Penmaen Burrows monument (GLA 5).

Parc-le-Breos-Cwm, although originally thought until 1937 to be enclosed within a circular barrow is, in fact, trapezoidal in form and resembles a number of Cotswold-Severn tombs found in Gloucestershire and Oxfordshire, such as Belas Knap and Notsgrove. The site was discovered and excavated in 1869, after the northern part of the cairn had been used as a quarry for road construction. The following year the southern end of the monument was excavated by Sir John Lubbock and Lord Swansea. A funnel-shaped forecourt, passage (gallery) and four side-chambers were revealed and led for many years to the view that this layout represented a gallery grave with 'two pairs of transepts' (Daniel 1950, 210). However, from excavation it is clear that the chamber of the monument is constructed of a passage and a series of chambers. At least 24 skeletons that were 'much broken and in no regular arrangement' were also found. However, Lord Swansea wrote (1887, 198):

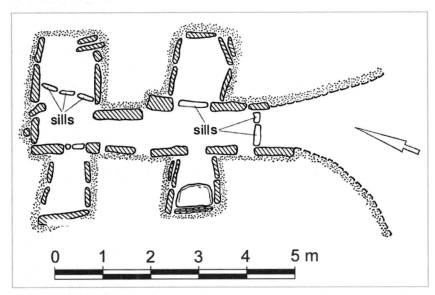

Parc-le-Breos: passage and chambers (after Daniel 1950)

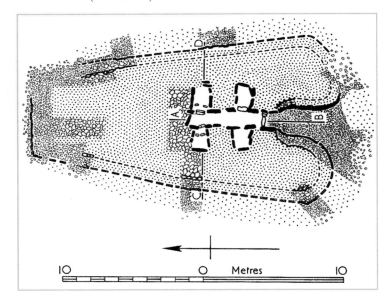

Parc-le-Breos: showing limit of excavation (after Atkinson 1961)

Each set of bones was found in a small confused mass, just as would be if a body in a sitting position had collapsed, as it were, vertically within its own area.

The bone piles, although overlying each other, suggest that a crouched-burial tradition prevailed. The bones found represent three children aged 8–10 years old, and at least 19 adults, both male and female, aged 25–45 years. Two other skeletons were of people aged over 45. The human remains from this monument suggests that it appears to be a corporate monument serving the community as a whole, rather than special individuals within it, although the interred may represent a dynasty that used the monument over a long period of time. Some of the human remains, originally found in the north-west and south-west chambers were recently radio-carbon dated by Whittle and Wysocki (1998) and gave a date range of between 3,705±55 bp (OxA-6495) and 4,875±55 bp (OxA-6491). The bones of a badger and large ungulate, possibly an auroch, found in the passage area possessed much earlier dates of 7,665±65 bp (OxA-6499) and 10,625±80 bp (OxA-6500) respectively (see Appendix II). It is quite possible that the deposition of the auroch's bones is a result of ritual feasting. Also recovered from the first excavation was a small assemblage of pottery including two rim sherds of so-called western-style pottery.

The second excavation undertaken by R.J.C. Atkinson in 1960 showed that the cairn at the southern end of the monument was constructed of limestone rubble (Atkinson 1961). The passage, measuring 5.25m in length, and the chamber walls were made of locally quarried limestone slabs and drystone walling. Between the two horns, a deep, funnel-shaped forecourt led to a small passage (oriented south-south-east/north-north-west). Both horns and inner forecourt were formed of rough drystone walling. Unlike other hybrid tombs of this size and form, Parc-le-Breos-Cwm had no false portal. Instead an entrance leading to a passage and four side-chambers was revealed, a low sill-stone forming the threshold at the entrance. Three of the four rectangular chambers have sillstones of a similar size, each measuring around 0.9m x 0.9m. Interestingly, many monuments of the type possess polygonal rather than rectangular chambers, such as Notgrove (GLOU 4) in Gloucestershire, but a similar sill arrangement is found at Hetty Pegler's Tump (GLOU 14) and Nympsfield (BRK 1). The chamber floors may have been cobbled (Daniel 1950, 35). Evidence for the capstone (or capstones), which may have measured up to 7m x 5m, has long since disappeared.

In the 1960 excavation, finds included several pieces of undecorated Neolithic pottery described by Lynch (1969b, 171) as hard clinker-like and that may have been influenced by Abingdon and Ebbsfleet wares (Corcoran 1969, 102). Similar pottery has been recovered from Ty-Isaf and a number of other Welsh tombs (Peterson 2003).

As part of the final phase of the monument, the entrance, forecourt and external limit of the outer cairn were filled in with limestone blocking material. This probably occurred during the Late Neolithic/Early Bronze Age when the cairn appears to have been finally abandoned; not uncommon with other trapezoidal monuments in Wales and western Britain.

Parc-le-Breos-Cwm looking north towards the upper valley

73

Maen Ceti (GLA 3; SS 4913 9055), also known as Arthur's Stone, Cefn Bryn and Coetan Arthur is located 147m AOD on the northern slopes of Cefn Bryn, a central upland area extending along the spine of the Gower Peninsula as far as Rhosilli Down in the west and the western outskirts of Swansea in the east. The site is not on the highest point within the landscape but is in full view of the Bristol Channel and Afon Llwchwr (River Loughor) inlet. To the west, located on the same ridge are two cairns which are Bronze Age in date. The RCHAMW record up to 14 cairns/barrows and ring cairns along the Cefn Bryn ridge (1976, 50–51).

This monument, classified by the RCHAMW as a double-chambered megalithic tomb, is one of a handful in Wales that have never been fully investigated (1976, 31). The capstone — described as an unshaped glacial boulder (Castlelden 1992, 382) — is estimated to weigh between 30 and 35 tonnes, originally measuring 4m in length by 3m in width and 2.25m in thickness. A large angular slab, partially submerged in a hollow at the southern side, may have broken off from the capstone, possibly leading to the abandonment of construction (ibid., 382). The monument may, therefore, be unfinished. The RCHAMW (1976, 31) suggests that the capstone derives from local conglomerate containing quartz.

According to the RCHAMW (1976, 31) the monument consists of a centrally-placed double chamber with supported capstone set within a circular cairn. The northern chamber, covered by this massive capstone, is roughly rectangular in shape and is oriented east-west. The chamber measures 1m x 1.8m and is delineated by four uprights. Between this chamber and the southern chamber are a further three angular uprights which separate both chambers.

Immediately to the west of both chambers are a number of large stones that probably once formed various sections of the chamber architecture,

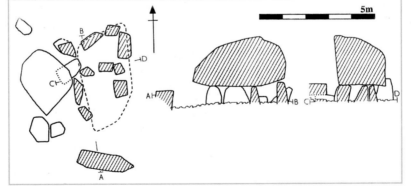

Plan and elevation of Maen Ceti (after RCAHMW 1976)

including a possible capstone measuring 2.2m x 3m. The uprights and surrounding cairn appear to be set in a hollow, which may have provided some of the cairn material. The hollow is around 15m in diameter and is usually seasonally water-logged. The depth of the hollow is unknown although the bedrock may lie close to the present surface. Further remains of the chamber could, however, exist. The cairn, circular in shape measures approximately 23m in diameter. It has been suggested that the cairn would have covered the capstone that stands around 3m above the existing ground level (ibid., 31). However, the upper section of the capstone appears to be more weathered than the lower section suggesting that the upper section may have been exposed during its use.

The uprights, ten in total and measuring on average 1.15m in height, form two chambers. Corcoran (1969, 17), however, suggests that only one simple chamber is present. This is probably based on the present condition of the monument and the extensive cairn in the chamber area. The southern chamber, forming the larger of the two chambers and measuring 1.2m x 2.3m is rectangular in shape. This chamber is delineated by six uprights, five of which support the massive capstone. The southern extent of the chamber is open and probably has up to three uprights missing — presently forming a gap of around 1.2m. This gap may have formed a doorway into the chamber.

The recent history of the monument is very interesting. The capstone appears to have been restored to its place during the 16th century and is quoted in the *Myvyrian Archaeology of Wales* (1870) as 'one of three mighty achievements of the isle of Britain'. In 1695, Edward Lhwyd, who uses the English name of Arthur's Stone, noted that the site was used by 'the common people' as it stands on common land and was (and still is to this day) accessible to anyone.

Maen Ceti, also called Arthur's Stone, looking north towards the south Wales mainland

The Sweyne's Howes North monument, located about 140m AOD on the eastern slopes of Rhossili Down within open heathland. Like its compatriot, Sweyne's Howes South, it has been robbed and heavily disturbed, leaving an extensive cairn rubble spread around the remains of both chambers.

According to Wendy Hughes (1999, 35) the name 'Sweyne' is derived from the name of a legendary Viking warrior. The word 'Howe', which means 'mound', has Norse origins. According to ancient legend, Sweyne, a Viking warrior, is buried here. Place-name evidence suggests that the name actually means 'swine's houses', so named because of its (Sweyne's Howes North) physical similarities with a pigsty.

Sweyne's Howes North (photograph by Laurie Waite)

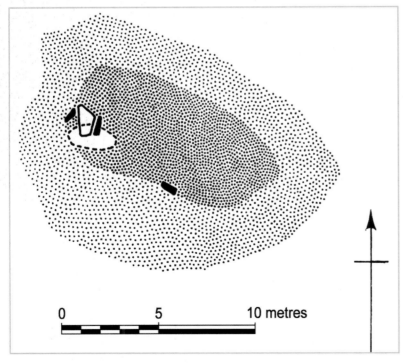

Plan of Sweyne's Howes North (after RCAHMW 1976)

0   5   10 metres

This northern monument is roughly similar in size to its southern neighbour, measuring 18.3m x 13.1m with a cairn height of 0.6m. This monument also has two possible phases of construction, an inner and outer cairn. A much denuded rectangular chamber, measuring 1.1m x 2m, is located on the north-west side of the monument and consists of three uprights which are partially covered by a small capstone. The uprights measure 1.3m in height. Within the chamber area are a number of loose stones that may have once formed cairns.

The Sweyne's Howes South monument is located at around 136m AOD and is arguably constructed similarly to Sweyne's Howes North (GLA 1), 100m to the north. It appears to have been oval in form and built of local sandstone conglomerate (RCHAMW 1976, 30). This monument, along with its neighbour, is laterally-chambered. There is no evidence of any passage.

The more disturbed of the two monuments, Sweyne's Howes South was first investigated in 1869–1870 by the antiquarian Gardiner Wilkinson. The cairn, constructed in possibly two phases of construction, measures

Sweyne's Howes South (photograph by Laurie Waite)

20.7m x 15m x 0.7m and is oval in form. Contained within the inner cairn are a number of loose and earth-fast boulders. One of the boulders may have formed part of a capstone. The inner cairn is delineated by a series of possible kerb stones. The RCHAMW (*ibid.*, 30) suggests that the inner cairn may be wedge-shaped. Within the north-west area of the cairn are the remains of a possible chamber, represented by five recumbent slabs.

Both monuments stand 1.3km east of Rhossili Bay. Although close to the coast, they appear to ignore the sea, as if purposely seeking shelter from the prevailing winds (Daniel 1950).

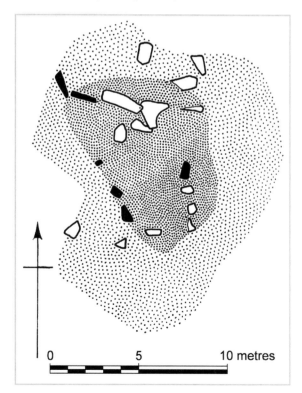

0   5   10 metres

Plan of Sweyne's Howes South

This denuded monument (GLA 5; SS 5315 8813), located 46m AOD among sand dunes, consists of two rectangular chambers with supporting uprights and an entrance passage. The chambers seem to be constructed differently, the materials including limestone, sandstone and sandstone conglomerate. The use of different stones may have socio-symbolic importance (see Tilley 1993).

The site was investigated in 1860 and later in 1881 by W.L. Morgan (1894, 1–7). The remains inside the chambers and surrounding the monument were removed during excavation in 1893 when the original ground surface was exposed. This disturbance resulted in several stones, possibly kerbing, being removed. Since then the site has been covered by wind-blown sand, which has increased the protection of the monument.

The excavation revealed the height of the chambers to be 1m, so rituals would have been performed with the participants squatting, kneeling, sitting or crouching (RCHAMW 1976, 32). It appears that the passage was slightly lower, the height decreasing at the entrance. This passage, opening out towards the east, measures around 2m in length. Powell suggests that the chambers are transepted terminal chambers, similar to those at Parc-le-Breos-Cwm, the idea originating in south-west Wales (1969, 16–17). This is supported by Castleden who suggests the monument is of the Cotswold-Severn tomb type (1992). Corcoran (1969) argues that the monument is not trapezoidal despite the fact that its mound has not been excavated.

The southern chamber, measuring 1.2m x 2.3m and constructed of three uprights, is rectangular. The western chamber, also rectangular in plan, is constructed of two transverse uprights that open out into a passage to the east. There appears to be no trace of any sill stones that would have delineated the space between the chamber and passage. The capstone appears to be dislodged (RCHAMW 1976, 32). It is possible that a third chamber may have existed to the north of the western chamber and passage, thus forming a cruciform-shaped chamber alignment. However, this cannot be proved until further excavation takes place. A number of loose stones in the area of the monument probably represent cairn or blocking material.

Artifacts recovered from the two minor excavations which were restricted to the southern chamber included a fragment of human jaw, animal bones and a fragment of bone tool handle. The jaw bone probably represents the remnants of a human burial. This assemblage was located within a series of residual deposits that underlay wind-blown sand. A further bone assemblage was found beneath two paving slabs along with a small selection of 'brown pottery'. It is probably the latter material that is contemporary with the monument's use.

I would argue that the architecture of the Penmaen Burrows belongs to the long mound tradition which was in use during the middle to late Neolithic, and has some similarities with nearby Parc-le-Breos-Cwm (GLA 4) and the Sweyne's Howes monuments on Rhossili Down (GLA 1 and 2).

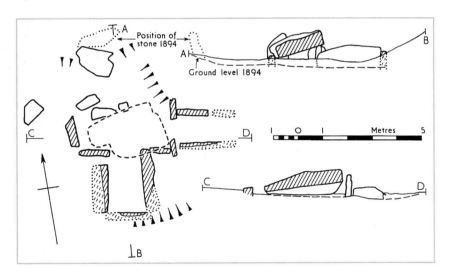

Plan of Penmaen Burrows

Penmaen Burrows looking west (photograph by John Swann)

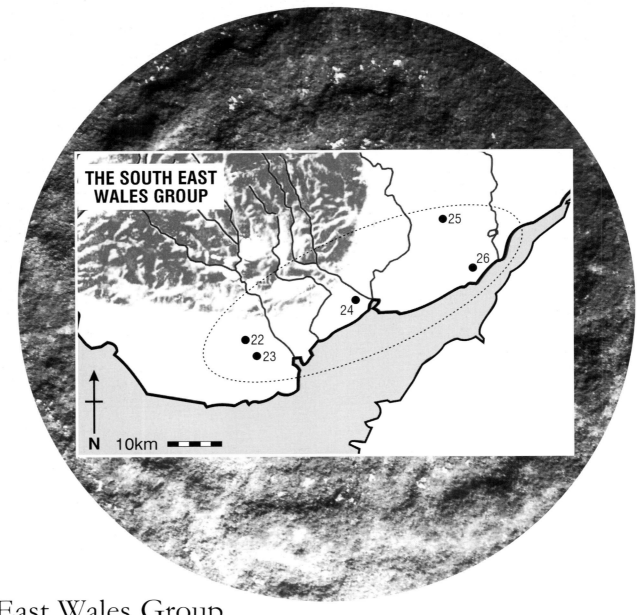

THE SOUTH EAST WALES GROUP

The South-East Wales Group

Chapter Four: The South-East Wales Group

Within this chapter the South-East Wales group is limited to five monuments: Tinkinswood (GLA 9), Maes-y-Felin (GLA 10), Cleppa Park (MON 1), Gaer Llwyd (MON 2) and Heston Brake (MON 3). Others that have not been included are Coity (GLA 7), Pentyrch (Cae yr Arfan) (GLA 8) and the recently discovered Thornwell Farm (MON 4).[30]

Three of the Monmouthshire monuments are located close to the Severn Estuary/Bristol Channel whilst Gaer Llwyd lies some way inland. Unlike the core areas of the Black Mountains and South-West Wales Groups, there are no geographical sub-groups recognized.

Each of the monuments have been constructed using local stone, the predominant materials used being Old Red Sandstone and sandstone conglomerate. Although the sandstone conglomerate is a weak material, Neolithic builders must have seen the importance of texture and colour when using this type of stone for uprights. The white quartz, set into red and brown sandstone must have had a desired effect on the people who constructed and used these monuments. Even the greyness of the Gaer Llwyd monument would have dominated the immediate landscape.

Associated with these monuments are a number of stray finds that include prestige items such as polished stone axes and a number of small flint scatters. In the south and east of the area there have been twelve single prestige finds, consisting mainly of polished stone and flint axes, that indicate possible trading alliances or seasonal expeditions. At least two of these axes come from southern Sweden: a south Scandinavian flat-butted axe found in Benchwood, an eastern suburb of Newport (SO 33 88), and an identically shaped axe within the root system of an old yew on the Great Doward, close to the border with Herefordshire. Further axes originate from Cornwall and Cumbria: an axe from the Scafell Pike axe factory was found on English Newton Common (SO 52 15), whilst two fine examples of Greenstone axes, originating from the Penzance area, were discovered close to the M4 Motorway, north-west of Newport (SO 30 88). A further three axes were discovered in Newport (SO 29 86).

The three monuments MON 1 to MON 3 have been discussed by a number of antiquarians and eminent archaeologists over the past two centuries, but the Thornwell Farm monument (ST 539 917) is a recent discovery and deserves some comment here. It stands on the western banks of the Wye Estuary and was discovered as a result of a housing development and excavated in 1990–1991. The monument has a similar landscape position to nearby Heston Brake and at present lies within the middle of the housing estate, its location marked by a large 300-year-old oak tree. The monument contained the remains of four adults and two children and associated grave goods dating to the Early Neolithic. The human remains appeared to have been disarticulated. A large assemblage of bones from birds of prey was also found. The rectangular chamber contained a port-hole[31] which may have divided the chamber into two areas. There was a substantial blocking deposit and evidence of secondary deposition in the form of two Early Bronze Age cist burials, each of a crouched male with associated grave goods including a barbed and tanged arrowhead and a corded ware beaker pot. Several Bronze Age barrows exist close by suggesting a long burial continuity over time.

Of the three other Monmouthshire monuments, two are classified as Portal Dolmens and the third a possible gallery grave, all of which lie in various states of destruction.

The sites of Tinkinswood and Maes-y-Felin are intervisible. Both monuments are truly megalithic in stature with Tinkinswood arguably having the largest capstone in Wales (Caselden 1992). Maes-y-Felin, which consists of three large uprights which support a rectangular capstone would have been covered with an enormous mound, similar in shape and design to those found within the Cotswold-Severn region in south-west England. Tinkinswood, which was restored by Ward early in the 20th century, still retains much of its architecture and is one of only a handful of sites in Wales providing an insight as to how the architecture may have interacted with the ritual performances of the Neolithic and Early Bronze Age periods.

This monument (GLA 9; ST 0921 7331) and nearby Maes-y-Felin (GLA 10) are similarly placed within a slightly undulating landscape, Tinkinswood standing on a small knoll. Located at around 75m AOD, it lies on a south-westerly slope at the head of the River Waycock. The monument appears to have been investigated prior to 1875 when Lukis claims that the 'contents of the Tinkinswood chamber had been thrown out many years ago' (*Archaeologia Cambrensis* 1875, 171). Lukis goes on to say that he dug in the debris outside the monument to find human teeth, unburnt bone and 'rude pottery'.

The monument was excavated and carefully restored in 1914 by the archaeologist John Ward (1916, 242–264). The excavation revealed a number of phases that included construction, utilization, abandonment in the form of a blocking deposit in front of the eastern chamber and later secondary use. The monument consists of a chamber constructed of five uprights supporting a huge capstone at the eastern end of a large rectangular, east/west oriented mound measuring 40m x 17m. A small stone cist or drystone walled pit, roughly 3m square and lined with nine upright slabs, was also incorporated within the cairn fabric at the northern end of the mound. This structure appears to date after the construction of the mound and may be late Neolithic or Early Bronze Age. Within this cist, the Ward excavation found a large quantity of domestic animal bone, including those of horse, cattle (*Bos primigenius*), sheep or goat and pig, which may represent a purpose-built repository for feasting remains, probably utilised during ceremonial funerary rites (Grimes 1951, 33). Also found was a small assemblage of wild animal bone.

The wedge-shaped mound is supported by a drystone revetment wall, which, according to Ward, was well laid and appears to be of locally quarried limestone. The mound rubble also consists of locally quarried limestone and mudstone blocks, the largest of which lie close to the eastern chamber. At the western end of the monument are up to seven upright stone alignments which originally formed three or maybe four linear stone settings, oriented north/south, their purpose unknown.

The monument also possesses the distinctive horns associated with all trapezoidal monuments in Wales, forming a cuspate forecourt (Corcoran 1969, 43). The horns are located to the north and south of the main chamber. The eastern chamber, rectangular in plan, is constructed of five unworked stone uprights and measures 5m x 3.6m. Between the uprights is drystone walling. The chamber is covered by a very large capstone estimated to weigh 40 tonnes (Grimes 1951, 31), partly supported by a recently inserted pillar. The original height of the chamber was 1.5m, suggesting that ritual activity could be conducted standing up. Between the horns, the forecourt area and the chamber there would have been a narrow passage possibly measuring around 1m in length which leads to the entrance of the chamber. The entrance itself is constructed of a large door-stone, flanked by two smaller uprights separating the chamber from the forecourt area.

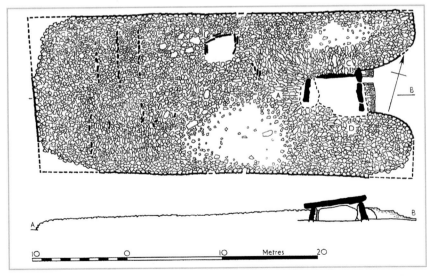

Plan of Tinkinswood and detail of chamber (after Ward 1915)

Ward's reconstruction tastefully extends the stone revetment in front of the portal stones, a feature not seen on any other trapezoidal monument that has a chamber within the forecourt area. The idea that portals are hidden by a revetment wall is also supported by Corcoran (1969, 43). Prior to excavation the monument appears to have been robbed for building stone.

The excavation produced a remarkable assemblage of bone and associated artifacts with the remains of at least 50 people found in the chamber: 21 women, 16 men, 8 children and a number of unidentifiable remains (Grimes 1951, 152–153). These individuals were disarticulated and found within three distinct areas of the site: the chamber, the forecourt blocking, and within the southern section of the cairn fabric of the mound. According to Sir Arthur Keith (in Ward 1916) the remains represented people aged between a few months and 70 years.

A large assemblage of Late Neolithic pottery was also recovered, some of which was found on the floor of the forecourt in front of the entrance. All the pottery from this period were round-bottomed bowls, much of it found embedded in the floor of the forecourt, Ward (1916, 260) rightly suggesting that the pottery and the human remains were contemporary. The Neolithic pottery from this site was identical in type to that found in other Cotswold-Severn Tombs (Grimes 1951, 32). Fragments of a Beaker vessel decorated with alternating bands of continuous chevrons and straight lines were also recovered, suggesting that the monument was in use during the late Neolithic period and the Early Bronze Age. A large flint assemblage that included a finely-worked leaf-

Tinkinswood chamber and façade looking west

shaped arrowhead or what Grimes (1951, 330) calls a lance head, lay in a trench beneath the original surface of the cairn, some 8.5m from the western end of the barrow.

The monument appears to have been used, possibly as a shelter, during the early Iron Age and the Romano-British and medieval periods, because a selection of artifacts including a bone gaming die and pottery from the three periods were found.

T his monument (GLA 10; ST 1009 7230), also known as Gwal-y-Filiast and Llech-y-Filiast (by Rees in 1815) is located on a small knoll within open pasture and has intervisibility with Tinkinswood (GLA 9). The two monuments were first compared with Cotswold-Severn monuments by Sir Henry Rolleston and W. Greenwell in 1877, whose work helped extend the geographical range of the Cotswold-Severn classification, developed in the last century by Thurnam and refined by Daniel (1950). Daniel identified a number of tombs with terminal chambers in this area, including Maes-y-Felin, which he labeled the Tinkinswood-Manton Down type.

The site was examined by J.W. Lukis in 1875, who reported finding fragments of unburned human bone and coarse pottery outside the chamber (Lukis 1875). This material may represent a clearance dump, formed when the contents of the tomb were cleared away to make room for further burials (Daniel 1950). However, it is more than probable that the clearance dump represents antiquarian activity or stone robbing during the recent past.

This unexcavated single-phase tomb stands 70m AOD on a gentle north-western slope near the head of Waycock Valley, where the soils are light and easily worked. Tombs in this area are usually located close to the boundary between areas of freely-drained soils and those with impeded drainage (Corcoran 1969).

A rectangular chamber is set at the eastern end of an eroded long mound, measuring 27m x 11m x 1m and oriented roughly east/west (RCHAMW 1976, 39). The precise form of the mound is unclear, but is probably rectangular or even trapezoidal, similar to nearby Tinkinswood, although there is no trace of a revetment. According to a plan of the site published in the RCHAMW (1976, 39), the mound may have resembled Parc-le-Breos-Cwm (GLA 4), with horns either side of the uprights within the eastern section of the mound.

The chamber measures 2.6m x 1.3m, and consists of three large unworked uprights that support a large capstone. The chamber is set on top

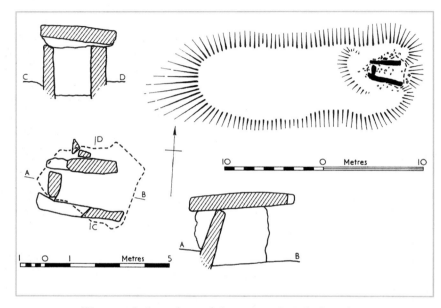

**Plan and elevation of the mound and chamber
of Maes-y-Felin
(after RCAHMW 1976)**

of a small platform within the fabric of the mound, traces of which lie close to the uprights. The chamber appears to be cut some 0.7m into the surrounding geology. There is no trace of any door-stone between the chamber and the eastern side of the mound. In my opinion, there would have been a small forecourt flanked by horns, similar in design and size to Parc-le-Breos-Cwm and Tinkinswood. The capstone, measuring 4.2m x 3.3m by 0.7m in thickness, is of mudstone, the same material used for the capstone at Tinkinswood. To the north of the chamber are two further uprights that may represent further chamber architecture.

Maes-y-Felin chamber looking east

Cleppa Park (MON 1; ST 2740 8571) also referred to as Gwern-y-Cleppa and Gwern-y-clepai is located on a south-east facing ridge and stands at around 43m AOD. This monument, named after a nearby farm, has been classified as a Cotswold-Severn long chambered tomb. The form of this monument is much disturbed but there are still traces of a mound, approximately 40m long and oriented roughly east/west.[32] The remains consist of one fallen capstone and six other stones, three of which are uprights (one now recumbent), the largest of these standing over 1.3m high. A possible fourth upright, now dislodged, measures around 1.5m in length and lies underneath a siliceous grey sandstone capstone that measures approximately 2.5m by 1.7m. The uprights are made from locally quarried conglomerate sandstone or millstone grit.

It was reported in 1897 that three uprights were in place forming what may have been a simple terminal chamber (Bagnall-Oakeley 1899, 11–12).[33] It is in the chamber that the fallen capstone lies and partly buries what was once a large chambered area. A plan of the site, made by Bagnall-Oakeley, suggests that the three uprights form a rectangular chamber, a shape concurred with by Daniel (1950, 67), who thought it formed the remains of an eastern lateral chamber.

Cleppa Park may once have formed part of a ritual landscape that incorporated a nearby Early Bronze Age standing stone (ST 2430 8347). Other monuments, now long since destroyed, would have dominated the lower Usk Valley. This slightly undulating landscape is similar to that of the nearby Tinkinswood (GLA 9) and Maes-y-Felin (GLA 10) monuments, with the monument positioned between the mountains and the flood plain of the lower Usk valley to the east, the alluvial flats to the south and the Severn estuary/Bristol Channel beyond. The Bristol Channel, approx-

The Cleppa Park monument looking east

imately 4.8 km away to the south, cannot be seen from the monument, whilst the uplands of south-east Wales are in view to the north and west. The M4 now blocks the view of the Severn estuary.

Two kilometres to the north-east at Gaer, within the city boundary of Newport, are several Neolithic findspots. These, together with others located either side of the River Usk, suggest that the river estuary and its hinterlands were probably utilised for settlement.

This monument (MON 2; ST 4476 9678), also known as Gaerllwyd and Garnllwyd (meaning 'grey cairn'), stands at approximately 209m AOD on well-drained soils, to the north of the village of the same name. The monument, classified by Powell *et al.* (1969, 288) as a possible Portal Dolmen, is located within a small area of rough scrubland and bush, close to a hedge boundary, and is now much disturbed.[34] The hedge boundary, which is of unknown date, may have served to preserve some of the monument. However, the road on the other side of the boundary may ironically have destroyed the south-western part of the mound. According to an unpublished account:

> ... that road cut into the field in which the cromlech stood, and which itself bounded on its eastern side, by the old trackway from Shirenewton over Earlswood Common, by Mynydd Bach to the great camp further to the north called Gaer-fawr. Until that new road was made, the cromlech lay entirely secluded and out of the way of tourists, or indeed of any ordinary communication; and though the Gaer-fawr is described by early writers, the cromlech appears to have been long unknown to, or unrecognized by, archaeologists.

Similar to other monuments in this group, Y Gaer Llwyd occupies a unique setting. According to the regional SMR, very little in the form of monuments and find spots contemporary with this monument have been found. However, 3km to the south on Gray Hill are a series of Early Bronze Age monuments, including two stone circles and a standing stone (ST 438 935). To the south-east and within Wentwood are several Bronze Age mounds located at ST 415 946 and ST 417 946 (Children and Nash 1996, 52).

The historical evidence for this site dates to at least 1613 when it is first described as Garne Lloyde. This place-name formed part of a survey of the parish of 'Sherenewton' (Crawford 1925, 157). According to Crawford, the site is first mentioned by a Mr Wakeman, who in 1846 in *Archaeologia Cambrensis* (1846, 277) produced a woodcut engraving of the site,[35] which was reproduced in 1848 in Cliffe's *Book of South Wales*. According to the engraving, the morphology of this monument has changed little since, although two further uprights are shown and what can be suggested as a circular enclosure made from loose stone. However, it is more than prob-

Y Gaer Llwyd looking east

able that these loose stones are the result of historical disturbance. Cliffe adds that a trench and bank were present around the site, Crawford suggests that this feature was the remains of a fossilised field enclosure. In addition to the observations and Crawford's notes, Mrs Bagnall-Oakeley in 1915 observed the presence of a mound within the north-eastern part of the site which, according to Crawford, would have been oriented north-east/south-west with the chamber at the north-eastern end. The outer cairn has been destroyed by road-building and stone-robbing.

The plan and form of Y Gaer Llwyd, and in particular, two transverse portal stones, suggest that it is linked to a western tradition — possibly the Irish Sea Group of monuments (Houlder 1978, 139). The remains now comprise a series of uprights, three of which support a large collapsed capstone (3.2m x 2.5m). Two of the uprights either demarcate an entrance or divide two parts of a rectangular chamber (Corcoran 1969, 21). Around the chamber area are a series of fallen uprights that possibly demarcate a now destroyed passage/entrance area. Several stones from this monument may have been incorporated into the sructures of nearby modern buildings (Castelden 1992, 386).

Heston Brake (MON 3; ST 5052 8865) is one of the Cotswold-Severn Group of monuments, as identified by O.G.S. Crawford (1925, 153–155). Later, Powell *et al.* (1969, 289) notes that this denuded tomb was possibly constructed in two phases.

This monument, standing at around 35m AOD, is located on the upper terracing of the Gwent Levels and has views of the Bristol Channel to the south. The soils surrounding the monument are associated with the flood plain of the River Severn and, during the Neolithic, would no doubt have been used to grow crops. Similar to nearby Tinkinswood (GLA 9) and Maes-y-Felin (GLA 10) monuments, Heston Brake is set within an undulating landscape.

The place-name appears not to have a Welsh origin; a Mr J.G. Wood, commenting in Crawford's volume (1925, 155), suggests that Heston Brake, along with Harpson Barn, are corruptions of a settlement known as Herberdston:

> A Welsh knight's fee, which was held within the lordship of Striguil, 13th century in date (Matthew Daneband of 'Portskewet and Herberdson').[36]

The chamber was exposed on 22nd August 1888 by members of the Monmouthshire and Caerleon Antiquarian Association (MCAA) and the Clifton Antiquarian Club. Notes of the investigation were made by Mrs Bagnall-Oakeley, who also made a plan of the chamber and passage that suggests that this monument may be a gallery grave, one of only two in Wales. The plan clearly shows evidence of a door-stone — stone 6 — and a kink between stones 14 and 15, located halfway along the stone alignment. She recorded that the largest upright within the monument — stone 1 — was located at the entrance to the passage and measured 1.3m in height. This and other stones were made from conglomerate sandstone (*cf.* Children and Nash 1996, 35). According to Crawford (1925, 153), stones 2, 3, 4 10, 12 and 19 were missing when the initial investigations were undertaken and that the positioning on the plan by Bagnall-Oakeley of these stones is therefore purely conjectural. Crawford appears to be concerned about the investigation of this monument and feels that Heston Brake had been excavated by antiquarian enthusiasts rather than archaeologists.

Nevertheless, the human remains recovered from the east corner of the western chamber included teeth and finger bones. Also noted within the same area were some bones of an ox and two smooth stones. Bagnall-Oakley (1889, 18–20) states that:

> On the north side of the mound, the workmen came upon three pieces of broken pottery; one of these was black and soft burnt, easily cut with a knife; another was grey, hard burnt, with lines upon it and near them lay a small piece of burnt bone. A third piece of pottery was very hard red ware, somewhat like Roman Samian ware.

Also found were part of a shaft of a human femur and part of a jaw of an (unspecified) animal. It was noticed during the investigation that the mound had been opened previously, Crawford suggesting that this may have been for a secondary burial as found within this context was a sherd of medieval green copper-glazed pottery.

The supposed chamber and passage are set within a long cairn aligned east/west, the cairn measuring roughly 23m in length. The chamber (3m × 1.4m), now without a capstone, is set within the eastern section of the mound, the chamber and passage forming an eastern lateral structure. Formed from nine upright stones, the chamber lies off-line in relation to the

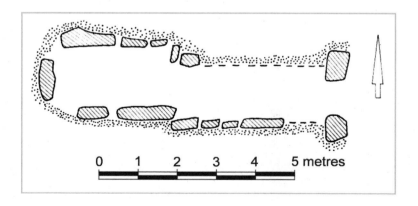

Plan of Heston Brake

passage. Two uprights mark the point of transition between the passage and the chamber entrance — both of which are 1.5m wide. However, the passage entrance is demarcated by two large uprights that stand 0.9m apart. The width of the chamber plus the kink in the internal arrangement of the chamber/passage alignment may suggest some form of restricted visual access between outside and inside of the monument.

The merging of the chamber and passage certainly suggests the monument may be a gallery grave. In terms of architecture, the builders of Heston Brake and Y Gaer Llwyd (MON 2) may have been influenced by a western style, rather than the Cotswold-Severn tradition (Houlder 1978). Similarities with the chamber of Ffostyll South (BRE 4) in the Black Mountains have also been noted (Corcoran 1969, 45).

The entrance stones at Heston Brake

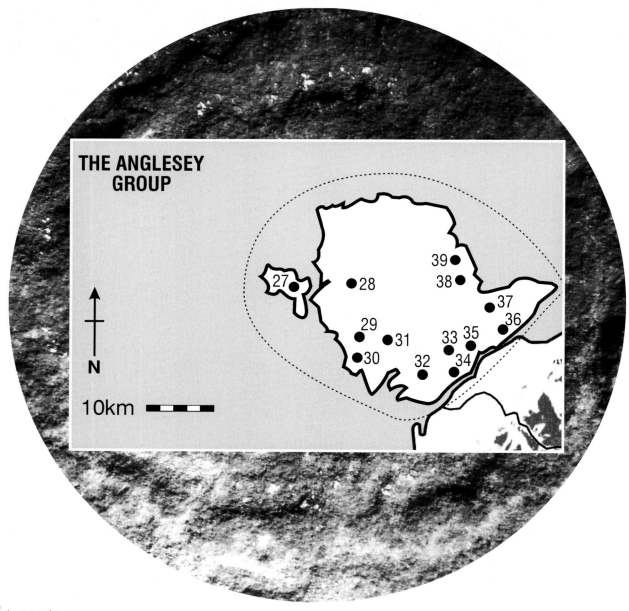

The Anglesey Group

Chapter Five: The Anglesey Group

Anglesey, lying north of the Lleyn Peninsula and separated by the Menai Straits from the North Wales mainland, covers an area of roughly 310 sq. km. Topographically, the island can be described as undulating but possessing a rugged, mountainous coastline, especially in the north-west. According to Lynch (1969a, 108) little or no change has occurred to the coastline since the Neolithic,[37] with the majority of monuments lying within a 5km wide coastal zone. Inland are a number of marshy areas which may have some ritual-symbolic association with nearby monuments, especially the vast expanse of marshland that lies in the south-west of the island, referred to as Malltraeth Marsh.

Where monuments are sited, the soils are divided into two main types: slowly permeable, seasonally waterlogged Palaeozoic fine loamy soils which occupy the north-west of the island, and deep well-drained Palaeozoic coarse loamy soils occupying the central and south-eastern areas (Soil Survey of England and Wales 1983). Interestingly, the majority of sites are located in the south-eastern part of the island where the soils are much deeper and according to Lynch (1969a, 109) monuments are usually sited on the lighter soils (Grimes 1945). It is more than probable that settlement lay close by.

The Anglesey Group comprises at least 29 sites, 13 of which have been classified as either lost, damaged or doubtful (Lynch 1969a, 108–124, 1970; Powell et al. 1969, 296–300).[38] Importantly, antiquarians such as the Reverend John Skinner in his *Ten Days Tour in Anglesey* of 1802 noted and sketched a number of monuments which have been since destroyed or damaged. Given the number of monuments that were in use, this Neolithic core area has the highest concentration of monuments per square kilometre in Wales.

For this volume I have chosen the following sites that have a diverse architecture and unique dating range: Trefignath (ANG 1), Presaddfed (ANG 2), Ty Newydd (ANG 3), Barclodiad-y-Gawres (ANG 4), Din Dryfol (ANG 5), Bodowyr (ANG 6), Bryn Celli Ddu (ANG 7), Bryn yr Hen Bobl (ANG 8), Plas Newydd (ANG 9), Ty Mawr (ANG 10), Hen-Drefor (ANG 11), Pant y Saer (ANG 13) and Lligwy (ANG 14). Possibly associ-ated with the Anglesey Group are up to three monuments that are sited on the Welsh mainland, within the coastal hinterland of Caernarvonshire, viz. Sling (CRN 5) (covered in the North Wales Group) and the doubtful sites of Bryn (CRN 16) and Coetan Arthur (CRN 17).

Dominating this group, both in architecture and size, are the two passage graves of Barclodiad-y-Gawres and Bryn Celli Ddu. Associated with both monuments (and the Calderstones in Liverpool) is a unique megalithic art style which consists of pecked chevrons, cup-marks, spirals and zigzag lines. According to Savory (1980, 222) the architecture is believed to have originated in Iberia during the 4th/5th millennium BC, later spreading northwards along the Atlantic coast of Europe to Brittany and Ireland before arriving in North Wales. Roger Joussaume suggests that both monuments, similarly constructed, date to the Middle Neolithic and are associated with the Breton and Irish passage grave tradition (1985, 71). Lynch argues that both monuments date to the Late Neolithic and, along with the sub-megalithic chambered tomb of Lligwy, are the last of the megalithic structures to be constructed in Anglesey (1969a). However, despite the passage grave tradition being a late phenomenon, Bryn Celli Ddu has a much earlier phase, in the form of a henge monument which is delineated by the ditch of the outer extent of the later passage grave phase. Further, passage graves in Brittany and within the Channel Islands have much earlier dates for construction and use. I am inclined to suggest that the passage grave tradition in North Wales, occurring sometime after 2,700 BC is the last bastion of this way of burying the dead.

Many monuments earlier in date than the two passage graves exist on the island, including the recently excavated sites at Din Dryfol and Trefignath (Smith and Lynch 1987). These early multi-phased monuments, their use extending into the Middle Neolithic, along with other Neolithic monuments, suggest that there was a continuous Neolithic presence in Anglesey for some 2,000 years. Whether the island experienced indige-nous or imported culture is not clear. However, Anglesey appears to lie at the centre of a complex contact/exchange area whereby ideas as well as commodities were moving around the core areas of the Irish Sea Province.

The Trefignath monument (ANG 1; SH 2590 8051), one of the most complex and most important chambered tombs in Wales, is also one of only a small number of Neolithic monuments to have been totally excavated in Wales using modern techniques. It is also one of only a handful of monuments which has produced secure radiocarbon dates. The following description of the site is taken from the most recent source, Christopher Smith's excavation report (1987). Importantly, Lynch (1969a, 114) proved that this as a composite, or multi-phase, monument, with complexity similar to that of Dyffryn Ardudwy (MER 3).

The name 'Trefignath' is derived from a nearby farm of the same name and means 'the settlement in the marshes'. The site is located at around 19m AOD, on headland close to the port of Holyhead, 'over a cleft in a knoll of outcropping rock' (Lynch 1969a, 113). Prior to C.A. Smith's excavation the site was described as 'one of three long graves' in Anglesey (ibid., 113).

The antiquarian history of the site is extensive. The site was visited by John Aubrey in the mid-17th century (either 1656 or 1660) who described it in *Monumenta Britannica*. This description is the earliest on a megalith in Anglesey:[39]

> In Anglesey, about a mile from Holyhead, on a hill near the way that leads to Beaumaris, are placed certain great rude stones much after ye fashion of this draught [drawing] here ...There is about a mile from Holy-H[ea]d a monument wch I conceive to be yt meant in yr paper [description] of great rough stones about 20 stones in number and about 30 paces from one of ye roades leadinge from Holy H[ea]d to Beaumaris, between 4 and 5 foot high, at ye Northern End where of stand two stones on End, about two yards high above ground. The fashion of them can hardlie be exactlie described, by the reason some are sunk deep and some fallen flat w[hi]ch are almost overgrown w[i]th earth and grasse.

A later description of the monument utilising Aubrey's text is made in Gibson's edition of Camden's *Britannia* (1695). Many years later the site was visited by Nicholas Owen[40] who first drew attention to the state of preservation and noted the morphological complexity of the site (1775, 33–36):

> ... some rude stone monuments supposed to have been three cromlechs; they join each other, though the upper stones are now fallen of their supporters.

During this period the site was something of an enigma, the morphology not being known. Then in 1789, R. Gough, following Lewis Morris, supported the idea that the site consisted of two or maybe three cromlechs, in other words three separate chambered tombs. In many respects this assumption was partially correct. It was not until 1870 that W.O. Stanley recognised not three cromlechs but three chambers (1870, 58). If there were three chambers then there may have been three phases of construction and use. However, it should be noted that this early phase of the assessment of the tomb's complexity was also the time when the monument was under the greatest threat of destruction. According to Stanley, much of the cairn and some of the uprights had been removed by the late 18th century. Complete destruction of the monument was averted by the intervention of Lady

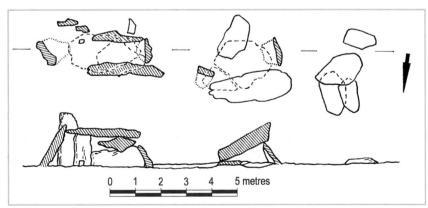

Plan (after Lynch 1969), prior to excavation by Smith 1977–1979

Trefignath looking west

Stanley around 1790. However, between Stanley's engraving in 1874 and 1971, the monument has changed little.

The monument was classified by E.N. Baynes in 1910 as a gallery grave, and this description remained current until 1971 when revised by Lynch who had always expressed reservations regarding this view of the monument (Lynch 1987). It was in 1971 that the capstone over the central chamber collapsed, and as a result the site was temporarily restored. However, by 1976 a timber support used to prop-up the capstone had begun to rot away and it was decided to fully restore the monument once a full excavation had been undertaken, the first to be conducted on any Neolithic monument in Anglesey with full modern rigour.

The excavation was directed by Christopher Smith and took place over three seasons between 1977 and 1979 (Smith 1981). Following the excavation, a post-excavation programme and consolidation of the monument followed in the years up until 1982. The excavation programme initially concentrated on the eastern chamber and its forecourt. The following year saw the excavation of the central chamber and cairn either side of the eastern chamber. Smith also excavated the western section of the site in order to establish the extent of the cairn mound. The final excavation season concentrated on the western chamber and its forecourt, and deter-

Trefignath western chamber

mined the northern and southern limits of the cairn. The cairn, once covering the three chambers, had been robbed within the recent past, probably for building stone.

From the excavation, Smith recognised three building phases as well as a further four activity episodes. The full sequence included pre-cairn activity, followed by the construction of the western chamber which was within a circular cairn; the construction of the central chamber; the use of both chambers; construction of the eastern chamber and the closure of the central and western chamber; closure of the eastern chamber; and finally, the abandonment of the monument.

Excavation Detail

The pre-cairn ground surface was sealed by the primary cairn and a radio-carbon date of 5,050±70 bp was obtained from a piece of charcoal from this surface. Scattered across the surface was a large selection of pre-monument artifacts including chert tools and debetage, flint tools and debetage, pottery, a sandstone disc and a chert hammer stone. These artifacts may suggest the presence of a small temporary settlement in existence prior to the construction of the monument (*ibid.*, 11). In contrast, it may be the case that these domestic items are derived from the phase of

Trefignath eastern chamber

preparation of the ground prior to construction of the monument, therefore suggesting ritual rather than domestic deposition. The flint from this phase, according to Elizabeth Healey (1987, 12) possibly dates to the Late Neolithic, which, confusingly, is not consistent with the radiocarbon dates associated with the same phase.

The western chamber was the earliest structure and was originally incorporated in a circular mound. A Post-Medieval road surface had damaged much of the cairn, but it was noticed that this phase consisted of a small simple passage grave and that little time had elapsed between the deposition of charcoal found within the pre-cairn surface and the construction of this chamber. This phasing is consistent with a date of between 3,750 and 3,500 BC for its construction.

Based on pollen evidence, Smith suggested that there was a considerable passage of time between the first use and subsequent abandonment of the western chamber and the construction of the central chamber. This chamber, rectangular in form and measuring 2.8m x 1.25m, had an entrance which opened towards the east. The uprights stood directly on the underlying bedrock, lodged in natural fissures, which gave some stability. During this phase the cairn mound was completely re-planned, being modified from a circular shape to that of a wedge. To the east of the central chamber was a deeply recessed forecourt area, the walls constructed of drystone walling. Incorporated into this architecture were horns, constructed either side of the forecourt and entrance. The southern side of the forecourt was, according to Smith, nine courses high, measuring up to 0.3m in height (ibid., 21). Petrological evidence suggests that the stone was locally quarried. Smith postulated that the cairn over the three chambers had architectural similarities with the trapezoidal cairns at Capel Garmon (DEN 3) and Carnedd Hengwm North and South (MER 5 and 6), themselves having architectural affinities with the Cotswold-Severn group of monuments. The demise of this monument phase is witnessed with a carefully laid blocking.

Due to the poor state of preservation very few Neolithic deposits were found within the central chamber. Neolithic pottery was, however, found in the vicinity of the chamber and was dated to the pre-cairn phase. Later historical disturbance in the chamber was proved by the discovery of a sherd of Medieval pottery, and it is thought that human remains were removed from the chamber about 1790. The dating of the chamber was based on a number of small Neolithic pottery sherds found on stone ledges

Trefignath looking west

in its walls. This consisted of Irish Sea carinated ware, which dated to the 4th millennium BC.

The third and final phase of construction consisted of the erection of the eastern chamber and associated portal arrangements. Pollen evidence from underneath the cairn suggests that the environment at the time of construction was open. This chamber, rectangular in form and measuring 2.5m by 1.1m, is the best preserved of the three and is constructed of two large capstones. The chamber opens towards the east. The portal arrangement consists of two sets of stones, one inner set standing around 1.2m in height, whilst the outer set stands around 2m. According to Smith, the cairn surrounding this chamber may not have covered the capstones. The cairn, supported by drystone revetted walling, would, however, have extended further to the east, north and south. The shape of the final phase cairn has similarities with other horned monuments in North Wales.

Located within the central area of the eastern chamber forecourt were four post-holes, arranged in an arc that indicate the structure may have had some ritual significance. Evidence was also found of a fire that dated to the 1st millennium BC. A Romano-British coin was also recovered.

South of a marshy lake (Llyn Llywenan) and built within a gently undulating landscape are two polygonal burial chambers, some 2m apart, forming the Presaddfed monument (ANG 2; SH 3486 8091). This monument stands on a small rise at around 20m AOD. The site was recorded and sketched by the Reverend John Skinner in 1802, when on Tuesday 12th December 1802 he described it thus:

> ... turning off into a field to the left we approached one of the finest and most finished cromlechs we have yet seen in the island, the cap stone measuring four yards and a half long, four yards wide and two yards thick, its three supporters each about a yard and a half high. Indeed there is a fourth nearly of the same height but it does not touch the stone above. Under this cromlech we were informed a whole family who had been ejected from their habitation sought shelter during the last winter. There was another cromlech close at hand but the cap stone had been forced down and rests in a slanting direction against the supporters; the top stone of this measured three yards long and two yards and a half wide and its supporters nearly two yards high.

According to Daniel (1950, 146) this monument has affinities with those found in Brittany and the Iberian Peninsula. I would also suggest that it has architectural similarities with the chambered tomb at Plas Newydd (ANG 9) and also with the now destroyed double dolmen at Trefor. Each monument possesses double polygonal-shaped chambers.

The south chamber, the larger of the two, has four uprights supporting a large capstone (approximately 3.3m x 2.5m) which slopes slightly to the south. The northern chamber has two uprights which support a probable capstone measuring 2.8m x 2.2m. The uprights and the capstone that form the chamber have collapsed inwards. Although the mound has disappeared, it seems it may originally have been oriented north/south. Presaddfed has been listed as an unclassified monument (Lynch 1969a, 123) but it appears to be a double dolmen of the Dyffryn Ardudwy type. Others have suggested the monument is actually two passage graves which face east (Daniel 1950; Powell et al. 1969). In his research into Welsh megalithic tombs, Wheeler (1925) has categorised this monument along with Longhouse (PEM 18) and the Hanging Stone at Burton (PEM 24) as part of the polygonal and circular dolmen group. However, in Lynch's plan (1969a, 123) the chambers appear to be rectangular.

The RCHAMW report for Anglesey postulates that Presaddfed represents 'a much ruined gallery grave', similar to that of nearby Trefignath (1937). I would suggest that Lynch's theory that it belongs to the long mound tradition, similar to those monuments on the Lleyn Peninsula, is plausible. However, Daniel (1950, 59) identifies the monument as a round barrow which may suggest a later date. However, no trace of this mound survives.

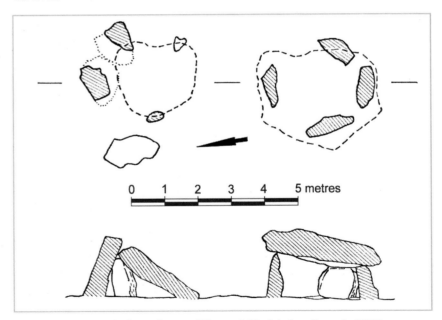

Plan and elevations of Presaddfed (after Lynch 1969)

The double dolmen at Presaddfed looking north

This monument (ANG 3; SH 3442 7386), lying approximately 3km north-east of Barclodiad-y-Gawres (ANG 4), is sited on the northern slope of a broad ridge, around 37m AOD. The sea is in full view to the west.

The site was visited by the Reverend John Skinner on Monday 6th December 1802 and described briefly thus:

> Hence continuing our walk to the northward we passed through the parish of Llanfaelog and about half a mile beyond the church came to a very perfect cromlech. The capstone is rather of an oblong shape and measured sixteen feet long, six wide, and three thick. It only rested upon three supporters each about three feet high although there were four placed in the ground. Near the cromlech were lying two large stones, the one seventeen feet long and three thick.

The monument still consists of three large uprights supporting a large, sub-angular capstone (4m x 1.5m). However, during the mid-20th century, two brick column supports were added to the chamber area. According to the excavator C.W. Phillips, the capstone had slipped to the north and did not cover the chamber area (Phillips 1936). The passage appears to be elongated, with a possible entrance at the south or south-east. Evidence of a fire of hazel wood within this entrance area was also found. However, no firm dates could be ascertained at the time of the excavation.

The idea that this monument belongs to the passage grave tradition has been given strong support by the discovery of a low stone within the northern part of the chamber which appears to form part of a passage approach (Lynch 1969a, 116). Skinner (1802) also mentions stone settings within the south-eastern part of the chamber. Lynch postulates that the chamber, in keeping with the passage grave tradition, was covered by a round cairn which, given the monument's position, is a possibility.

When excavated by Phillips in 1935, the monument produced up to 110 fragments of broken, white quartz, along with charcoal (Phillips 1936). These were found over the floor of the chamber, within black humic earth 50mm thick and may represent some deliberate ritual act that revolved around the whiteness of the quartz. It should be noted that quartz is naturally found in the vicinity. A fire-damaged barbed-and-tanged arrowhead, a polished flint axe fragment and a small assemblage of five tiny pieces of Beaker pottery were also found, suggesting either that the monument was constructed during the Late Neolithic or Early Bronze Age, or that it was at least in use during the Early Bronze Age. The fabric of the pottery is a typical fine, grit-less ware with a coarse, sandy surface. One sherd was decorated with two finely impressed twisted cord lines. Also recovered was a small rim forming part of a Bell Beaker or Short-Necked vessel, of either the B3 or Cord Zoned class. I would tend to agree with Lynch in that these artifacts are not primary in context but were deposited later. Other finds included a small chip from a polished flint axe which could not be properly identified, but may be similar to types found at Ty Isaf (BRE 5) in Breconshire and the passage-grave cemetery at Loughcrew in County Meath, Ireland.

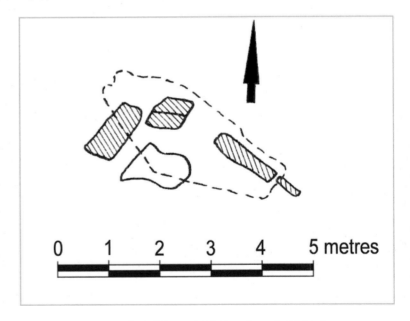

Plan of Ty Newydd (after Lynch 1969a)

Ty Newydd looking north

This passage grave (ANG 4; SH 3290 7072) also referred to as Mynnedd Cnwc or Mynydd-y-Cnwc, lies 19m AOD on the southern part of a short promontory overlooking a small inlet known as Porth Trecastell. From the passage area, the monument looks over the rugged north-western coastline of Holy Island. To the north and east is a series of small undulating hills. Due to its proximity with Ty Newydd (ANG 3) and Din Dryfol (ANG 5), it is possible that these monuments may have had some contemporary association.

The monument appears to have suffered the usual pillage of previous centuries. Used as a stone quarry in the 18th century, most of the contents, including archaeological deposits from the chambers, were removed. However, the monument did receive some archaeological recognition in 1799 when a 'note' was published by David Thomas in the *Cambrian Register* listing the Cromlechau or Druidical Altars of Anglesey. One of the first accounts of this monument was given by the Reverend John Skinner, who on Monday 6th December 1802 described it thus:

> Instead of a cromlech at Mynnedd Cnwc we found the vestiges of a large carnedd; many of the flat stones of the cist faen or chamber are still remaining but the small ones have been almost all removed to build a wall close at hand. On another fork of the peninsula about a hundred yards distant we observed the traces of another carnedd of much smaller dimensions [this is now regarded as a Bronze Age cairn]. From the nature of their situation, the bay, the earth work andc. it is possible to suppose that an engagement here took place with the natives wherein some principal officers were slain and interred on the spot.

In 1869 Prichard published a full description of the site including a plan of the passage and part of the chamber, but made reference to the destruction of the monument. It was photographed in 1900 by J.E. Griffith. In 1910, E.N. Baynes concluded that Barclodiad-y-Gawres was a small cairn, and it was not until 1937 that the full extent of the chamber area and the mound was exposed in the plan made by W.F. Grimes. In his research, Grimes concluded that the monument was a passage grave of the style 'of Newgrange and other Irish sites'.

Terrance Powell and Glyn Daniel excavated this large, impressive, now reconstructed, Late Neolithic passage grave, the only attested example of

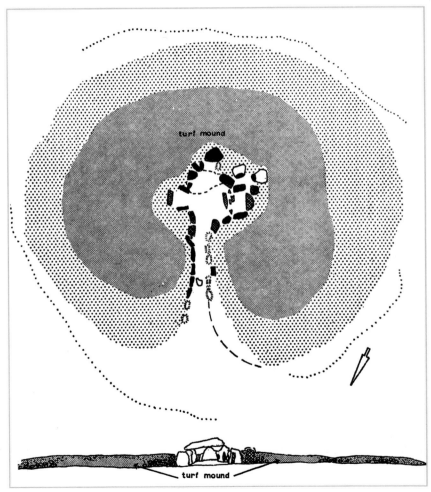

Plan of Barclodiad-y-Gawres (after Powell & Daniell 1956)

a cruciform type in North Wales, in 1953 (1956). The reconstruction sadly incorporates a concrete dome and drystone walling around the passage area. Set in a dramatic coastal landscape, the monument now has all the appearance of an air raid bunker. However, set within the reconstructed fabric is one of the most impressive decorated megalithic monuments in north-western Europe. The passage, measuring approximately 6m, leads to a cruciform chamber which has a series of uprights decorated with chevrons, lozenges, spirals and zigzag designs. These designs, which have been pecked rather than carved, are similar to decorated uprights found in association with the Bryn Celli Ddu (ANG 1) monument, on the Calderstones monument in Liverpool and monuments found in the Boyne Valley of central Ireland (Lynch 1967, 1–22).

Carved decoration occurs on Stones 5 (L8), 6 (C1) 8 (C3), 22 (C13) and 19 (C16) (Shee-Twohig 1981, 229). These stones have been discussed by Lynch who looks at the possible relationship with decorated stones from Brittany and Ireland, in particular the time, effort and style (167, 1–22). On Stone 5 are lozenges and vertical zigzags; Stone 6 exhibits a conjoined circular motif, lozenges and vertical zigzags; on Stones 8 and 19 are a series of spirals and a series of unrecognisable motifs. Finally, on Stone 22 is a spiral with supporting motifs, lozenges, a horizontal chevron band and a series of vertical zigzags. This particular stone bears some resemblance to the decorated Pattern Stone found at Bryn Celli Ddu. All five stones have their decoration facing into the chamber rather than being hidden, as found at monuments in the Boyne Valley.

Regarding the cruciform chamber area, it is probable that different strata and gender of society were ritualistically deposited in different chambers, with, for example, male and female remains being placed in separate chambers. The chamber area was once roofed over by several enormous capstones, and although the chamber and passage architecture was not

Decorated stone C16 from Barclodiad-y-Gawres (after Powell & Daniel 1956)

covered prior to excavation it is considered that when constructed it was probably covered by a large turfed mound. The forecourt area opens out onto views across the western coast of Anglesey.

The profile of the passage appears to narrow as one progresses into the chamber area, an arrangement unlike passage tombs elsewhere. However, one should be cautious in so far as the true lines of both passage walls may no longer be in their original positions. It is clear that passages in all other passage graves provide some form of restricted visual access to the chamber area. One further missing element is the height of the passage uprights. It could be the case that these stones were set in such a way as to again afford restricted visual access.

Within the central chamber was discovered a hearth approximately 1m in diameter which contained a mixture of charcoal and stone chips. Also recovered was an assemblage of shells, fish bones, amphibia, reptiles and small mammals.

The cremated remains of two young adult males were found in the western chamber during the 1953 excavation. According to Powell and Daniel (1956) no primary pottery was found, but there was one artifact which may be contemporary with initial use of the monument. This was a bone or antler pin which was found in fragments that had been burnt, presumably in association with the cremation burials in the western side chamber where they were found. The pin was similar to skewer pins found at Loughcrew and Fourknocks in central Ireland. The location of a cinerary urn above the collapsed roof area suggests that the deposition of this cremation was subsequent to the initial use of the tomb. The urn had a decorated bevelled rim made up of a series of lines of plaited cord impressions.

The carved stones located in the inner passage and chamber areas appear to be strategically placed so that they can be viewed only by people using these areas. It is probable that they were incorporated to form part of

View of façade inside the mound, looking north

Barclodiad-y-Gawres: view of the reconstructed entrance and mound which forms a shell around the original monument

a ritual procession way between the façade area and the chamber. Metaphorically, this art would have been viewed by the dead as well. Subtly-pecked designs are carved on the uprights which form the side chambers and these could only have been viewed by an artificial light source. The subtleness and position of the art suggests that only certain living members of a stratified society viewed it. As they made their final journey from one familiar world to another which was not, those who had died would also see it. The chamber area would have provided a resting area before the final journey when the spirits of the dead travelled onwards. The archaeological evidence indicates that excarnation was used and, therefore, the physicality of the deceased would have changed from a recognisable form to a loose pile of bone. The transformed body would then be taken from the façade, along the passage to the chamber. An array of grave goods, including pottery vessels and tools, would accompany the dead on these series of journeys. The art with its secret meanings and symbolism may have assisted the smooth transition from this world to the next.

A visit in March 2006 by a team from the Department of Archaeology and Anthropology at the University of Bristol has rediscovered unrecorded rock art on Stone C2. The designs are being studied at present and they include a complex chevron design. It is clear, from this and other Neolithic burial sites in Wales that archaeologists are not looking hard enough.

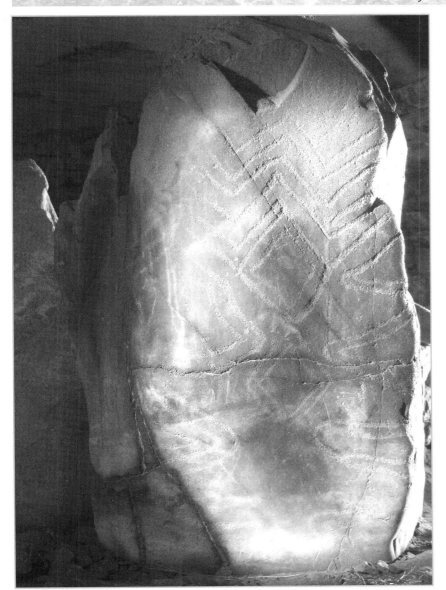

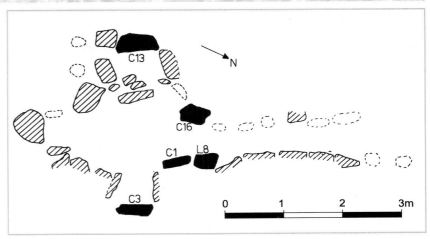

Plan showing the locations of the decorated stones

Stone C16, facing the chamber and hidden from view from the passage (photo: Adam Stanford)

Stone C3, hidden inside the eastern chamber (photo: Adam Stanford)

The following description of the site (ANG 5; SH 3963 7254) is taken from the text of Frances Lynch's excavation report (1987). Din Dryfol is one of several monuments in North Wales that have been investigated using modern excavation techniques.

This early Neolithic monument, excavated between 1969 and 1970 and again in 1980, is located in the south-west part of Anglesey and stands around 18m AOD. All that survives of the internal architecture is a rectangular chamber constructed of three uprights and a small capstone to the west; little of the cairn survives. It is more than probable that the cairn was robbed for building stone. According to Lynch, up to four chambers existed, all aligned roughly east-west. The arrangement of these chambers suggests a gallery-type monument (rather than a passage grave), similar in form to the much damaged Cerrig Llwydion monument (CRM 10) in Carmarthenshire. If this is the case, Din Dryfol may also have similarities with the destroyed Llanymynech Hill monument in Montgomeryshire.[41] Further similarities are to be seen with the two- and four-chambered court tomb monuments found in Ireland. From Lynch's excavation report, there appears to be no formal division between the chamber compartments.

Situated some 6km from the south-west coast, this monument forms part of a small group including Ty Newydd (ANG 3) and Barclodiad-y-Gawres (ANG 4). The monument is situated on a south-west facing slope within a rocky landscape overlooking the Afon Gwna. Between the monument and Ty Newydd, approximately 4km to the north-west, is a large area of marsh known as Llyn Padrig. To the south-west is a small lake known as Llyn Coron. It is probable that these two natural features would have had some ritual or economic significance at the time that the monument was in use.

The earliest reference to Din Dryfol was made by the Reverend H. Longueville Jones in 1865 when he suggested that it was two separate monuments: a chamber to the north-west and a standing stone to the north-east. This interpretation remained current until the early part of the 20th century. Later, Prichard (1871, 310–311) suggested the presence of two monuments on the basis of stone alignments, and his engraving and plan of the site shows a clear chamber. He also records the presence of two large holes (or depressions) which may represent the settings of two uprights. However, excavations by Lynch in 1980 did not find any evidence for these latter features. Neil Baynes's survey *The Megalithic Remains of Anglesey* (1911) suggests that the two monuments at Din Dryfol are in fact one when he says that the menhir 'may have formed the end of a long chamber' (Baynes 1911, 75). Further, he compares the western section of the monument with Trefignath, classifying both as gallery graves.

According to the RCAHM inventory of Anglesey (1937), investigations revealed that a possible missing portal stone approximately 2m north of the present standing portal indicates that an unusually wide entrance existed which may have formed part of a passage grave. Packing stones, according to Hemp (1935), were found in the location of the missing portal. Furthermore, investigations also showed that at some time during its use, possibly during the Early Bronze Age, the entrance was blocked, as a ridge of cairn material was found in front of the portal area which turned out to be a Post-Medieval track. Lynch agrees with Daniel that this monument is a gallery grave and is similar to tombs such as Cashtal-yn-Ard (MAN 1) on the Isle of Man and Trefignath (ANG 1).

The eastern and southern sections of the chamber (Lynch's Chamber 4) were excavated in 1969, and the following year the capstone was lifted so as to fully excavate the chamber area. Further work was undertaken in 1980. The trenching was carried out in five areas and showed that the monument, this was constructed over a rock shelf; in places this shelf was exposed and suggests that any stratigraphy within the area of the tomb was shallow.

The number of finds from the three excavation seasons was small, but included assemblages of Neolithic burnt bone, flint, pottery and stone implements from the chambers and Romano-British pottery, slag and stone from inside and outside the cairn. The earliest pottery helped to provide a rough date for the construction of the monument of around 3,000 bc. The absence of later pottery suggests that Din Dryfol was not in use during the Late Neolithic. Also recovered from each of the chambers was a small assemblage of bone, of which 12 fragments were identified as human. According to T.P. O'Connor, the human bone assemblage represented two individuals. Other identified bone included those of sheep/goat, pig and a large ungulate, either cattle or horse (1987, 129).

The monument consists of four uprights, two of which support a small capstone. The distance between the chamber and a large portal stone measured approximately 3m in length (Lynch 1987, 123).

Oriented roughly east/west, there appears to be little cairn present. The plan of the monument in some ways replicates the chamber and portal stone of Arthur's Stone, in Herefordshire (HRF 1), whilst Lynch (1969a, 114) suggests that there are some architectural characteristics in common with Hen-Drefor (ANG 11). Uncovered through excavation were the remains of a multi-chambered tomb with the eastern upright representing a door-stone to a chamber. Lynch suggests that chambers 3 and 4 are the earliest, followed by chambers 1 and 2 (1987, 123). This is partly based on two deliberately filled-in post-holes located either side of chamber 3. Chamber 3 may have been added after several generations of use of the original chamber 4. Between chambers 3 and 4 Lynch uncovered blocking material, whilst to the east of chamber 3 was a possible façade that was partially delineated by uprights on the south-east side of the chamber.

According to Lynch (1987, 123), this monument, classified as a long mound, has its architectural emphasis placed on the tall portal(s) around the entrance and the rectangular chambers. Based on archaeological evidence, wood was also used in its construction. These features are present in other monuments within the northern part of the Irish Sea province. Because of previous damage, especially during the Romano-British period and also during the 19th century, Lynch concludes that any full interpretation is inconclusive. It is certainly multi-phased, although the number of phases is unknown.

Din Dryfol chamber looking west

This monument (ANG 6; SH 4632 6825), also referred to as Bodower,[42] is located 38m AOD on a lightly undulating south-eastern slope that overlooks the Menai Straits and the dramatic peaks of Snowdonia. Close to the monument and slightly later in date is a series of standing stones that lie on the north-western slopes of the small valley of the Afon Braint. Both sets of monuments were once probably intervisible. Approximately 2km south-east of Bodowyr is Perthi Duon (ANG 17), located at SH 480 668. It is probable that both these two monuments were in contemporary use during the Early Neolithic.[43]

This simple monument consists of four upright stones standing approximately 1.5m high supporting a mushroom-shaped capstone measuring 2.45m x 1.75m. Located around the monument are the possible remnants of a mound. Two uprights towards the east of the monument form a possible entrance, whilst a single upright oriented to the north-east forms part of a possible passage and is referred to as a sill-stone. An example of a sill-stone was also found, according to Prichard, in 1873 (22–27) at Ty Mawr (ANG 10), also located close to the Menai Straits. The Reverend John Skinner visited this site and produced several sketches of the monument, one including the now demolished Bodowyr House and another possibly showing himself sketching the monument. According to his sketches, little has changed with the monument since 1802. However, Skinner does show it to be located on a pronounced mound of which little survives today. In his useful description of Thursday 2nd December 1802, Skinner remarks:

> Here we were gratified of a very perfect cromlech standing in a field to the north-west of the house [Bodowyr House]. The upper stone terminates in a ridge like the roof of a building and measures seven feet four inches long, three feet deep and four wide: this is sustained by three supporters, each three feet in height and nearly the same in thickness. That cromlechs were not always used (if they were at all) as altars for sacrifice I think may be demonstrated by the one before as its Pyramidical form is by no means adapted to the purpose. Indeed there is a tradition amongst the Welsh that this rude memorial was erected over the grave of a British princess named Branwen who flourished in the year of the world 3105!!!! [a date derived by those who believed in a literal theory of creation].

In plan, the uprights of Bodowyr form a polygonal chamber, referred to by Daniel as a B-Dolmen (1950, 9).[44] Lynch has suggested that this monument has close similarities with monuments such as the Hanging Stone (PEM 24) at Burton, Pembrokeshire and simple passage graves at Carrowmore, County Sligo (Lynch 1976, 75).

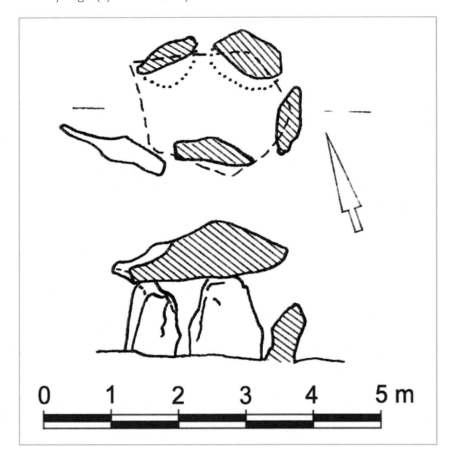

Plan of Bodowyr (after Lynch 1969a)

Bodowyr looking north

This monument (ANG 7; SH 5086 7023), one of two known passage graves in Anglesey, can be considered as one of the most important Neolithic monuments on the island. Located on a low ridge of glacial moraine at around 33m AOD and close to the Menai Straits, it has extensive views of the Snowdonia peaks. To the north and west is a slightly undulating landscape. Approximately 1.5km south-east of Bryn Celli Ddu is the large dolmen of Plas Newydd (ANG 9), whilst Bodowyr (ANG 6) and Perthi Duon (ANG 17) lie approximately 4km south-west of the monument.

Bryn Celli Ddu dates from the Late Neolithic and probably has some temporal association with the nearby Bronze Age monuments such as the standing stone that is located in a field some 200m west of the monument (SH 5063 7010). Also worth noting is the recent discovery of 26 cup marks on rock outcropping that lies roughly 250m north-west of Bryn Celli Ddu (at SH 5062 7024) Both the site, the rock-outcropping and a standing stone located 330m west of the monument are visible. These sites along with other finds appear to delineate an area of ritual activity. (Nash et al. forthcoming).

Within its recent history, the monument has been restored. However, one can get a glimpse of its original appearance by following the Reverend Skinner's account of his visit in 1802. He entered the passage and chamber on Friday 3rd December and made a number of important, detailed and sometimes rather quirky observations which included the (poorly punctuated) following:

> But in this parish we were fully recompensed for all our former disappointments by the site of the Carnedd at Bryn Celli. Accompanied by a young farmer who procured a lanthorn for the purpose we walked nearly a mile south-east of the church to the spot where in Mr Rowlands's time there were two carnedds remaining, having two rude stone pillars placed between them but these stones have been employed for the purpose of building a wall near this place as well as a great part of the western carnedd which is nearly destroyed for the same purpose about twenty years ago [1782] when the labourers went digging towards the centre discovered a flat pan about ten inches overturned bottom upwards and under it a wedge of gold as they pretend the size of the heater of an iron with a piece of wire passing through the smaller end of it. The father of the young man who was with us happened to be one of the workmen employed at the time, but as what they found was immediately taken by Colonel Peacock the proprietor of the ground, the man could give no further account of the circumstance. I should imagine that what they called the wedge of gold was no other than one of the brazen celts or sacrificial instruments used in former times which have been discovered in great numbers in Cornwall and other parts of the kingdom. Whilst a farmer was removing some of the stones from the north-east side of the larger carnedd to employ them in his repairs he came to a mouth of a passage covered with a square stone similar to that at Plasnewydd, anxious to reap the fruits of his discovery he precured a light and crept forward on his hands and knees along the dreary vault, when lo! In a chamber at the further end a figure in white seemed to forbid his approach. The poor man had scarcely power sufficient to crawl backwards out of this den of spirits as he imagined. However in a course of a few days instigated by the hopes of riches and the presence of many an assistance he made his second entrance into the cavern and finding the white gentleman did not offer to stir he boldly went forward and discovered the object of his apprehensions was no other than a stone pillar about six feet in height standing in the centre of the chamber. His former consternation could now only be exceeded by his eagerness to see what contained beneath the stone which he shortly overturned but treasure there was none, some large human bones lying near the pillar sufficiently testifying the purpose for which the structure was intended. This is the substance of the account we received from the young man whose father was one of Colonel Peacock's labourers and on the premisise at the time of the discovery. The superstition of the common people still supposed this to be the habitation of spirits. Our two conductors seeming rather to compliment each other about precedence, I took the lanthorn and crawling for about twelve feet long a narrow passage got into a more capacious chamber, my companions followed close at my heel and we assembled to the number of six in this singular scpulchre. The passage by which we entered is about three feet high and a little more in breadth and was formed like that we noticed at Plas Newydd with flat stone stuck endways and covered with others of still greater magnitude laid across. I have still my doubts that if the former was further explored it might terminate in a similar vault

to what we are now speaking of. The height of the chamber is nine feet, its form nearly triangular some of the sides being about three yards long and four or five feet high. The intermediate space up to the roof is filled with stones placed one above the other in the manner they build walls but without any kind of cement. Two prodigious flat stones covered the whole one about three yards in length and two in breadth the other not quite so large. These are of a gritty substance not like any other stone found in the vicinity. The pillar stone lying in the cavern is a kind of freestone and seems to have been rounded by the tool.

An antiquarian engraving of the site published in *Archaeologia Cambrensis* in 1847 portrays Bryn Celli Ddu as much ruined, consisting of a confused entrance and passage and an exposed chamber. There appears to be little or no trace of any mound. Therefore much of the destruction had occurred sometime after Skinner's visit in 1802.

The site was first excavated by Captain F. du Bois Lukis in 1865. In letters to his brother, the Reverend W.C. Lukis, the captain describes how he excavated the chamber area and found a small piece of lead and a flint 'instrument'. After the death of his brother, the letters were obtained by the British Museum, who found among them a fragment of pottery, a strip of lead, a broken flint flake (possibly part of a tranchet arrowhead) and 'colouring matter' (*cf.* Daniel 1950, 122). This 'colouring matter' proved to be jasper that according to Hemp occurs frequently on the site (1930).

Later excavations by Hemp between 1925 and 1929 revealed a complex history to the site. Beneath the mound was a possible circular henge consisting of 14 upright stones, some of which were broken, others leaning outwards, and within the centre of this was a pit which was covered by a recumbent stone slab. During excavation, socket holes were found which might represent the position of further uprights. Underlying some of these socket holes was evidence of cremation material, which may suggest that the earlier henge monument deliberately included human burials during the period of its construction. Covering the area of the henge monument, but underlying the present mound, was a purple coloured clay which Hemp suggests may represent a ritual floor. However, Lynch (1969a, 112) argues that it is a palaeo-turf line, the colour of which has been affected by drainage conditions from the overlying mound. This being the case, Lynch suggests that grass was covering the henge before the construction of the passage-grave, indicating a time lapse between the abandonment and the construction of the henge (*ibid.*, 112). I am inclined to think that the excavation process was less than rigorous and as a result the henge, which is also considered a later Neolithic monu-

Entrance to the tomb looking west

ment is, in fact, kerbing belonging to the passage grave (Julian Thomas: a pers. comm.)

Outside the upright stones were the remains of a silted, flat-bottomed ditch approximately 6m in diameter and 2.2m in depth. It is this feature that is considered to be the henge, and to predate the mound. Within the entrance area of the passage-grave phase were the sockets of five post-holes that may represent a possible burial platform for human excarnation. Immediately behind this structure was a shallow pit containing the remains of an ox. Also within the entrance area were two hearths. The presence of the post-holes, the burial pit and the two hearths suggests that some form of ritual activity was being conducted within the entrance and forecourt area. The remains of the ox may suggest an offering for the dead to consume during their journey to the other world; an act widely noted in the ethno-graphic record.

Finds from the 1925–1929 excavation are meagre, but included a petit tranchet (transverse arrowhead) which is probably Late Neolithic in date, a rounded scraper (thumb-shaped end scraper), a small lithic assemblage numbering 20 pieces and a mudstone bead which was found within the turf line of the ditch, south of the passage. According to Lynch it is probable that this artifact belongs to the passage grave builders rather than the henge users (1969b, 160). However, previous anti-quarian interest in this monument (dating to at least the early 19th century) has probably seen the removal of much of the artifactual evidence.

The mound, now 26m in diameter, may have been larger, but during part-restoration by the Ministry of Works the monument could have been severely altered. The entrance with its two uprights (without capstone) is located on the eastern side of the mound, and leads into a slab-roofed passage approximately 7.5m in length. Intriguingly, the southern wall of the passage is straight, whereas the northern wall is not (Thomas 1988, 45). To the west of the monument and almost in line with the alignment of the walls

Plan of Bryn Celli Ddu (after Daniel 1950)

of the passage is a standing stone, suggesting some planning of the monu-ment. The passage leads into a polygonal chamber roughly 2.5m across.[45] Between the entrance and the passage are two sets of kerbing, which suggests two phases of building during the passage grave phase. Within the chamber area is a single pillar-stone which has no structural use and there-fore may be considered as possessing some ritual or, at least, an aesthetic significance.

Considering the design and the presence of an ox burial Lynch suggests that this monument has a greater association with passage graves in Brittany than with monuments in the Boyne Valley in southern Ireland (1969a, 111).

Along with Barclodiad-y-Gawres (ANG 4), this monument has two stones decorated with megalithic art, one within a pit, the other in the chamber. Decoration on one stone includes an anti-clockwise spiral approxi-mately 13cm in diameter. The other stone, known usually as the Pattern Stone was found in a possible ritual pit in the centre of the monument. The stratigraphic rela-tionship between this stone and the surrounding soil deposits suggest that it belongs to the henge phase of the monu-ment, yet it has similarities with other decorated stones in passage graves throughout north-western Europe which were constructed as single-phase monu-ments. It could be the case that the stone that formed part of the henge was left in situ while the passage grave was being constructed.

The complex decoration of the 'Pattern Stone', confined to three faces on the upper section of the stone consists of a clockwise spiral which is linked to a meandering curvilinear pattern, referred to by Shee-Twohig as a serpen-tine form (1981, 230) which covers both faces of the stone. Also present is a cup-mark. The simple spiral may have direct similarities with stone C16 within the chamber of Barclodiad-y-Gawres. There are also design similarities with the megalithic art of the uprights of the Calderstones, Liverpool, (see page 26).

The name of this unusual monument (ANG 8; SH 5190 6900) that forms a kidney-shaped mound approximately 5.5m in height and 13.5m in diameter, translates as the 'Hill of the Old People'. Bryn Yr Hen Bobl, standing around 33m AOD, has been classified as a passage grave and, although not similar to nearby Bryn Celli Ddu (ANG 5), it does share a similar landscape, standing a few hundred metres from the Menai Straits. To the north-west, Bryn Celli Ddu is 1km away, whilst to the south-west and north-east are further Neolithic chambered monuments. Bryn yr Hen Bobl is also sited close to a series of standing stones running from north of Bryn Celli Ddu to the south of the Bodowyr monument (ANG 6). Prior to the monument becoming included within a late 18th-century walled park, Bryn Yr Hen Bobl may have had even more outstanding views of the North Wales mainland, including Snowdonia, as well as views to the south which include the open sea.

The site was visited by the Reverend John Skinner on Friday 3rd December 1802, when he produced several sketches and remarked:

> From hence we pursed our walk across the park towards Lord Uxbridge's house, stopping in the way to examine a very large Carnedd or artificial hillock formed of loose stones but now overgrown with turf and trees. This remain is one of the most considerable in the island, measuring one hundred and thirty-four paces in circumference. On walking around it we observed a square opening on the south side which I entered on my hands and knees and found it about ten feet long, four wide and three high, the sides formed of three large flat stones placed edgeways in the ground supporting the roof, which consists of only two. I have endeavoured to be as exact as I could in my drawings of this cistfaen (which without doubt it was) and employed as the grave of some considerable personage in ancient times, though Mr Rowlands appropriates the carnedd to a very different use and connects it with the religion of the Druids. In his time three skeletons were discovered in digging near the surface of the carnedd, which gave him an idea of its being a place of sacrifice; but as he had never an opportunity of viewing the interior (the opening having been discovered within these few years) he was unable to speak with certainty on the subject.

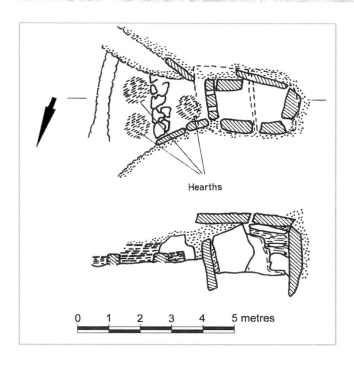

Hearths

Plan and section of Bryn yr Hen Bobl (after Hemp 1937)

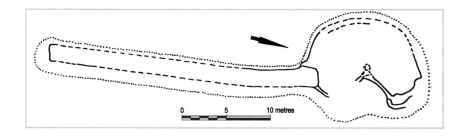

Plan of Bryn yr Hen Bobl (after Lynch 1969)

The monument consists of a damaged stone-lined entrance that is incorporated into the mound on the eastern side. There are also several trees, (one dead), on the mound. The burial chamber, measuring 2m x 1m and 1.6m high, is constructed of a series of uprights supporting a large capstone. The remains of at least 20 individuals including adults and children were discovered in the chamber; all were disarticulated. There was also a small assemblage of burnt human bone found outside the southern end of the terrace, which may be associated with a later Bronze Age urn burial associated with the monument (see later).

Bryn yr Hen Bobl was excavated by W.J. Hemp between 1929 and 1935 (1935). The sides of the forecourt were found to be constructed of uprights and drystone walling. In front of the entrance was an extensive blocking deposit of large stones and soil; Lynch (1970, 47) suggests that the drystone walling was also used to block the forecourt. Within this blocking were fragments of Neolithic pottery, lithics and charcoal, the origin of which is unclear. However, similar deposition has been found in blocking material in the forecourt areas of other passage graves and may

Bryn yr Hen Bobl chamber looking west

represent some form of ritual activity, whose locus was on top of the monument. A few sherds of pottery were also found in three ritual fire pits in the forecourt area. In addition to the excavation of the chamber and forecourt area, Hemp also considered that a side chamber may have existed. However, this was never found.

Located around the southern part of the mound, and now almost undetectable, was a stone-revetted platform or terrace measuring 100m x 5m. This is referred to by some as the 'tail'. Excavators deduced that this was constructed after the mound and may have been part of an architectural trend that was associated with the construction of the horns, located either side of the entrance. The terrace, which is aligned north-south, had small pieces of pottery within its foundation material, and was later replaced with a drystone wall. Beneath the foundation material there appeared to be a specially laid primary deposit consisting of clay and charcoal. Remarkably, within this clay surface were a number of footprints probably belonging to the builders or users of the monument. The various suggestions as to what this platform may represent include Hemp's idea that it is a deliberate addition to the monument, which transforms the plan of the tomb and the surface into a phallus. However, this shape can be only be viewed from above or in plan, and a more likely origin of the terrace is that it forms part of a prehistoric field system which may pre-date the monument. To support this idea the break in the slope continues north of the passage grave and the plan of the terrace. However, within this area there is no trace of any drystone walling or clay foundation and, as Castleden (1992, 365) suggests, no ritual significance can be attributed to this feature. Indeed, I would further add that no other monument in Wales has this type of feature running away from the cairn. However, it should be noted that an inverted cinerary urn and associated cremation were found at the southern end of the tail and it could be the case that both the monument and the possible wall form part of a later ritual sequence that incorporates Bronze Age ceremonial rites. Furthermore, the tail may have acted as a procession route that linked the lands of the living with the mound of the dead (Children and Nash 2001).

The finds from the ritual hearths and blocking material make Bryn yr Hen Bobl one of the richest pottery and flint sites in Anglesey. More remarkable is that the majority of these finds are not associated with the actual monument, according to Lynch (1969b, 161), except for a broken bone pin which was found in the chamber.[46] Such a pin, not usually associated with the Irish Sea Zone long cairns, is nevertheless linked within the passage grave tradition of which this monument is one. Concerning the pottery, of which there is decorated and undecorated types, it appears that the assemblage was not provenanced and co-excavator Colin Gresham formally dissented from Hemp's findings, producing an alternative report on the pottery finds, that offers a different account of their locations and associations in the site chronology.

The only pottery, therefore, that can be specifically assigned to a location within the mound was that found in the south-eastern corner of the terrace (Hemp 1935, 269) where the fragments of two shouldered bowls were unearthed. Other pottery from across the site included fragments of decorated Peterborough Ware and undecorated wares of Western Neolithic derivation. The Western Neolithic types were found beneath the main structures of the monument and both types were allegedly found within the chamber area. Up to six pots with slightly different fabrics were linked to the Western Neolithic pottery group. The most complete vessel was a lugged bowl, the fabric of which was very hard and pitted, black to brown in colour throughout and measuring up to 25.4cm in diameter. The Peterborough Ware types comprised a series of sherds that included shoulders and rims decorated with whipped-cord and square-toothed comb designs. Also

Bryn yr Hen Bobl looking south towards Snowdonia

recovered was a single sherd which may belong to a beaker, suggesting that the monument was in use, or at least known about, during the Early Bronze Age. Along with pottery, there was a comprehensive assemblage of lithics and stone, including scrapers, awls, leaf-shaped arrowheads, end scrapers and transverse arrowheads (Petit Tranchet derivative). Associated with the diagnostic lithics was a large assemblage of waste material, including stone flakes which are believed to come from polished stone axes (Daniel 1950, 139). Probably the most interesting finds were four complete polished stone axes, three of which were recovered from the terrace and the other from the northern horn of the cairn. A roughed-out stone axe was also found at the base of the outer wall within the forecourt area. Three of these axes had pointed butts and convex cutting edges and appear to be made from local Anglesey dolerite, while the rough-out is made from Graig Llwyd diorite, and almost certainly is a product of the well-known axe manufacturing centre near Penmaenmawr, North Wales. Other finds included an Iron Age bead which was found within the disturbed filling of the chamber, and two small balls, one of bone, the other of stone, which may be associated with the Irish Passage Grave tradition.

Located on top of the cairn was evidence of Iron Age or early Medieval burials, again suggesting the monument's continuing sanctity as a place of burial, which 'aura' included the forecourt area and entrance.

This possibly much-modified monument (ANG 9; SH 5203 6972) stands in the formal gardens in front of the National Trust-owned property of Plas Newydd. During the Neolithic period, this monument may have enjoyed extensive views across the Menai Straits. It is located approximately 250m north of the shores of the straits within an undulating landscape both to the north and west, and stands around 30m AOD. Approximately 2km to the north-west is Bryn Celli Ddu (ANG 7). Further Neolithic activity is presumed both north-east and south-west of the monument, but whether or not these monuments were in direct association either spatially or temporally, remains the subject of debate. Bryn Yr Hen Bobl (ANG 8) stands some 300m to the south-west of the Plas Newydd site. It would appear that its architecture, consisting of ten uprights, supported two massive capstones.

Although Lynch has described this monument as 'unclassified' (1969a, 123) due to the site being unexcavated, I would suggest that this monument has similar architectural traits to Trefignath (ANG 1) and Presaddfed (ANG 2).

The Plas Newydd monument has functioned as a parkland folly for well over two centuries. The Reverend John Skinner, when visiting the site on Friday 3rd December 1802, remarked:

> From hence we proceeded to look at a very large cromlech or Druidical altar preserved in the Park near his lordship's stables (which still stand) ... However I made a drawing of the cromlech, which is nearly four yards long and above a yard thick, the supporters at the north end nearly five feet high; a smaller stone lying close to the other extremity measuring three feet long and two and a half thick has also its small supporters and is to all appearance intended as a separate cromlech.[47]

The tomb in fact consists of two chambers, the largest of which measures 3m x 2.7m and which supports a large capstone measuring 3.5m x 3m and 1m in thickness. It is considered that the entrance was located to the south-west where an ante-chamber with supporting capstone is located. Both chambers appear to be circular in plan and are separated by a large stone that restricts access between the two. The capstone of the larger chamber slopes towards the north-east, where three large uprights are aligned

roughly east-west. It is probable that the central upright within this alignment was a closed portal similar to that at Pentre Ifan (PEM 5). Both the eastern and western sides of the large chamber are missing.

Due to the lack of excavation, one can only imagine what the monument looked like during the Neolithic. Hemp (1935) suggested that the monument consisted of a large single chamber with associated ante-chamber or passage, whereas Daniel (1950, 57) suggests that the southern chamber is, in fact, a side chamber. The passage, according to Daniel, is located at the east. I am more inclined to think that the two chambers, which are oriented on roughly a north/south axis, form a continuous chamber set. The mound would have only partially covered the chamber leaving much of the capstone exposed.

Plan and elevation of Plas Newydd (after Lynch 1969a)

Plas Newydd chambers looking south-west

This much-damaged monument (ANG 10; SH 5390 7224), drawn by H. Prichard in 1873 (1873, 22–27), lies between the Menai Bridge and Llanfair Pwllgwyngyll and has identical landscape affinities with nearby Plas Newydd (ANG 9) and Bodowyr (ANG 6), and commands outstanding views of the mountains of Snowdonia. The monument, standing around 73m AOD, overlooks the north-eastern reach of the Menai Straits (and the open sea of Conwy Bay beyond), whilst to the north-west lies an undulating, marshy landscape. The location of this monument is interesting in that it sits on the interface between two contrasting landscapes.

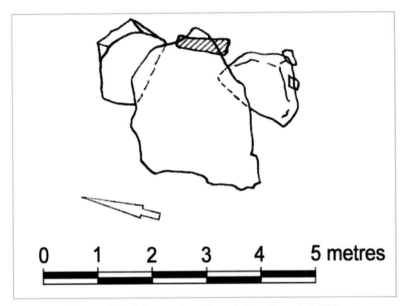

Plan of Ty Mawr chamber (after Lynch 1969)

The much damaged site of Ty Mawr, looking west

Lynch (1970) has suggested that, although badly damaged, the capstone would have formerly been supported by three to four uprights, one of which stood up to 1.5m high. The capstone measures 2.5m east-west by 3m north-south and appears to slope from east to west. Between the two fallen uprights at the eastern end is a sill-stone measuring 0.75m in height, believed to be one of the architectural traits associated with the passage grave tradition (e.g. Bodowyr).

It is suggested by Lynch (1969a, 117) that Ty Mawr, along with Bodowyr, represents a simple passage grave type similar to those found at Carrowmore, County Sligo and Burton, Pembrokeshire. When visiting this site, no particular form could be discerned. Although much of the monument may have been removed, one could be looking at a simple earth-fast type monument. It is clear that no uprights to the west of the capstone are present, unless they have been either removed or are buried.

Hen-Drefor (ANG 11; SH 5512 7731) is located approximately 6km north-west of Bryn Celli Ddu (ANG 7) and is one of a group of monuments which appears to visually acknowledge the hinterlands of the Menai Straits. This monument, approximately 2.5km north of the Straits, is located on the intermediate slopes of an undulating landscape, standing around 112m AOD, whilst to the north and west is a series of bogs. This monument therefore occupies the interface between two distinct landscapes. Similar with other chambered tombs within the Menai Straits area, Hen-Drefor lies close to a number of Early Bronze Age monuments, including four standing stones. Hen-Drefor would have been a striking visual monument during the Neolithic.

This monument was first described in 1783 when Thomas Pennant, in his *Tours in Wales*, noted that it was a 'sad monument'. In 1802 Hen-Drefor was visited by the Reverend John Skinner who echoed a similar opinion.

The monument consists of two groups of what are termed by Lynch (1969) as 'fallen stones', roughly 8m apart. Included in the eastern group of stones is a tall portal stone, close to which are a recumbent capstone and a possible upright. Lynch (1970, 34) suggests that the western group may have formed a rectangular chamber. According to the literature, there appears to have been no evidence of any stone in antiquity between the two groups. If this is the case, one can assume that this is a double chambered monument similar to that of Dyffryn Ardudwy (MER 3) in Gwynedd, nearby Din Dryfol (ANG 5) and Trefignath (ANG 1); it may even represent two monuments. However, surrounding the monument are slight traces of a cairn. According to Lynch (1969a, 115), Hen-Drefor has collapsed at some time within the last two centuries.

Lynch (1969 and 1970) places Hen-Drefor within the long-mound tradition. However, Daniel (1950, 150) suggests that it belongs to a terminal-chambered long barrow belonging to the Irish Sea group of monuments, even suggesting that it is a gallery grave without forecourt or side chambers, similar to that of Bedd yr Afanc (PEM 27), Pembrokeshire, and Trefignath (ANG 1). What is clear is that the two piles of stone represent chambers. It is also clear that these chambers are incorporated into a mound, traces of which are still visible. It is probable that each chamber would have been

Hen-Drefor: the eastern chamber looking south

entered either via a passage or forecourt. This being the case, the appropriate classification is that it belongs to the long-mound tradition, i.e. of Cotswold-Severn type, and that, if passages or entrances were present, the monument conforms to a group of monuments which are indigenous to North Wales and Anglesey. The site is difficult to assess because of its condition.

Hen-Drefor: the western chamber looking south

Hen Drefor: view of the two chambers, the eastern chamber is on the left side of the picture

Pant-y-Saer (ANG 13; SH 5097 8241), located 0.75km north of the Glyn monument (ANG 12) and within the town of Benllech, possesses dramatic views west over north-east Anglesey and east over The Wirral and Conwy Bay. The monument, standing around 99m AOD, occupies a ridge of a limestone escarpment, close to a small stream on uncultivated ground. It is one of a group of three chambered-tomb monuments that that are architecturally similar along this part of the Anglesey coast. Recent development of the area has partly obscured the landscape vista of this monument and the nearby Glyn monument at SH 5142 8172[48] and a doubtful burial chamber[49] at Benllech (ANG 26) at SH 5190 8267.[50]

Pant-y-Saer consists of a rectangular chamber, which opens at the south-eastern side. The chamber, consisting of a rock-cut pit measuring 4m × 3m × 1m and three uprights, is covered by a large capstone measuring approximately 4m × 4m, and is set within a kidney-shaped rubble cairn or mound, presumably formerly similar in form to that at Bryn yr Hen Bobl (ANG 8). The cairn is defined by a low limestone and gritstone block wall. At the north-eastern end of the monument, excavation has revealed an original edge to the cairn.

Lynch states that excavations carried out in 1875 were primarily concerned with the chamber and its contents, and may have destroyed a rectangular Beaker cist that contained at least two crouched burials (1969, 119). These burials, dating to the Early Bronze Age, were of secondary deposition. More discoveries were made by Scott (1933), when the bones of at least 54 individuals were recovered, of which some 18 were children. Also included within this skeletal assemblage were at least nine full-term foetuses. Osteological analysis revealed that there were not enough skulls to match the long bones, which may suggest that human remains were being deposited from other sites, with Pant-y-Saer acting as an ossuary. It could be the case, however, that bone material from the 1875 excavation has been mislaid. Alternatively, the deliberate removal of cranial material may have formed part of a religious act, similar to that observed with undisturbed material found at West Kennet Long Barrow in Wiltshire. The large number of people buried within the small chamber suggest this monument was being used over a long period of time by either high-status individuals

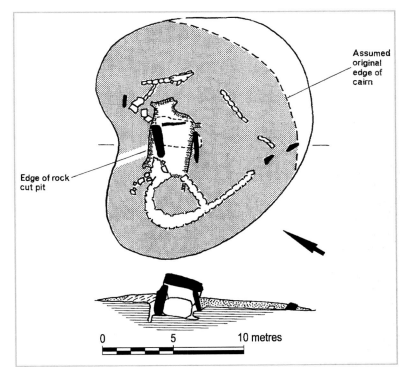

Plan and elevation of Pant-y-Saer

or that a corporate approach to death was in vogue, in which all members of the community were interred together.

Finds included an assemblage of Neolithic pottery representing at least nine vessels of Western style pottery (Daniel 1950, 140). At the western end, between the horns and the cairn, were the remains of a forecourt area. There appears to be no direct entrance to the chamber from the forecourt and it is probable that one of the large uprights may have been periodically moved in order to deposit more remains. However, Lynch (1969a, 119) has made the point that serious disturbance caused by the excavators may have distorted the stratigraphy inside the chamber.

Pant-y-Saer looking east

Pant-y-Saer revealed a typical homogenous Neolithic assemblage that included undecorated or shell grit-ware pieces. The majority of the finds came from within the forecourt area and the chamber. It is probable that the finds from the forecourt are the result of the spoil which was removed from the chamber during the 1875 excavations. However, Lynch (1970, 46) mentions that within the forecourt there was a small assemblage of pottery, a scratched pebble and a section of human skull along with animal bone, which appears to have been a deliberate deposit, possibly an offering made in front of the tomb's entrance. Like most monuments the deposit was covered by an extensive blocking deposit, which is probably Bronze Age in date. Also included in the finds inventory was Beaker pottery, a selection of worked flint including four leaf-shaped arrowheads, scrapers, two stone discs and an antler-point. The largest arrowhead, made from chert, is believed to derive from a type found in Ireland, suggesting some form of contact/exchange network between communities on either side of the Irish Sea. The pottery assemblages, which are very fragmentary, are interesting in that they appear to embrace pottery traditions that are both local and regional. Lynch (1969b, 172) suggests that the pottery has affinities with the Irish Sea traditions, as is seen with pottery from Dyffryn Ardudwy (MER 3). It is worth noting that a small nodule of pyrites was also found, believed by Lynch (1969b, 157) to be associated with burial activity, possibly dating to the Beaker Phase.

As Lynch rightly points out (1970, 97) much of the upper stratigraphy of this monument was probably disturbed during the 1875 excavations, while what was then recorded was not fully understood. According to the excavators Williams and Prichard, the rectangular stone Beaker cist covered by a capstone (2m x 0.75m) lay diagonally across the chamber and cut into earlier deposits. The cist walls were constructed of drystone blocks, while the floor was laid with a bed of shingle. According to Lynch, this type of architecture is unique (1969a, 118). Inside the cist were two skeletons, which according to the published plan in *Archaeologia Cambrensis* were arranged in a confused form. The bones were also crushed due to the collapse of the walling. However, it is interesting to note that the plan places the skeletal remains in the north-western part of the cist only. In my opinion these remains had been moved to this area in order to make way for more human remains. Lynch states that as there were no finds in the cist other than the bones, that dating these burials to the Late Neolithic/Early Bronze Age is difficult to substantiate (1969b, 159). The later 1933 excavation did uncover sherds from a long necked beaker in the areas of the cist which had not been disturbed by the earlier Williams and Prichard excavation.

Otherwise known, in common with many similar genuine and spurious sites, as Coetan Arthur (Arthur's Quoit) (ANG 14; SH 5014 8604), this monument, located 1.5km east of Moelfre, has extensive views across the North Wales coastline and the northern coastline of Anglesey. The monument, standing at 63m AOD, is located in an undulating landscape and shares a similar landscape position to two other monuments in the locality, Pant-y-Saer (ANG 13) and Glyn (ANG 12).

The site was visited by the Reverend Skinner on Saturday 11th December 1802, when he made a sketch and provided a brief description:

> Not far distant facing the ocean is a cromlech the upper stone six yards long, five yards and a half wide and three yards thick. One end rests upon a bank of earth and the other is supported by four or five small upright stones, leaving a hollow beneath about two feet high.

This chambered tomb is classified as a sub-megalithic type monument and is considered to be a Late Neolithic or transitional development. Lynch's description suggests a structure that was not intended to be visually impressive, but which served the purpose of providing a makeshift burial chamber with minimal effort. Both Daniel (1950) and Lynch (1970) suggest this monument type appeared late in the megalithic sequence and was a 'degenerate' form representing the waning of the megalithic tradition. Other monuments within this classification include Glyn and Gop Cave (FLT 2). However, I feel that this monument is extremely megalithic and very visible. The size of the capstone, weighing at least 25 tonnes, implies that the monument can surely not be makeshift or degenerate.

The tomb comprises the massive capstone, measuring 5.5m x 4.5m x 1m, beneath which is a series of eight rough stones — some upright, others laid horizontally — and a rock-cut pit. The three supporting stones rest either on the edge of the pit or on drystone walling. The chamber is some 2m in height, measured from the underside of the capstone to the base of the pit. Lynch (1970, 52) suggests the entrance was on the east and that the tomb never had a formal passage and although stones can be seen around the chamber, this is not taken as firm evidence for the existence of a cairn.

The chamber was partially excavated in 1908 by E.N. Baynes, who found, beneath a layer of sterile soil, an undisturbed burial deposit comprising two layers which were separated by a series of flat stones. Within the chamber he found the remains of up to 30 individuals including men, women and children. The upper part of the deposit, which was covered by a layer of limpet shells, contained fragmentary unburned human and animal bone, as well as black earth, some flint and several pottery sherds. More black earth and a greater quantity of bone was discovered in the lower layer, together with further pottery and flint, above a quantity of mussel shells. According to the excavator, many of the human bones had been deliberately broken and trampled. The later burials, located above the paving, probably date from the Late Neolithic or Early Bronze Age period, i.e. what Lynch refers to as Beaker in date (2,000–1,800 BC).

During the excavation, there appears to have been no stratigraphic record of where 40 pieces of pottery were found, which is frustrating

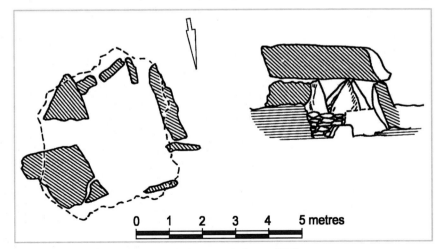

Plan and cross-section of Lligwy
(after Daniel 1950)

considering that this monument appears to have been in use during both the Neolithic and the Bronze Age. The pottery was subsequently analysed by Stuart Piggott in the 1930s, who found that all but two sherds belonged to a Western Neolithic pottery type, now referred to as Groove Ware. Some were decorated with grooves, of a type that suggested a Scottish connection (Lynch 1969b, 172), others which came from above the paving had cardium shell impressions. In general, the pottery showed marked affinities with sherds from Pant-y-Saer. Among the flint finds was a 'slug' (plano-convex) knife said to resemble those found in the court cairns of Northern Ireland (*ibid.*, 159). Also found was a polished bone pin that has been compared with examples from Loughcrew in Eire and Yorkshire.

Lligwy sub-megalithic chamber looking east

40 Letty'r Filiast

41 Maen y Bardd

42 Porth Llwyd

43 Sling

44 Hendre Waelod

45 Tyddyn Bleiddyn

46 Capel Garmon

47 Gop Cairn

48 Gop Cave

49 Tyn-y-Coed

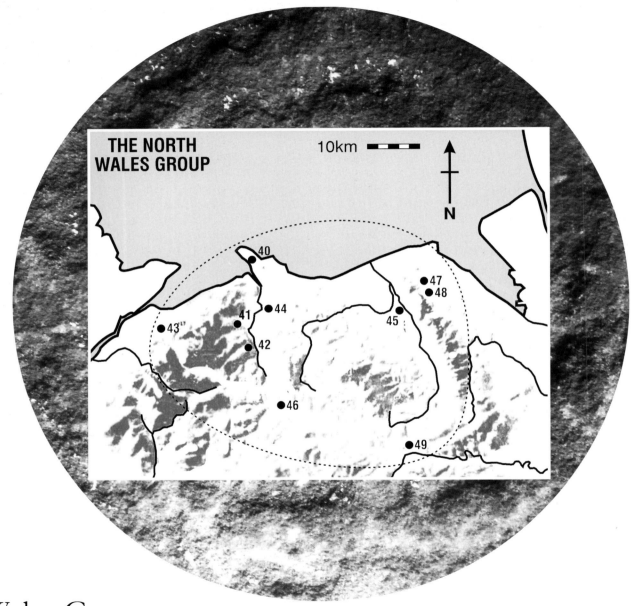

The North Wales Group

Chapter Six: The North Wales Group

Each of the ten monuments discussed in this chapter is located within a very distinctive landscape and includes Lletty'r Filiast (CRN 1), Maen-y-Bardd (CRN 3), Porth Llwyd (CRN 4), Sling (CRN 5), Hendre Waelod (DEN 1), Tyddyn Bleiddyn (DEN 2), Capel Garmon (DEN 3), Gop Cairn (FLT 1), Gop Cave (FLT 2) and Tyn-y-Coed (MER 7). Monuments within the eastern part of Denbighshire and Flintshire lie within secluded undulating valleys, whilst inland monuments such as Capel Garmon lie close to the mountains of Snowdonia. The Hendre Waelod monument, along with the Portal Dolmens of Maen-y-Bardd and Porth Llwyd lie next to or within the hinterlands of the Conwy valley.

Gop Cairn (and neighbouring Gop Cave) lie some 8km south of the North Wales coastline and have extensive views to the north, south and west. Its architecture, consisting of a large limestone-block cairn, is very different from the small chamber located within Gop Cave, some 100m below the cairn (RCAM 1912). Gop Cairn is extremely visible within the landscape, although the cave and its surrounding rock outcrop is arguably hidden by merging into outcropping within the area. Close to Gop Cairn was found an occupation site which had a series of finds indicative of the Neolithic, including leaf-shaped arrowheads and diagnostic flint scrapers and knives, as well as a flint borer and a large number of worked flint flakes. Visual features together with nearby Neolithic artifacts could suggest that Gop Cairn dates around the Middle to Late Neolithic, when the position of monuments was changing from intermediate slope locations to hilltop sites.

South-west of the Gop sites is the much-ruined site of Tyn-y-Coed. This monument can be described as an inland site which lies on the lower western slopes of the Berwyn Mountains overlooking the River Dee. The monument lies within a fragmented late Neolithic or Early Bronze Age landscape; to the south-east is a stone circle and beyond this are several cairns. Its situation is similar to that of Hendre Waelod and is classified as a Cotswold-Severn type monument (Lynch 1969a, 147).

Located close to the famous Middle Palaeolithic cave site of Pontnewydd is Tyddyn Bleiddyn, which lies on the eastern slopes of Cefn Meiriadog within a secluded valley, similar to that of a doubtful monument known as Maen Pebyll, oriented north-west/south-east. This laterally chambered Cotswold-Severn tomb was excavated by Boyd-Dawkins in 1874 and is now in a poor state of preservation (RCAM 1914). To the south-west is an extensive upland area which forms the southern extent of the Snowdonia mountains. Arguably, Tyddyn Bleiddyn has a landscape affinity with the nearby Capel Garmon monument that lies some 19km to the south-west. Capel Garmon, located some 300m AOD, also occupies a valley location and is sub-megalithic in form, having extensive views to the north and west, but again is hidden from lower ground.

For most members of the group, the visitor has to be in close proximity in order to see the monument's architectural form. During the Neolithic, most if not all the monuments were covered with an earthen mound or cairn and visibility would, therefore, have been even more restricted.

Located within the central region of Great Orme's Head, a limestone headland, and close to the famous Great Orme Bronze Age copper mines, is the Lletty'r Filiast monument (CRN 1; SH 7722 8295). Standing around 165m AOD, this lies on the edge of a small depression and has restricted views of the immediate landscape. However, open sea to the east, north and west plus the Conwy estuary to the south-west are all within close proximity. According to Lynch (1969a, 140) the situation of Lletty'r Filiast is similar to those of the Portal Dolmens in Ireland. However, it is worth noting that its position, enclosed within a restricted space, bears similarities to the small polygonal-chambered monuments found in southern Scandinavia, in particular, the monuments in Bohuslan in south-west Sweden, as well as several monuments in south-west Wales, particularly St Elvies (PEM 20) and Twlc-y-Filiast (CRM 6).

The monument, described as a terminally chambered long barrow (Daniel 1950, 86), consists of an oval barrow approximately 25m in length. Near the southern end of the monument is evidence of recent quarrying. The chamber itself, originally rectangular in form, is set within the south-eastern part of the mound and comprises a dislodged and broken capstone supported by a series of uprights which may themselves have been dislodged. The uprights form a polygonal chamber with a large entrance located at the eastern end. The size of the entrance may be the result of an upright being removed and, according to Lynch (1969a, 140), the chamber was probably rectangular in plan.

According to Daniel (1950, 141), the site was visited by members of the Cambrian Archaeological Association in 1911 where they referred to

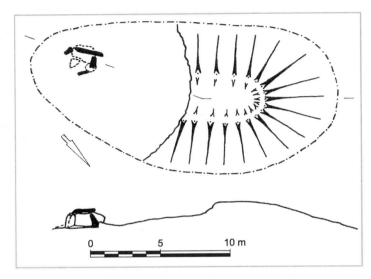

Plan of Lletty'r Filiast (after Lynch 1969a)

it as the Great Orme's Head site. The meeting deduced that excavations had previously taken place and they themselves found various objects including a dark brown pottery sherd and a bone pin. It was later noted by Grimes (1936a, 106–139) that the mound was at least partially natural bedrock and that much of the 'barrow' might indeed be natural. However, Lynch (1969a, 140) argues that the cairn has been 'greatly robbed' to reveal the natural bedrock.

Lletty'r Filiast, Llandudno

This Portal Dolmen (CRN 3; NGR SH 7416 7188) is located near the village of Ro-wen. It was formerly known as Cwrt-y-Filiast (translated as, 'the kennel of the greyhound bitch'), and is located on open grazing close to a track leading to Tal-y-fan and the mountains beyond. The track is arguably a Bronze Age route and definitely the line of the Roman road via Abergwyngregin to *Canovium*, a Roman fort at Caerhum, beside the River Conwy in Caernarvonshire. It has extensive views across the eastern, northern and southern extents of the Conwy Valley, being sited on an exposed plateau at the foot of Tal-y-Fan and standing approximately 305m AOD. Indeed, this monument is unusual in that it sits within the upland zone, unlike many Neolithic burial monuments in this area, and lies within a very much fragmented Late Neolithic/Early Bronze Age landscape. Several kilometres to the west and north lies a series of cairns and standing stones, including the 'Giant's Stick' (SH 738 717). According to Castleden (1992, 394) both the monument and the standing stones appear to be on a roughly east/west alignment. It is interesting to note that Mean-y-Bardd also lies quite close to the Graig Lwyd Neolithic axe factory (SH 717 750), some 3.5 km north-west of the monument.[51]

The monument, incorporated within a later field bank, consists of a large capstone which measures 4m x 2.2m x 0.7m, and four upright stones. The rectangular chamber and uprights sit within the traces of a long cairn, the entrance probably located within the western part of the chamber.

Interestingly, Daniel (1950, 191) notes another monument, Ro-wen East (CRN 2), located at SH 7754 6604. This questionable megalithic site, approximately 18m east of Mean-y-Bardd, consists of an east/west oriented long barrow measuring approximately 10m long.[52] A small rectangular possible chamber is located at the eastern end, also described as a cist (Bezant-Lowe 1912, 40).

Plan and cross-section of Maen-y-Bardd (after Lynch 1969a)

Maen-y-Bardd looking north

Similar to Hendre Waelod, this much-ruined monument (CRN 4; SH 7703 6777), once a possible Portal Dolmen, is sited within the Conwy Valley, approximately 8m AOD on the valley floor, close to Porth-Llwyd Falls. The monument lies close to Dolgarrog on the western side of the valley along the flood plain and may have had extensive views to the north and to the hills on the east. It is one of a group of four monuments associated with the Conwy valley and Creuddyn Isthmus, the others being Lletty'r filiast (CRN 1), Maen-y-Bardd (CRN 3) and Hendre Waelod (DEN 1).

This monument consisted of four stones, of which three are incorporated into a field bank. One of the three remaining uprights was displaced by a flood in 1925, a result of the Dolgarrog dam burst. The largest stone is the capstone which sits on its edge on the southern boundary of the field bank, whilst a recumbent stone lies within a field immediately north of the field bank. The site is spread over a five square metre area. However, it should be noted that according to Daniel (1950, 191), the surrounding fields were 'boulder strewn' which suggests that parts of the monument are scattered far and wide.

Lynch has considered that only two stones remain *in situ*, and these are considered to be uprights (1969a, 142). It is believed that the uprights were at least 1.5m high and that the monument may be similar in plan to the Carnedd Hengwm South chamber (MER 6). However, the upright arrangement suggests that the chamber may, in fact, resemble the chamber at Cist Cerrig (CRN 10). If the original position of the western upright is correct as illustrated in Lynch (*ibid.*, 142), the south-eastern upright may be a partition-stone dividing a rectangular chamber. It may also form an H-shaped entrance, leading into a former chamber located west of the *in situ* uprights. Crucially, the site was drawn by Bezant Lowe in his *The Heart of Northern Wales* (1912), where it appears that the uprights formed a rectangular chamber. Later, the monument was recorded by the Office of Works List of Scheduled Monuments as 'presumed destroyed by flood'.

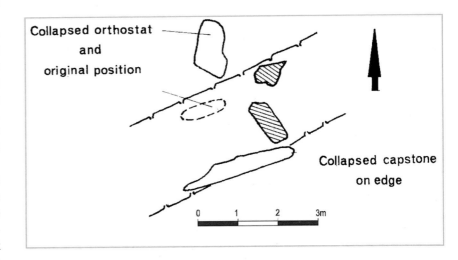

Plan of Porth Llwyd (after Lynch 1969a, now descheduled)

Sling, Llandegai

This much-ruined monument (CRN 5; SH 6055 6696) lies close to the town of Bethesda within the village boundary of Tregarth, standing around 210m AOD. The Sling tomb, also known as Yr Hen Allor (meaning 'Old altar'), is located on a north-facing slope of Careg-y-gath. Standing west of the Afon Ogwen, it has extensive views across the North Wales coast between Bangor, Llanfairfechan and the southern coast of Anglesey. The upland peaks of Moel Wnion and Gyrn Wigau to the north-east are also in view.

Sling and the doubtful sites of Bryn (CRN 16), near Llanfair (SH 5154 6604) and Coetan Arthur (CRN 17), near Llandeiniolen (SH 5550 6485), form part of a series of Caernarvonshire monuments which face others along a southern ridge in Anglesey, between Brynsiencyn and Beaumaris.

The monument consists of a large rectangular capstone measuring 4.8m x 1.9m x 0.35m and several uprights, one of which supports the capstone, part of which is embedded in the ground. A recumbent stone found close to the capstone appears to belong to a collapsed chamber (Lynch 1969a, 148). Although unclassified by Powell *et al.* (1969, 301), the remains are probably those of a small Portal Dolmen. There is, unfortunately, no trace of a mound. Daniel (1950, 14) suggests the monument is earth-fast (or sub-megalithic), in which case it would have had no mound, but I would disagree with this interpretation as no other earth-fast monuments are known in North Wales, apart from the possible Ty Mawr (ANG 10). The site is evidently disturbed, and much of the original structure, including any cairn material, has been taken for re-use elsewhere.

The Sling capstone, supported by one upright looking north-west

This monument (DEN 1; SH 7931 7487) with its large capstone and cairn occupies a north-west facing slope overlooking the mouth of the Afon Conwy, on the eastern side of the valley. Below the monument is an area of salt marsh and open pasture. West of the river are the mountains of North Wales, where, based on the archaeological evidence, little Neolithic ritual activity occurs. This monument, standing at 21m AOD, appears to be strategically located in that it commands extensive views of the mouth of the Afon Conwy and the mountains to the west. It would also have had extensive views of Great Orme's Head to the north. It should be noted that the Afon Conwy is tidal at this point and that a multitude of economic resources would have been available to the people utilising the area.

Hendre Waelod, also known as Allor Moloch (Molloch's Altar), comprises a short rectangular chamber with an entrance at the south-east, flanked by two portal stones which stand to a height of around 1.7m. The chamber, which measures roughly 4.1m x 3m, is set within an elongated cairn. The cairn itself sits on a slight shelf in the hillside. The portal stones on the eastern side are embedded in the cairn material. The capstone, measuring 4m x 3.2m x 1.4m, is supported by three uprights on the southern side of the chamber. This arrangement of uprights and capstone, also found at Gwern Einion, has been termed a 'portalled A-dolmen' (Daniel, 1950, 150).

The passage consists of two uprights approximately 1.5m apart and a series of scattered stones (which are not cairn material). Located to the south-east of the southern upright is a possible door-stone that separates the passage from the chamber. How far the two uprights are embedded into the hillside is not known. To the north, a number of uprights appear to have been removed.

Hendre Waelod looking north

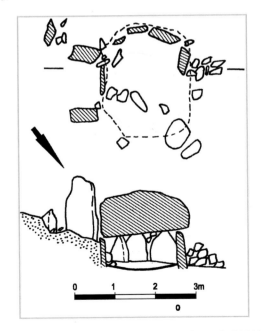

Plan and cross-section (after Lynch 1969)

This sadly neglected monument (DEN 2; SJ 0104 7203) is often referred to as a passage grave (Powell *et al.* 1969). With its mound aligned along the valley, it sits within a hilly landscape close to the Afon Elwy and stands at around 122m AOD. To the south-east and north-east of the monument is an extensive limestone rock outcrop.

This monument, regarded as the only true megalithic structure in the Clwyd Valley, has, like Capel Garmon, been linked with the Cotswold-Severn tradition owing to its lateral chamber arrangement. The present state of the monument is such that only one intact chamber can be identified at the north-western side of an ovate mound oriented north-west/south-east. The chamber measured 2.7m x 1.8m wide. Discovered between the passage and the chamber was a partition which consisted of a series of transverse jambs and a sill slab, measuring 0.45m in height. The chamber, which contained the remains of at least 12 people, includes a short passage (measuring 1.8m in length and 0.6m in width) to the south-west. However, Daniel regards the chamber as opening to the east (1950, 88), and also describes the north-western chamber as having a projecting jamb and a septal slab which lies between the passage and chamber (*ibid.*, 45). Both passage and chambers are constructed from locally quarried limestone slabs.

The mound, constructed of a stony-earth material, measures around 26m in length x 12m wide x 0.8m in height. The monument was saved from total destruction after the site had become a quarry for road repairing (Britnell 1991, 59).

When Boyd-Dawkins excavated the monument in 1869 and 1871, he identified a second chamber (referred to as the southern chamber), roughly parallel with the first and sharing a north-east/south-west orientation, at right angles to that of the mound. The chamber measured 3m in length by 1.8m and was triangular in shape. A jamb or sill lay between the

chamber and the passage, which was entered from the north and measured 3m in length and 0.7m in width. The chamber was said to contain a large quantity of human bone, along with the bones of dog, pig and roebuck. Also present was an assemblage of unworked flint pebbles and numerous pieces of quartz, but no pottery. Both chambers, according to Boyd-Dawkins, were full of remains of 'people of all ages', many of whom were placed in a 'sitting posture', with their backs to the sides of the chambers (1901). This statement is indeed interesting in that the preferred method of internment within the Cotswold-Severn tradition was disarticulation. Furthermore, Britnell (1991, 60) suggests that the visible chamber is similar to the two opposed chambers at Ty Isaf (BRE 5) and the chambers at Penywyrlod (BRE 14).

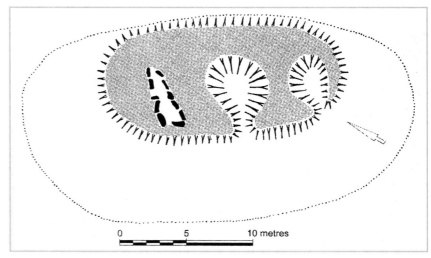

Plan of Tydden Bleiddyn (after Brittnell 1991)

Tydden Bleiddyn looking north-west, regarded as a true megalithic structure, but sadly neglected

The monument (DEN 3; SH 8182 5441) lies within a natural hollow behind Tyn-y-Coed Farm and stands at around 264m AOD. Specific features have persuaded some authors that this monument is a northern outlier of the Cotswold-Severn distribution (e.g. Grimes 1936b; Lynch 1969). It has little or no affinity with other monuments in the Conwy Valley, its closest relative being the multi-phased monument of Ty Isaf (BRE 5) in the Black Mountains (Lynch 1969a, 143). Both monuments possess a wedge-shaped cairn, transepted lateral chambers and a fore-court with blind entrance.

At Capel Garmon, two slate uprights form a simple doorway set in a deep forecourt measuring 5m east-west. Access to the chamber is from the south side of the mound, through a curved passage 4.5m in length and just over 1m in height. Despite the monument possessing horns, the location of the chamber within the wedge-shaped mound suggests that it has more in common with western monuments such as King Orry's Grave (MAN 2) in the Isle of Man (Daniel 1950).

In 1924 it was decided by the Ministry of Works to excavate this monument as the site was in such a poor state of preservation, with trees growing out of the mound. W.J. Hemp, who excavated the monument in 1927 in order to secure the chamber from further damage, found the corbelled passage to be blocked, and took this to indicate that the tomb had been used once only and then sealed. According to Hemp, some of the stone in the chambers was dressed (Hemp 1927).

A small excavation south of the western chamber was undertaken in 1989. The excavation area measured roughly 2m × 2m (Yates and Jones 1991, 1), in which were recognised three broad phases of activity: pre-monument activity, monument construction and post-construction disturbance. A single fragment of human skull was found within a well-sealed context underneath the monument, and may be associated with the construction process (*ibid.*, 4).

A passage leads to a tripartite chamber arrangement, emerging into a rectangular central chamber roughly 3m × 2m flanked by two circular chambers. The central chamber is partially divided by slabs projecting from the north wall and separated from the other chambers by door jambs. One of

Capel Garmon: the southern chamber

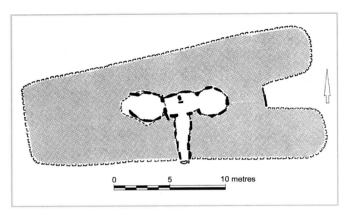

Plan of Capel Garmon

The north-south chamber alignment of Capel Garmon

the chambers was in use as a stable in 1853. As a result of measures to clear the chamber, the remaining two chambers were discovered. Today the site has only one original capstone covering part of the central chamber.

As at Bryn Celli Ddu (ANG 7) and Bryn yr Hen Bobl (ANG 8) the floors of the chambers were found to be of 'prepared clay' extending beyond the kerbing, Grimes (1950, 41–42) argued that the builders did not see the kerbing as the termination of the barrow area. In all three sites, the revetment material was firmly embedded into what Grimes calls a prepared clay floor.

The majority of the mounds of long chambered monuments in Wales are oriented north/south. However, the mound of Capel Garmon is aligned east/west, suggesting that local landscape features played an important role in the siting and alignment of this monument.

The cairn measures 27m x 12m and narrows towards its western end. The wider eastern end consists of a horned forecourt area, a false portal consisting of two uprights located between the two horns. This architectural trait features prominently in the Cotswold-Severn group of monuments.

Regarding finds, a single rim-sherd of Ebbsfleet pottery was found in the passage (Grimes 1951, 35). There were also traces of small fires, an unworked flint flake and human bone. Five sherds belonging to two Late Neolithic/Early Bronze Age Beakers were also discovered, suggesting either periodic or continuous use of the monument for at least 1,500 years.

Lynch (1969a, 139) suggests that Capel Garmon has no connection with monuments further down the valley such as Maen y Bardd (CRN 3), Porth Llwyd (CRN 4) and Hendre Waelod (DEN 1). If this is correct, then Capel Garmon is isolated and penetration of the Conwy Valley and the subsequent settlement and construction of the lower Conwy Valley monuments was self-contained. Savory (1980, 222) tenuously suggests that the rounded transepts imply that the builders were influenced by the Boyne Valley passage grave tradition in central Ireland. However, I believe that the design is essentially a Cotswold-Severn trait with local idiosyncratic additions in order to personally place one's 'signature' on to the monument and make it different from others nearby.

Gop Cairn (FLT 1; SJ 086 802), also referred to as Gop-y-Goleuni ('well-lit summit' [as being less densely-wooded]), lies within an extensive Neolithic landscape. Close to the cairn and within fields to the north and west, a large assemblage of Neolithic flint was found, including a number of leaf-shaped flint arrowheads, scrapers, knives, a flint borer or awl, as well as a large number of worked flint debitage. Many researchers consider that this enormous cairn, located on the brow of Gop Hill, is in fact Bronze Age in date (Britnell 1991, 61). However, its sheer size, which is unlike any other Bronze Age cairn in Britain, suggests a Neolithic date.

The cairn, approximately 12m in height and 100m in diameter, stands around 250m AOD with outstanding views in all directions, but appears to dominate the landscape to the south. At its base is an extensive natural scree deposit. On top of the cairn is a doughnut-shaped indention — evidence of antiquarian excavation. Recent disturbance around the southern base of the cairn has revealed a section of a limestone revetment wall (Britnell 1991, 62) which may be contemporary with the construction of the cairn. A similar revetment wall, constructed of chalk blocking, is present at Silbury Hill in Wiltshire.

The cairn was excavated in 1886–1887 by Boyd-Dawkins and this revealed that the mound was constructed of a limestone rubble core. The excavation cut a single vertical shaft and two galleries. A large bone assemblage, including ox and horse, was uncovered within the mound's core but there was no trace of any human remains. However, its English counterpart, Silbury Hill, whilst considerably larger, showed similar finds and deposition. It is suggested by Castleden (1992, 372) that the cairn may house a passage grave which is comparable to passage graves in Anglesey and within the Boyne Valley in Ireland. However, the Boyd-Dawkins excavation revealed no evidence of any passage or chamber architecture, and his excavation tunnelled to the bedrock/cairn interface.

It is more than probable that Gop Cairn, whatever function it fulfils, is directly associated with nearby Neolithic activity within the Gop Cave system; and what one is probably looking at is a complex Neolithic landscape which involves both burial and ritual practices. The extensive flint scatters would also suggest that a Neolithic settlement was close by.

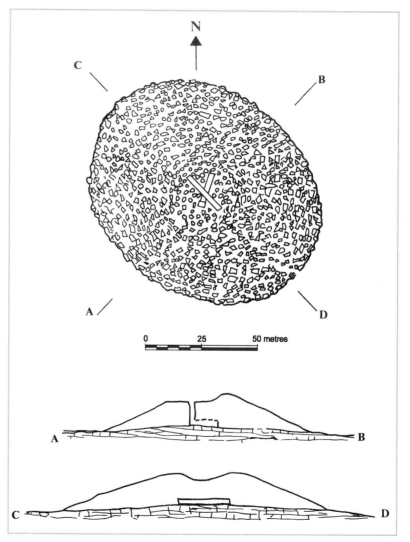

Plan and cross-section of Gop Cairn (after Boyd-Dawkins 1901)

Two limestone caves (FLT 2; SJ 086 800), located on the south-facing slopes of Gop Hill command outstanding views to the south and stand around 215m AOD. Approximately 35m north of the caves and up-slope, is Gop Cairn. The south-eastern cave was excavated by Sir William Boyd-Dawkins in 1886.

Immediately in front of the cave entrance is an extensive lip that partially hides the cave from view when viewed from the valley. It is difficult to assess whether this lip forms part of the natural topography, was constructed during the Neolithic or is merely spoil from the 19th-century excavation of the site. Daniel regards the cave, which he classifies as a sub-megalithic tomb, as the only authentic Neolithic burial site in Flintshire (1950, 196). I would add that the Gop Cave site is probably the most unusual Neolithic burial site in Wales as it utilised a natural feature to replicate an artificial construct.

According to the excavation report, several significant features and structures that date from the Neolithic, including a burial chamber, were found inside the cave. Excavation revealed the remains of at least 14 individuals, some of whom were placed in a crouched position. Found in the assemblage of skeletal material were a number of decorated pottery sherds with a herring-bone pattern, possibly of the Peterborough type. A polished stone axe from the Graig Lwyd axe factory near Penmaenmawr was also recovered. This important artifact was located close to the entrance to the cave. Other finds included a large assemblage of broken and burnt domestic animal bone, a discoidal polished flint knife, some white quartz pebbles and the possible remains of a jet slider or necklace (Boyd-Dawkins 1901, 330). The jet slider, although illustrated, is now lost. Also found was a possible Beaker-type dagger, allegedly sold by one of the workmen to a visitor!

The burial chamber, rectangular in form, is constructed with three stone walls, the fourth wall being part of the northern wall of the cave. The roof of the chamber was likewise formed from the roof of the cave. The chamber lies some 2m inside the cave entrance and overlies a series of cave earth deposits. According to

Boyd-Dawkins, the chamber entrance was buried in (natural) spoil that completely covered the entrance to the cave.

It is probable that the site belongs to a Late Neolithic burial tradition, referred to by Britnell (1991, 64) as sub-megalithic in character. Daniel (1950, 153) regards Gop Cave, along with Glyn and Lligwy, as late, degenerate types of his Gwynedd Group, due to its sub-megalithic nature. This later date is reinforced by the enormous cairn that lies above the cave and that is roughly of the same date. Other cave sites in Flintshire such as Perthi Chwarae (Llanarmon) and Rhosddigre (Llandegla), both in the Alyn Valley have yielded similar burial assemblages that date from this period.

Gop Cave looking north-east. One of a number of Neolithic burial sites located in a cave

This much-ruined monument (MER 7; SJ 048 396) is located close to the valley floor of the Afon Dyfrdwy (River Dee), at approximately 154m AOD on a west-facing slope. Directly behind the monument are the Berwyns, a range of mountains which extends to the east and the south. To the west are the hinterlands of the mountains of Snowdonia.

The monument is located outside the village of Rhyd-y-Glafais, and lies close to two doubtful sites known as Branas Uchaf and Maen Egryn. The monument sits within an elongated cairn, 30m in length, with a capstone lying at one end, embedded within cairn material (Bowen and Gresham 1967). The capstone measures 3m in length by 0.45m in thickness and is supported by at least one upright. Bowen and Gresham concluded that there is a possible passage leading to the chamber area from the side and Britnell concurred with this (1991, 60), suggesting that the passage possibly measured around 3m in length. However, Lynch (1969a, 147) suggests that the passage may be a result of extensive disturbance. This site is clearly a terminally chambered monument, indicative of the Cotswold-Severn group of monuments.

This monument can be regarded as being unusual in its geographical location, in that little other monument evidence is present within the inland area of central and North Wales, although its position within the landscape is typical of other Neolithic monuments *per se*. Lynch has suggested that this monument is significant in that it may have been constructed by people from the Cotswold-Severn area who may have used the route over the Berwyns (1969a, 147). However, as suggested throughout this book, it is not people who were moving, but ideas and it is more likely that the long cairn design 'blueprint' was transmitted between groups. This monument, along with the Portal Dolmens of

Gwern Einion (SH 587 286), Mean-y-Bardd (SH 741 718) and Porth Llwyd (SH 770 677), is located along a large river valley. Colonisation of this area would have probably come via the exploration of the streams and river valleys by hunter-gatherers or early Neolithic groups.

The capstone and chamber of Tyn-y-Coed, set with a large cairn mound.

50 Gwern Einion

51 Bron-y-Foel-Isaf-West

52 Dyffryn Ardudwy

53 Cors-y-Gedol

54 Carneddau Hengwm North

55 Carneddau Hengwm South

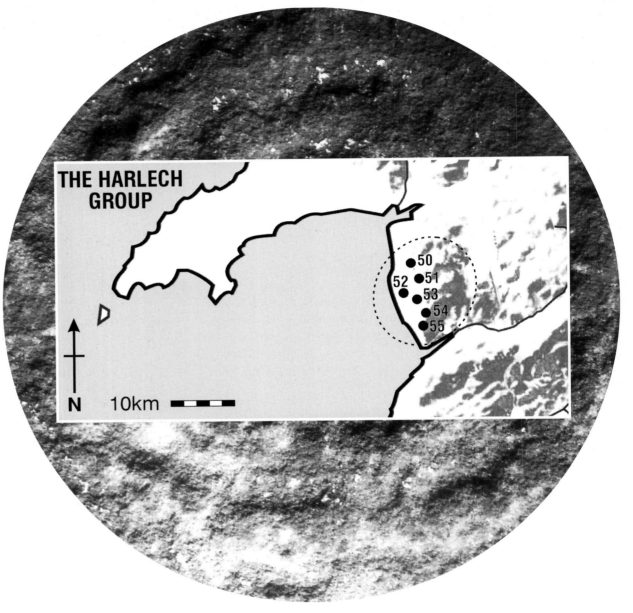

The Harlech Group

Situated south of the Lleyn peninsula — between Traeth Bach and north of the Afon Mawddach — are seven monuments that lie on the western intermediate slopes overlooking the Irish Sea and the Lleyn Peninsula. The six monuments listed within this gazetteer are architecturally diverse and all lie in different landscape settings: Gwern Einion (MER 1), Bron-y-Foel-Isaf-West (MER 2), Dyffryn Ardudwy (MER 3), Cors-y-Gedol (MER 4), Carneddau Hengwm North (MER 5) and Carneddau Hengwm South (MER 6). In this group, Bron-y-Foel-Isaf-East (SH 608 247) has been re-classified as of probable natural origin. Four of the sites are regarded as Portal Dolmens, the exceptions being the two Carneddau Hengwm monuments which, with their surviving cairn long mounds, are regarded as belonging to the Cotswold-Severn group (Lynch 1976, 69).

The orientation of all these monuments appears to be roughly consistent, in that their (Portal Dolmen) chambers and long mound axes are oriented approximately in the same direction, roughly east/west, thus pointing to the sea and the mountains. This emerging pattern, repeated elsewhere within the coastal Neolithic core areas of Wales, has potentially significant ritual-symbolic ramifications — see Tilley (1994); Children and Nash (2002); Cummings (2002); Cummings and Whittle (2004).

The most northerly of this group is the monument of Gwern Einion. This classic Portal Dolmen, incorporated into a farm wall, lies on a plateau that has no view of the sea, although this only lies approximately 1.75km to the west. Although only the chamber of the monument survives, it is probable that the orientation of the wall delineates the alignment of the mound. Lying close to this site is further evidence of late Neolithic/Early Bronze Age activity, which includes, on the western slopes of nearby Moel Goedog, two stone circles (SH 610 324). Between Gwern Einion and the stone circles are several standing stones that occupy the eastern slopes of Moel Goedog and Moel y Sensigl. Given their position there may be a monument association, albeit tenuous, between Gwern Einion and the standing stone and stone circles. The monument appears to be deliberately located to occupy the uplands that dominate the Harlech landscape.

The site of Bron-y-Foel-Isaf-West, lying north of the cairn circle at Tal y Ffynonau (SH 609 239) is much ruined (Powell et al. 1969, 303). The site lies on the intermediate slopes of Moelfre that rises to a height of 589m AOD and is at the same elevation as the two Carneddau Hengwm monuments.

Close to the Carneddau Hengwm monuments is Dyffryn Ardudwy and Cors y Gedol, each sited down-slope towards the coast. The double chambered monument at Dyffryn Ardudwy is approximately 1km to the west of the Cors-y-Gedol monument. Both chambers are incorporated into a stone cairn. The monument lies at the interface between the uplands and the coastal hinterland.

The Cors-y-Gedol tomb is located approximately 2.2km north of the Carneddau Hengwm monuments. Although much smaller, it nevertheless shows similar architecture and although regarded as a Portal Dolmen it is incorporated into a long mound and probably has some architectural traits with the Cotswold-Severn classification.

The Carneddau Hengwm monuments lie on the western slopes of Mynydd Egryn, close to a number of upland streams and bogs. They also lie within an extensive Late Neolithic to Early Bronze Age landscape. To the east and north of these monuments are a series of cairns and standing stones and two stone circles, Ffridd Newydd North (SH 616 213) and Ffridd Newydd South (SH 616 213) (Burl 1976, 370). Unlike the two Carneddau Hengwm monuments, the Bronze Age monuments are usually located on top of the highest points within the landscape, as typified by the Llanaber cairn at a height of 515m AOD.

This monument (MER 1; SH 5873 2861) is incorporated into a field and sheep enclosure wall, lying within the bounds of a small farmstead. The monument is a classic Portal Dolmen which has been linked morphologically with other early forms in the area, such as the west chamber at Dyffryn Ardudwy (MER 3). Once hidden among local rock outcrops, this monument is sited 106m AOD on an intermediate plateau above the Afon Artro. It lacks intervisibility with the nearby tombs of Bron-y-Foel-Isaf-West and Dyffryn Ardudwy as well as the sea, 1.9km away. Behind it, and dominating the view to the east, is the peak of Foel Ddu (473m AOD).

The closed rectangular chamber, which is oriented north-west/south-east, consists of a steeply sloping capstone supported by two portal stones standing to around 2m and resting at its western end on a third upright about 1m high. The portal

blocking slab rises to about 1.3m. Grimes (1936a, 120) suggests the chamber may originally have extended further back than at present.

Both to the south and the north is a series of monuments including standing stones and stone circles with associated settlements. This high concentration of sites dating from the Neolithic and Bronze Age suggests the presence of a ritual landscape along this intermediate slope. Gwern Einion, and possibly a now-destroyed monument 1km west of Harlech Castle, appears to mark the northern extent of this group of monuments.

Since the photograph of this monument was taken in 1993, a recent visit in December 2005 has wiitnessed the removal of the drystone SW wall, revealing a possible *in situ* cairn belonging the the mound. This was removed under archaeological supervision in order to visually enhance the monument (Mike Yates: pers.comm.)

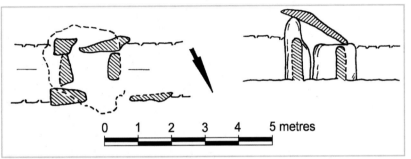

0   1   2   3   4   **5 metres**

Plan and cross-section of Gwern Einion (after Lynch 1969a)

Gwern Einion, looking south

Bron-y-Foel-Isaf-West (MER 2; SH 6088 2472), with its doubtful neighbour Bron-y-Foel-East,[53] stands on an upland plateau known as Moelfre and has uninterrupted views of the sea to the west and the mountains to the east. To the east of this monument is the peak of Moelfre which rises to 589m AOD. The monument — whose name means 'The Lower slope of the Bare Hill' — is located within a probable early Post-Medieval (or earlier) field system. The farms of Bron-y-Foel-Ganol and Bron-y-Foel-Uchaf lie close by.

Cors-y-Gedol (MER 4) and the cairns of Carneddau Hengwm (MER 5 and 6) are sited on the same plateau. Within this landscape are several monuments that date to the Bronze Age, including cairns, standing stones, a stone circle and evidence of associated settlement. Although these monuments occupy prominent locations, the siting of this tomb is such that it cannot be seen from the valley below.[54]

Bron-y-Foel-Isaf-West and Cors-y-Gedol are separated by the Afon Ysgethin from the two Carneddau Hengwm monuments to the south. This natural boundary may explain the change in tomb morphology between the two sets of monuments.

Bron-y-Foel-Isaf-West, oriented east/west and intervisible with both Dyffryn Ardudwy (MER 3) and Cors-y-Gedol, is sited on higher ground (at around 214m AOD), and located several kilometres further inland. The monument, initially classified as a laterally chambered long cairn, originally consisted of a closed portal with a rectangular chamber which was set into a mound measuring perhaps 18m x 9m. The chamber capstone is 3m x 2.5m and rests on an upright at the south, and on the ground to the west, and could be construed as being earth-fast in form. The height of the closed portal is about 1m, about the same as that of its nearest neighbour, Cors-y-Gedol, but only half that of Gwern Einion. As with Gwern Einion, the chamber has been incorporated within a field boundary wall. At present only three uprights of the chamber remain, whilst loose stone litters the area where the chamber was once sited. Two of the uprights appear to form an H-chamber setting and it is probable that the smaller upright — oriented north/south — was a doorstone at the entrance into the chamber from the west. Immediately to the east of the field boundary may have been a forecourt area. A low, crescent-shaped bank 3.5m in front of the chamber has been linked with similar features at Dyffryn Ardudwy and Cors-y-Gedol (see later) and considered 'a uniting element between these three tombs' (Lynch 1969a, 127).

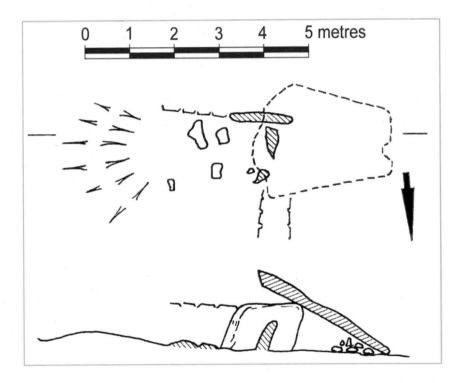

Plan of Bron-y-Foel-Isaf-West (after Lynch 1969a)

Bron-y-Foel-Isaf-West, looking south

The Dyffryn Ardudwy monument (MER 3; SH 5887 2294), lying within the village of the same name, is one of the largest in the Harlech Group and because of its meticulous excavation in the 1960s has received much comment. This tomb is located on the edge of the coastal plain. Because of its landscape position, it seems unlikely that there was any direct intervisibility with other monuments of the group. The earliest part of the monument, the western chamber, resembles other Portal Dolmens within the group such as Gwern Einion (MER 1). In addition its landscape position is similar to that of Cors-y-Gedol (MER 4) in that both are close to fresh running water, in this case the Afon Ysgthin, which flows south of Dyffryn Ardudwy.

The monument stands on a western slope at around 50m AOD and consists of two Portal Dolmen-type chambers that face up-slope to the east. The chambers are set within a well-defined cairn which is roughly rectangular in shape and aligned south-west/north-east. While the sea is only 1.8km away, and is clearly visible from the site, the monument forecourts are oriented inland and appear to visually ignore the coastal zone completely.

According to the excavator, T.G.E. Powell, two clear construction phases are evident, each phase consisting of a chamber and associated cairn (1973). It has been said of Portal Dolmens that their most striking components are monumentality and restriction of chamber access (Kinnes 1992, 122). At Dyffryn Ardudry, the original monument seems to have been a relatively modest structure, comprising a rectangular stone chamber 2.5m × 1m and closed off with a blocking slab. A V-shaped forecourt converged on two portal stones and contained what seems to have been a shallow ritual pit. Within the pit were found sherds of several fine Neolithic vessels constituting a single context and comparable in overall form with finds from the Neolithic settlement of Carn Brea in Cornwall. Pottery from the chamber consisted of a single stamped Beaker sherd, assumed to represent secondary deposition. The monument was enclosed in an oval cairn measuring 8.5m × 9m.

The western chamber was then superseded by a second, larger chamber, built about 10m to the north-east. This partitioned structure comprises a western compartment measuring 2.3m × 2m, and an eastern

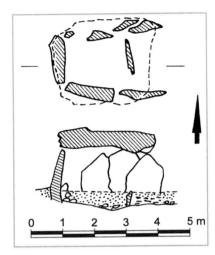

Plan of Dyffryn Ardudwy (after Lynch (1969a)

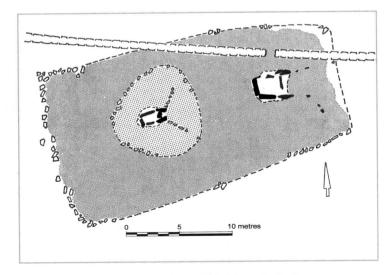

Overall site plan of Dyffryn Ardudwy

entrance area containing blocking stones. Lynch suggests that a gap in the north chamber wall provided a side entrance which could be easily reopened for the insertion of burials after the formal entrance had been blocked (Lynch 1969a, 134–135).

Uprights to the east and south-east of the southern portal stone have been interpreted as a vestigial forecourt (*ibid.*, 134), whilst a roughly rectangular long cairn 28m × 15m enclosed both chambers and the original oval cairn. The deposition of the chambers and blocking revealed crucially that the site had not been disturbed and that the cairn's stratigraphy lay intact (Lynch 1976, 66).

Pottery deposited in the forecourt and blocking area is dated to later than the construction of the western chamber. Largely undecorated sherds from the disturbed eastern chamber context have been compared with examples from Lough Gur in Limerick, southern Ireland.

Other fragments decorated with fingernail impressions may indicate the spread of Beaker influence into the area, as do small pieces of polished slate or schist, possibly belonging to a Beaker wristguard. A leaf-shaped arrow head was found beneath the cairn edge near the eastern chamber.

Recent research by Cummings (2004, 129) suggests that different landscapes are viewed from different parts of the monument. Whilst the sea can be viewed and experienced from both chambers, the eastern chamber has views of the southern Lleyn Peninsula, while the western chamber does not. The idea of different views may be extended to other large monuments in Wales. Thus, at Llech-y-Tribedd (PEM 1) the sea, just a few hundred metres to the west, can only be viewed from the top of the capstone; unlike the dominant views to the east and the Nevern Valley (Children and Nash 1997). A similar interplay with landscape is probably present at Dyffryn Ardudwy.

Dyffryn Ardudwy: western chamber, looking north

Dyffryn Ardudwy: looking east

147

The much ruined monument of Cors-y-Gedol (MER 4; SH 6033 2281) has been described by Daniel as a terminally chambered long barrow (1950, 86), with the remains of a Portal Dolmen located at the eastern end of the mound. This site has received much attention, especially by antiquarians during the late 19th century, whilst William Stukeley sketched both it and the Bron-y-Foel-Isaf (MER 2) monuments in the 18th century. Crawford (1920, 98) notes that a possible drawing of the monument was made in 1800, now housed in Devizes Library.[55]

The irregular, much denuded cairn mound and ruined chamber are all that remain. The site lies on the slopes of Moelfre and forms one of many belonging to the Irish Sea Group of monuments (Daniel 1950, 150). The position of the capstone, which measures roughly 3.5m x 3m, has its western end resting on cairn material. The mound is roughly 25m x 12m, and approximately 0.4m deep. The height of the upright supporting the capstone is about 1.5m. The present position of the capstone, resting on a single upright, gives the impression that it belongs to the earth-fast group monuments; but it is probable that the capstone has slipped off the two uprights which once formed the northern section of the chamber. The chamber appears to be polygonal in plan, although it is impossible to determine its size from the position of the two remaining uprights. The general orientation of the chamber, which is located at the eastern end of the cairn, appears to be north-east/south-west. The upright north-east of the capstone may in fact be part of an entrance or forecourt area that opened out towards the east, similar to that of nearby Dyffryn Ardudwy. Sited on the same plateau as Bron-y-Foel-Isaf and the two Carneddau Hengwm monuments (MER 5 and 6) this monument is the lowest at 191m AOD. It has a clear view of the coastal plain, the sea to the west, and the mountains — in particular the peak of Graig-y-Grut at 588m AOD — to the east. It also lies 200m or so from the Afon Ysgethin to the south.

A few kilometres to the east and in front of the mountain peaks are a series of standing stones and cairns, together with the Iron Age settlement of Craig-y-Dinas. The monument is located, as are others within the group,

on the interface between deep, well-drained fine loamy silty soils and the more shallow soils found on the slopes (Soil Survey of England and Wales 1983). Recent research undertaken by Cummings (2004, 129) using the view shed theory suggests that different landscapes are viewed and experienced from different parts of the monument. The sea can be viewed from both chambers. However, the earliest chamber has views of the southern section of the Lleyn Peninsula, while the western chamber does not. One can extend the idea of different views to other large monuments in Wales. At Llech-y-Dribedd (PEM 1) the sea, which is only a few hundred metres to the west of the monument can only be viewed if one is standing on top of the capstone; the dominant views are confined to the east and the Nevern Valley (Children and Nash 1997). Likewise a similar interplay with landscape is probably present at Dyffryn Ardudwy.

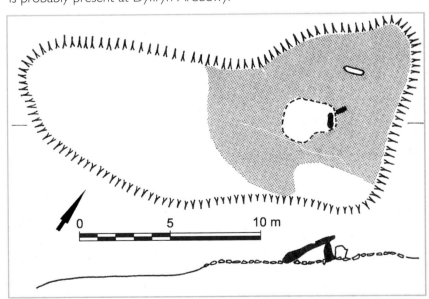

Plan and cross-section of Cors-y-Gedol (after Lynch 1969a)

Cors-y-Gedol looking west

The two Carneddau Hengwm monuments are sited on an upland plateau and overlook the Lleyn Peninsula, standing around 283m AOD. The translation of the monuments' name is quite simply 'Cairns of the Old Valley' (Olding: pers. comm.). This monument (MER 5; SH 6143 2058) along with its neighbour (the individual monuments are spaced some 35m apart) is one of a limited group of monuments which form a pair.

The Carneddau Hengwm monuments are constructed similarly and mark the southern extent of the Harlech Group. To the east of the monuments is the dramatic peak of Graig-y-Grut at 588m AOD.

Carneddau Hengwm North lies close to the top of a small river gully running roughly east/west. Between the monuments and the coastal zone some 2km to the west are extensive rock outcrops, whilst to the east of this site, at a point where the mountains and upland plateau merge, is a series of Bronze Age ritual monuments including several cairns, a cairn circle and standing stones. To the north-west is a small Iron Age enclosure known as Pen-y-Dinas (SH 6070 2081), at the highest point within the immediate landscape.

Carneddau Hengwm North is smaller than its neighbour and has been extensively robbed. However, two lateral chambers are visible and open from opposite sides of the cairn. The mound, oriented east/west and measuring around 33m x 18m, is much denuded and cairn material possibly spreads beyond the limits of the original cairn walls.

The chamber arrangement is rather complex and in some ways is replicated within the mound of the Carneddau Hengwm South monument. Three or perhaps four chambers are present within the mound. In my opinion and based on a recent site visit, the two eastern lateral chambers possibly mark the end of the mound. Each chamber, delineated by a series

**Plan and cross-section of
Carneddau Hengwm North**

of uprights oriented north/south, measures around 1m x 1m in plan. The chambers are spaced 6.7m apart. Between the chambers are up to three uprights which may indicate either a third chamber, or the possible denuded remains of a passage that may have led to the central chamber.

To the west of the two lateral chambers and within the centre of the mound is a drystone walled circular feature which Crawford (1920, 129) believed was another chamber. At present, cairn material has fallen into this void preventing identification. At the western end of the mound is a probable capstone that may have belonged to the central chamber. This large slab, measuring approximately 3.7m x 2.2m, overlies cairn material. Daniel (1950, 197) claimed that the slab overlies a further chamber. If this is the case, then a lateral chamber, possibly forming a Portal Dolmen, exists at the western end and it is probable that an entrance and forecourt area is present beyond this proposed chamber.

Corcoran (1969, 103) suggests that the remains of a drystone wall running east/west at the north-western end of the mound could indicate a cairn revetment and possibly reveals Cotswold-Severn or Wessex Culture influence. Corcoran (*ibid.*, 103) goes on to say that if the mound is trapezoidal in shape, then this site may have influenced monument construction in Ireland, in particular sites located within the Audleystown area, Co. Down.

Interestingly, the chamber arrangements of the monument are the opposite of those at Carneddau Hengwm South. This arrangement may have had significant implications with winter sunrise and sunset, in that light from the sunrise would enter the eastern chamber of the Carneddau Hengwm South monument, whilst light from the sunset would have illuminated the western chamber of Carneddau Hengwm North. However, it is unclear whether both monuments were in use at the same time.

This monument (MER 6; SH 6141 2052) and its neighbour Carneddau Hengwm North (MER 5) are, in my opinion, two of the most important monuments in North Wales. This egregious statement is mainly based on two factors, *viz.* landscape setting and the monument's state of preservation. The site was described both by William Stukeley and by Thomas Pennant (in 1783). Of particular interest is the utilisation of one of the chambers as a shepherd's hut. Pennant writes:

> Half a mile south of these [two stone circles], on the side of a hill, are two carnedds [cairns], of a most stupendous size, containing an uncommon assemblage of druidical customs, or religion, in form of Cromlech, Maen Hir and Cist Vaen. Both are of an oblong form, and composed of loose stones: the largest [Carneddau Hengwm North] is fifty-five feet long, and twelve high, in the middle. At the east end is a great Cromlech [chamber], composed of two sloping stones, one placed over the edge of the other, upon five flat upright stones, seven feet high in one part, and four feet ten in the lowest. About eight yards [7.5m] from this, is the upper stone of a Cromlech, lying flat on the carnedd, without the appearance of any other support.
>
> Eleven yards farther, in another great heap of stones [Carneddau Hengwm South], and in it a large Cromlech, supported by upright stones. It is now converted into a retreat for a shepherd, who has placed stone seats within, and formed a chimney through the loose stones above. In the same carnedd, a little farther on, is another magnificent Cromlech, whose incumbent stone is twelve feet by nine; four vast columns, or maeni hiron, three now fallen, and a third erect. The columns are from the height of ten feet four, to that of twelve feet eight; and each between four and five feet broad.

The isolation of both monuments has probably dissuaded many an antiquarian from excavation. The landscape setting of this monument is identical to that of its neighbour, although Carneddau Hengwm South is at a slightly higher elevation, around 283m AOD, and has a Post-Medieval drystone wall oriented north-south incorporated into the eastern section of the monument.

Carneddau Hengwm South appears to be a two-phase monument comprising, in its present form, a closed Portal Dolmen at the eastern end

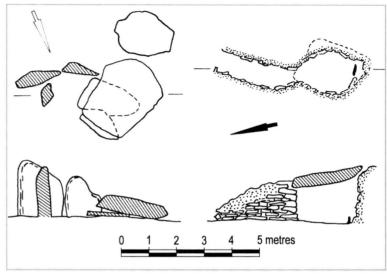

Plan and cross-section of the east and central chambers (after Lynch 1969)

of a long irregular mound; and a lateral chamber with a passage located towards the centre of the cairn (Lynch 1969a, 133; 1976, 70; Masters 1981, 109). The phasing of the monument is based on the difference in cairn material, with small to medium stones being used in the initial construction (*ibid.*, 69). Lynch (1976, 69) suggests that the initial mound may have only measured 16.5m in length, for distinctly larger cairn material is found within the remaining 27m of the mound.

The eastern chamber is now partially collapsed, but originally consisted of two overlapping capstones supported by five uprights, including the closing slab or doorstone. Pennant describes two capstones as being present, probably still in their original position (1783). Other antiquarian reports, compiled in the 18th century when the chamber was still standing, suggest 'the great cromlech altar' stood about 2m high at its eastern end, sloping down to about 1.2m at the west. The chamber, described by Powell *et al.* (1969, 304) as a ruined Portal Dolmen, measures around 3m x 2m

Carneddau Hengwm Sóuth: the eastern chamber is separated from the cairn by a post-medieval drystone wall (probably rectangular in plan). The surviving uprights once formed an H-shaped doorway; two of these lie underneath the capstone.

A central rhomboid chamber, measuring 2.5m x 2.5m, may have been constructed during the phase of cairn enlargement, which extended the overall length to 57m. This chamber is formed partly of drystone walling. A roofing slab stands to a height of 1.5m, and a passage measuring 3m x 0.9m curves north-west from the chamber to the edge of the cairn. The passage narrows to 0.5m towards the chamber entrance, suggesting restricted visual access (see discussion on Arthur's Stone, pages 64–67). It is this chamber that Pennant notes as having been taken over by a shepherd and used as a shelter during the Post-Medieval period. He believed that, in spite of some degree of rebuilding, the chamber was essentially as it had been at the time of construction, complete with a carefully worked recess in the southern wall and, possibly, a low bench of stone set in clay.

Several depressions between the central and eastern chambers may suggest further contemporary structures or stone robbing. Within the same area of the mound and located along the southern extent of the cairn, is probable evidence of mound kerbing. This kerbing, now consisting of three stones oriented east/west, probably delineates the extent of the mound.

Located at the western end of the monument and incorporated into the secondary phased cairn are up to four stones. These are set in a north/south line and may either be further kerbing or the remnants of a small cist-type structure, similar to those found within the eastern section of Carneddau Hengwm North.

Earlier references speak of additional chambers in the body of the cairn, one to the east of the central feature, another to the west (Pennant, 1783). However, little evidence of these remains today.

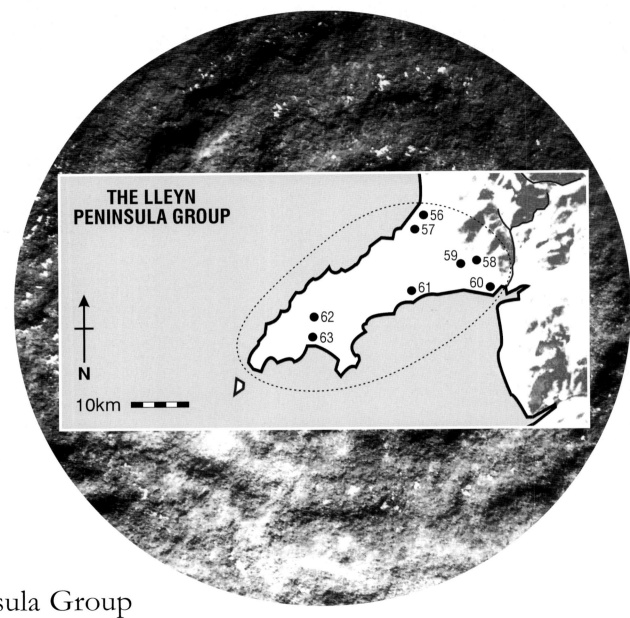

The Lleyn Peninsula Group

Chapter Eight: The Lleyn Peninsula Group

Lynch (1969a, 109) has included monuments within what I have called the Harlech Group — between Barmouth and Porthmadog — with monuments on the Lleyn Peninsula (referred to as the Lleyn-Ardudwy Group). However, each area has monuments with distinct architecture and are separated by a 10km corridor between Llanfair and Porthmadog, which, according to the Sites and Monuments Record (SMR) has little or no evidence of Neolithic activity. I have kept these two groups separate.

There are three distinct environments present: coastal, coastal plateau and uplands. The upland zone, which in places exceeds 300m AOD, is spread along the western coastal fringes and along the central spine of the peninsula. The coastal plateau lies immediately north-east of the upland zone and rises to around 150m AOD. The coastal zone does not exceed 100m AOD. The majority of the Lleyn monuments occupy the coastal and coastal plateau zones and appear to encompass and visually acknowledge but not encroach upon, the upland zone.

Most of the 13 Lleyn Peninsula monuments are classified as Portal Dolmens (Gwynedd Archaeological Trust SMR; Lynch 1969a, 108), and some are classified as either lost, possible or doubtful sites (Daniel 1950, 191–194; Powell et al. 1969, 300-8).The eight discussed in this section are Penarth (CRN 6), Bachwen (CRN 7), Ystum Cegid Isaf (CRN 8), Cefn Isaf (CRN 9), Cist Cerrig (CRN 10), Four Crosses (CRN 11), Mynydd Cefn Amwlch (CRN 12) and Tan-y-Muriau (CRN13). Unlike other core areas such as those of the Black Mountains Group and South West Wales there are no geographical sub-groups recognised, and they appear to be evenly spread throughout their landscape.

These monuments have been discussed by Daniel (1950), Lynch (1969a) and recently by Cummings and Whittle (2004). Lynch has concentrated on the morphology of each monument and has made an extremely useful synthesis concerning the architectural similarities and differences between various monuments within this group and others in North Wales. However, little or no recent intrusive investigation into these monuments has been undertaken. Cummings and Whittle have tended to concentrate on the landscape setting of each monument, particularly its orientation and visuality (2004).

The majority of the Portal Dolmens appear to conform to a series of basic rules. All have either rectangular or polygonal chambers, all have or have had a capstone, and all occupy one of three geographic locations: the valley floor, the intermediate slopes or the coastal plateau.

Monuments such as Cae Dyni (CRN 14),[56] located within the coastal zone east of Criccieth, have in the past been considered as cists and therefore wrongly classified as belonging to the Bronze Age (Powell et al. 1969, 306–307). I would suggest, however, that monuments of this size (which include a chamber measuring 1.3m x 0.80m) can still be considered megalithic and therefore valid in the context of Neolithic burial. The cha,mber is also set within a rectangular mound and measures around 13m x 8m.

Certainly, other monuments of this size and form found elsewhere within the core areas of Wales, such as Carn Besi (CRM 20), Bedd Taliesin (CRM 6) or the Eithbed complex (PEM 31) are given megalithic status, and are usually ascribed to the Late Neolithic. It is probable that Cae Dyni conforms with this date range, although there is no objective dating for any of these monuments. Other monuments, such as Ystum Cegid Isaf, have been identified as a passage grave with a large polygonal chamber (Powell et al. 1969, 301).

This monument (CRN 6; SH 4300 5117) is one of two megalithic monuments within the parish of Clynnog. The Penarth tomb is located in a field called Cae'r Goetan between a road and the mouth of the Afon Desach, approximately 0.5km from the coast and stands around 26m AOD on a gentle slope overlooking Caernarfon Bay. It is one of a number of monuments along the Lleyn peninsula that have similar landscape affinities to monuments found in south-west Wales. Penarth lies on the northern slopes of Bwlch Mawr, whilst the nearby Bachwen monument (CRN 7) is located on the lower slopes of this impressive mountain. The two monuments have some architectural associations.

The remains of the monument consist of three uprights which define the plan of a chamber, with a capstone that rests on two of them and measures approximately 1.8m x 1.6m. This may have been dislodged from its original position. The shape of the chamber is difficult to ascertain, but the three uprights could form a small rectangular or polygonal chamber which would

have been oriented roughly north-west/south-east (i.e. facing the sea). Surrounding the ruined monument is a large stone cairn deposit that is the result of successive field clearance.

Lynch (1969a, 130) has suggested that due to the ruinous state of this monument no classification can be applied. Nevertheless, it is probable that Penarth forms a small Portal Dolmen that was once laterally located within a long mound, although there is no evidence of any visible cairn (Daniel 1950, 192).

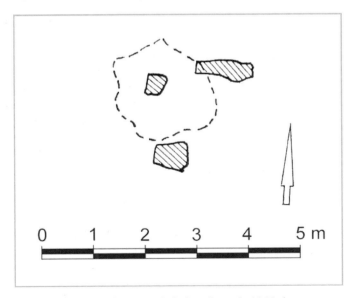

Plan of Penarth (after Lynch 1969a)

0   1   2   3   4   5 m

Penarth monument looking south

Bachwen, Clynnog

This Portal Dolmen (CRN 7; SH 4076 4957) is located approximately 200m from the sea and stands at around 24m AOD on the lower north-western slopes of Bwlch Mawr. As with the nearby Penarth monument, Bachwen would have had an affinity with the sea and its economic resources.

The site was investigated by Barnwell who describes in detail a large number of cupmarks which have been carved into the capstone (Barnwell 1867, 152; Lynch 1969a, 130) and has suggested that dry-stone walling was used to infill the spaces between the four uprights that each stand over 1m high and support a wedge-shaped capstone. The capstone, measuring 2.4m x 2.7m, is aligned east/west and dips towards the sea. It is probable that the covering mound, measuring approximately 14 x 7.5m and constructed of stone of which traces can still be seen, would have been oriented similarly. It has been suggested that further chambers once

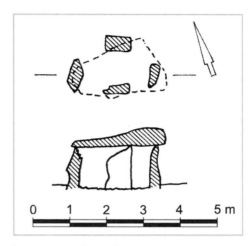

Plan and cross-section of Bachwen (after Lynch 1969a)

existed (Hemp 1926, 429), but the idea of a multi-chambered cairn is difficult to sustain. The notes of antiquarian observers, however, do suggest that traces of kerbing were visible in 1783 (Pennant 1783).

Up to 110 cupmarks, each measuring roughly 5cm in diameter and 2cm in depth, are present on the capstone; similar to those found on the upper section of the capstone at the Trellyffant monument (PEM 2) near Newport, Pembrokeshire (Barker 1992, 19).[57] Two shallow grooves on the upper surface of the capstone link three cupmarks together, whilst up to eight cupmarks are located on the northern ridge of the capstone The rest are on the southern side, facing the mountains to the south and the east. Similar groupings are found on Bronze Age rock-art panels in northern Britain. The eroded upper surface of the capstone does give support to the argument that capstones remained exposed during the period of use of the monument. It is even probable that the cupmarks date from the Bronze Age and represent a form of graffiti or 'statementing' of an ancestral monument. Alternatively, the cupmarks may have been hidden and were for the eyes of the ancestors only, as suggested for art found within the chambers at Barclodiad-y-Gawres in Anglesey (Chippindale and Nash, forthcoming).

The Bachwen monument: the capstone has up to 110 cupmarks

This monument (CRN 8; SH 5000 4132), also referred to as Coetan Arthur (Arthur's Quoit) and Ystumcegid ('Bend in the (river) Cegid') Cromlech, is located 0.7km east of the Afon Dwyfor within a marshy area and has a similar landscape position to the nearby Cefn Isaf monument (CRN 9). However, Ystum Cegid Isaf is very much larger. The monument, standing at around 99m AOD commands dramatic views of the uplands to the north and west.

A sketch by Richard Farrington published in *Snowdonia Druidica* in 1769, suggests that several large stones to the north are the remains of the passage. The drawing clearly shows further uprights and capstones ('triple cromlechs' as Pennant describes the stones in 1783) suggesting Ystum Cegid Isaf was originally a passage grave. According to Lynch (1969a, 139), during the 18th century there was a 5m long passage to the north of the chamber which was made of seven uprights supporting two capstones. The remaining chamber appears to have been rebuilt some time in the recent past, for J.G. Williams (in a notebook published in *Archaeologia Cambrensis* in 1903) records that the capstone was dislodged in 1863 and Barnwell's sketch of 1869 shows the chamber in a ruined state. It is clear that the chamber has been replaced since that date. The position of the passage is indicated by the location of a drystone wall and the lower section of the passage is probably incorporated in the wall.

The monument is located within an east/west drystone field boundary that appears to cut through the centre of the mound. In the field to the west of the site are the remains of a rubble stone heap, partly a result of modern field clearance. However, beyond the rubble is evidence of a possible long mound that was oriented east/west. If this small rise does represent the mound, then the chamber is laterally positioned. The chamber, possibly polygonal in form, has five uprights that stand approximately 1.1m high and which support a large capstone measuring 4.8m x 3.9m.

The monument has been compared morphologically with Bryn Celli Ddu (ANG 7) in Anglesey, which is regarded as 'the best example of a passage grave in England and Wales' (*cf* Daniel 1950, 55). However it should be noted that monuments of this size with a passage are usually incorporated into a circular mound (Grimes 1936a, 128–129).

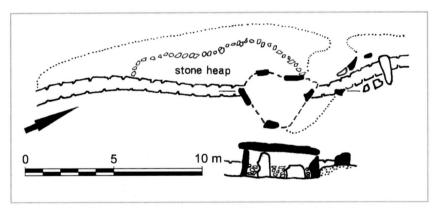

Plan and cross-section of Ystum Cegid Isaf

Ystum Cegid Isaf (*Archaeologia Cambrensis*, Volume XV)

Ystum Cegid Isaf looking north

This monument (CRN 9; SH 4846 4090), in terms of landscape position, stands close to an area of marshy land between the Afon Dwyfach and the Afon Dwyfor, at around 90m AOD. Approximately 0.75km to the east of the Afon Dwyfor stands the monument of Ystum Cegid Isaf (CRN 8). Both monuments have extensive views to the north and west — the upland rock outcrops of Bwlch Mawr and Garn Goch are clearly visible some 3.5km from the mouth of the Afon Dwyfor and the coast and may have landscape association.

Cefn Isaf, also referred to as Rhos-y-Llan and Rhoslan, comprises a substantial fine-grained capstone measuring 3.4m x 2.5m which is supported by three uprights. The site, classified by Powell *et al.* as a Portal Dolmen (1969, 301), has been damaged. Whilst the north-western side of the monument appears intact and is formed by a single stone lying on edge, the south-eastern side of the monument has been destroyed with all traces of the uprights gone (RCAHM 1960). The chamber, rectangular in plan, appears to be oriented north-east/south-west and was probably covered by a mound of the same orientation. The entrance to the chamber may have been from the north-east via a portal stone which is located between the north-eastern upright and the large slab which runs along the western wall of the chamber (Lynch 1969a, 129). This stone slumps in towards the chamber and seems to fit awkwardly if standing upright. West of Cefn Isaf is a recently cut field drainage ditch. Supporting the banks of this and other drainage ditching around the field are large quantities of stone, some of which may have originated from the monument.

It is suggested by Lynch (1969a, 129) that this monument, along with Four Crosses (CRN 11), is located close to a trading route which runs

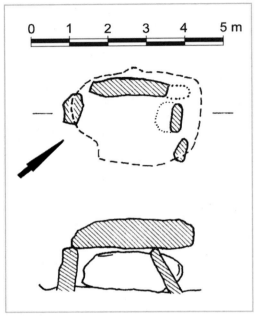

Plan and cross-section of Cefn Isaf (after Lynch 1969a)

across the Lleyn Peninsula. I would further suggest that the Afon Dwyfach and the Afon Dwyfor would have served as approaches to these sites. It is also worth considering that the marshy areas around this and the nearby Ystum Cegid Isaf monument would have restricted physical access to the monuments during use.

Cefn Isaf looking west

This monument (CRN 10; SH 5436 3845), also known as Cist Gerrig, stands on the lower slopes of Moel-y-Gest, close to Portmadoc and is similar architecturally to Hendre Waelod (DEN 1), Gwern Einion (MER 1), Bron-y-Foel-Isaf (MER 2) and Cefn Isaf (CRN 9). Approximately 3km to the south-east are the sand banks of the Afon Dwyryd, Afon Glaslyn and Tremadoc Bay and these rivers would have been economically important to Neolithic communities using this monument. More importantly, it would probably have been an island during the Neolithic. The monument stands within an enclosed valley at around 73m AOD. Exposed rock outcrops located 0.75km to the north were utilised during the Iron Age and form the Moel-y-Gest hill enclosure.

The monument consists of two uprights and a possible door-stone. The largest of these stand 2.2m above the present ground level. Although in a ruined state, it is possible to suggest that a rectangular chamber once existed, based on the existing H-shaped plan of the door-stone and associated uprights. Alternatively, it may be a false portal of a lost Cotswold-Severn monument. Yet again, the alleged door-stone may be an upright which separates a larger rectangular chamber. Lynch (1969a, 129) has suggested that the three stones once formed a small Portal Dolmen with a chamber to the west, facing uphill, 'since this is a very consistent feature of tombs of this class in North Wales', (ibid., 129). Inside the chamber area is an extensive rubble deposit which may be the result of field clearance or rubble packing. No evidence of a cairn or capstone survives.

Cist Cerrig is one of several megalithic monuments in Wales associated with a series of 12 cupmarks. These do not occur on the monument itself, but on a natural rock surface 23m to the south-east (Hemp 1938, 141).

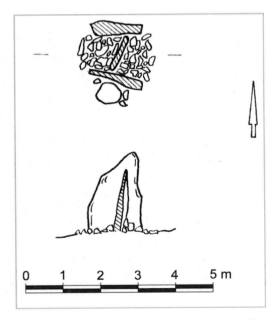

Plan and cross-section (after Lynch 1969a)

Cist Cerrig monument

Cist Cerrig

The monument (CRN 10; SH 3981 3858) stands in open pasture on a small ridge to the west of the Afon Erch at around 66m AOD. Close by, to the south of Rhyd-y-gwystl, are two standing stones each approximately 1.7m high (SH 400 389 and SH 400 388). The ridge was utilised to avoid extensive areas of marshland to the east and provides the best route across the Lleyn peninsula (Lynch 1969a, 129). This monument forms part of a small megalithic group within the area that also includes Cefn Isaf (CRN 9) and the small coastal megalithic chamber of Cae Dyni, east of Criccieth (CRN 14). Daniel (1950, 89) suggests that these monuments are similar in plan and can be linked architecturally to other Portal Dolmens in North Wales, for example, Hendre Waelod (DEN 1), Gwern Einion (MER 1), Bron-y-Foel-Isaf (MER 2) and Cefn Isaf (CRN 9). All these surviving structures have a single capstone which is supported by either three or four uprights, delineating a rectangular or polygonal chamber.

A plan of the site made by Barnwell in 1869 depicts the monument prior to its restoration in 1936 by the owner, Mr. William Evans. It appears that prior to this restoration the western upright had fallen on its side under the capstone. Nothing was found within the chamber area of the monument during the restoration (Grimes 1936a). A recent site visit in January 2006 shows the uprights are set into concrete. (Swann and Waite: pers. comm.) rightly suggest that the southern upright may actually be the capstone but when reassembled, Mr Evans was not sure of the original morphology of the monument. The shape and size are similar to nearby Cefn Isaf (CRN 9).

Lynch suggests that the siting of tombs within this area indicates the inland movement of people from the coast, probably using streams and rivers flowing south from the hinterland of the Lleyn peninsula. Lynch further considers that by the time the Four Crosses monument was constructed, the original architectural inspiration for this and other monuments had been lost (1969a, 129). I would further suggest that this monu-ment has architectural similarities with nearby Cefn Isaf (CRN 9). Both monuments, although classified generically as Portal Dolmens, have short uprights which support horizontally placed capstones, unlike Hendre Waelod (DEN 1) and Gwern Einion (MER 1).

The monument consists of a small enclosed rectangular chamber measuring approximately 1.3m x 0.8m x 1.48m, which would have once stood within a covering mound. The capstone measuring 2.3m x 1.4m x 0.6m is supported by three uprights, with an entrance probably located on the north-eastern side of the monument. A fourth upright stands approximately 0.20m short of the capstone.

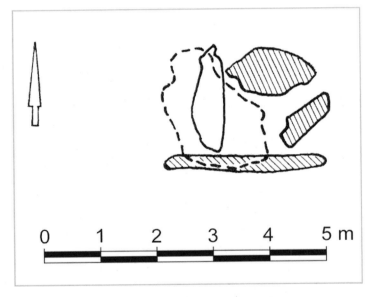

Plan of Four Crosses (after Lynch 1969a)

Four Crosses looking north east, showing the reconstructed monument

Standing on the north-western slopes of Mynydd Cefn Amwlch (CRN 12; SH 2301 3465), this tripod dolmen (Daniel 1950, 52), also known as Coetan Arthur and Tref-y-garnedd, shares a similar location to that of the Penarth monument (CRN 6). It lies approximately 2km from the sea at around 99m AOD. The Afon Soch flows to the east and would have provided a direct route between this monument and that at Tan-y-Muriau. According to Lynch (1969a, 132) there are 19th-century accounts of destroyed monuments within the surrounding area. Whilst Lynch has suggested that the area around Mynydd Cefn Amwlch was probably unpopulated (ibid., 131), these accounts show that it was clearly an important symbolic area, and certainly has one of the greatest concentrations of Portal Dolmens in North Wales.

This much ruined monument consists of a large capstone measuring 3.5m x 2.5m which is supported by three uprights, all of fine-grained sandstone. Located within the north-western area of the chamber is a possible recumbent sill-stone which probably would have allowed periodic access to the chamber. The original shape of the monument is unknown. However, the chamber, regarded by Lynch (1969a, 131) as featureless, may have been laterally placed within a long mound — similar to other dolmen-type monuments on the Lleyn Peninsula. Castleden (1992, 394) states that the chamber is rectangular, with which I would agree, and speculates that the monument was covered by a circular mound measuring 8.5m in diameter. However, the shape and size of the mound is difficult to determine. The present architectural form is similar to Bachwen (CRN 7), Lech-y-Tribedd (PEM 1), located within the Newport sub-group in south-west Wales. Daniel (1950, 193) notes that a large flat stone, possibly belonging to another chamber exists immediately west of the monument. This stone, made from white quartz veined sandstone, is large enough to be a capstone, however, it is more than likely to be later field clearance. The author is sceptical that it forms part of the monument architecture.

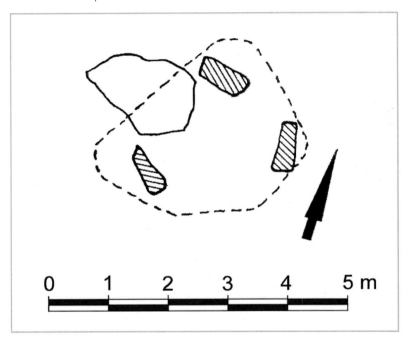

Plan of Mynydd Cefn Amwlch (after Lynch 1969a)

Mynydd Cefn Amwlch

This complex site (CRN 13; SH 2381 2886) is regarded as one of the Lleyn Peninsula's most important surviving monuments and stands on the eastern slopes of Mynydd Rhiw at around 132m AOD. It has extensive views across the eastern part of the peninsula and the northern coastline of Cardigan Bay. At the foot of Mynydd Rhiw is a large area of marshland and many small streams run off the mountain into the nearby Afon Soch. During the Neolithic these natural spaces may have been significant, perhaps dividing the landscape into social and symbolic areas.

The monument, classified as a laterally chambered long mound, has a Portal Dolmen-type chamber. The mound may have once been trapezoidal in form and, morphologically, Tan-y-Muriau may be similar to other tombs that follow the Cotswold-Severn monument tradition. It is possible that sometime during the Middle Neolithic there was a need to alter the form of existing monuments and Tan-y-Muriau may exemplify this process of architectural change. Similarly, at Ty Isaf (BRE 5) in the Black Mountains, the original round mound with central chamber and passage was later incorporated into a large trapezoidal monument.

The survival of this monument is mainly due to its being incorporated into a large field bank that runs down a ten degree slope, the unorthodox north-south zigzag line of the field boundary showing the probable north-eastern extent of the monument. During its construction and use the mound must have measured some 43m in length and 15m in width.

This monument, described by J.G. Williams in 1871 (*Archaeologia Cambrensis* 1903, 260), notes three chambers as being in a north/south line, 20 yards (9.5m) from each other.

The northern Portal Dolmen-type chamber consists of a large capstone measuring approximately 3.6m x 2.9m x 0.7m supported by four uprights (RCAHM 1956). The chamber floor, rectangular in plan, appears to be cut into the natural slope of the mountain with the northern three uprights banking into later, naturally accumulated soils. The centrally placed upright at the northern end of the chamber possibly forms a door, which was periodically moved in order to allow ritual deposition of human remains into the chamber area.

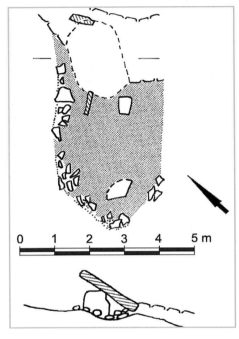

Plan and cross-section of the side chamber (after Lynch 1969a)

Plan and cross-section of northern chamber (after Lynch 1969a)

Approximately 7m south-east of the northern chamber, and incorporated into the mound, is a smaller chamber which Castleden refers to as a side chamber (1992, 394). This consists of a capstone measuring 2.3m x 1.5m leaning against two uprights. Located outside the western area of the chamber within the mound is an extensive rubble spread, which possibly represents a passage. The plan reproduced in Lynch (1969a, 131) suggests that the small chamber is centrally located within the mound

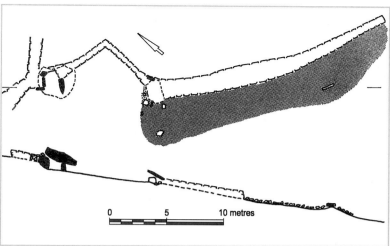

Tan-y-Muriau:
the northern chamber looking east

Tan-y-Muriau: overall site plan
showing the location of the two chambers

which would have been entered via the passage from the west. The large chamber at the northern terminal is believed to have formed part of an earlier monument, which may have been circular or oval in form. Lynch (*ibid.*, 133) associates the architectural form with other monuments such as Carnedd Hengwn South (MER 6) and Dyffryn Ardudwy (MER 3). Approximately 10m north of the southern end of the barrow was, according to Daniel (1950, 193), a heap of large stones which may have formed part of another chamber.

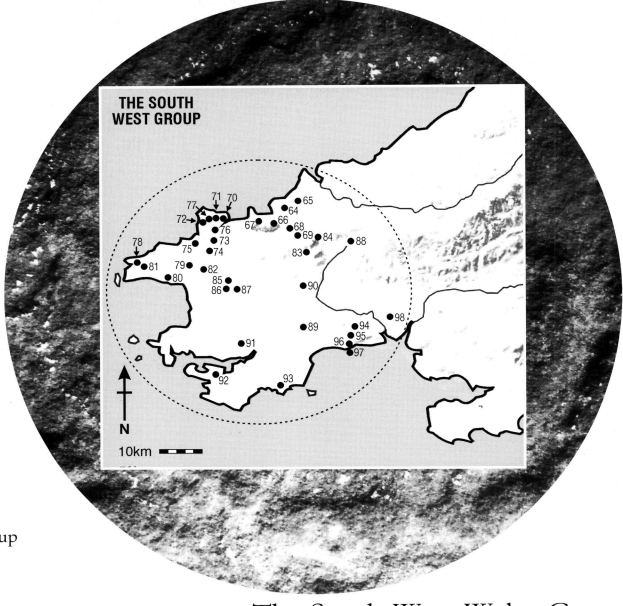

The South-West Wales Group

Chapter Nine: The South-West Wales Group

By far the largest Neolithic core group in Wales are the 50 or so monuments in South-West Wales.[58] These sites are located within the counties of Cardiganshire, Carmarthenshire and Pembrokeshire and have in the recent past been discussed in detail by Barker (1992), Children and Nash (1997; 2002), Figgis (2001), Cummings (2002), and Cummings and Whittle (2004). Up until 2004 only one site in this area — Carreg Coetan (PEM 3) — had been dated using radio-chronometric methods (see Appendix II). There is, therefore, a problem in assessing a chronology of architectural phasing of monuments within this group. However, based on the limited artifact evidence it is probable that the Portal Dolmen group of which Carreg Coetan is one, is the earliest and the earth-fast style monument the latest. No one monument group appears to be in use throughout the Neolithic, the duration of which spans between 1,700 to 2,000 years. In addition to morphology, the landscape position of each monument type varies through time and geographical area. Due to the size and distribution of these monuments, I have organised them into a series of sub-groups.

The overall group of monuments can boast the most diverse architecture. In particular ideas from central and southern Ireland appear to have reached the builders of some of the monuments helping to create an Irish Sea Portal Dolmen tradition (Lynch 1976). There is also a group of late Neolithic monuments referred to as earth-fast, where one end of the capstone rests in or on the ground, probably the only area in Wales to have such monuments. Unlike many monuments within this group these probably did not possess a covering mound. Also important to this group are the three axe factories located around and on Mynydd Preseli that encouraged the trade and exchange of exotic items, some of which were deposited in burial monuments. One should also remember that Mynydd Preseli is the area in which the Preseli blue stones of Stonehenge fame originate.

The location of many (but not all) of the monuments is based on a relationship with the sea, with several being close to the shoreline yet ignoring it. Arguably the Neolithic package, which includes burial monumentality, may include farming the sea. A similar geographic location is found in other core groups such as Anglesey and the Harlech Group. Tilley (1994), David and Williams (1995) and Children and Nash (1997) have suggested further that monuments were deliberately positioned in order to be visually associated with various local landscape features. In South-West Wales, such features can include mountains, rock-outcropping, naturally formed cairn heaps and water. Many monuments of this group are in fact sited within extensive rock outcropping, thus hiding the monument within the landscape.

The group includes some of the largest megalithic sites in Wales: the sites of Pentre Ifan (PEM 3), Garn Turne (PEM 11) and Carreg Samson (PEM 18) all possess massive capstones and large chamber architecture. The Garn Turne capstone weighs in excess of 60 tons and the size and weight of such stones would have probably required inter-communal co-operation. Indeed, this area contains two Neolithic settlements, Clegyr Boia and Coygan Camp, which allows researchers to associate settlement activity to burial activity. Throughout the rest of Wales there are many upland and lowland lithic scatters which could be deemed as settlement sites but Clegyr Boia and Coygan Camp both have the remains of house structures.

The Newport Sub-Group

The Newport Group comprises six monuments: Llech-y-Tribedd (PEM 1), Trellyffant (PEM 2), Carreg Coetan (PEM 3), Cerrig-y-Gof (PEM 4), Pentre Ifan (PEM 5) and Bedd-yr-Afanc (PEM 27) that encompass an area of around 40km². Other monuments may have existed, but due to intensive agricultural activity over recent centuries they are now long gone.

The area has a continuous early prehistory dating back at least to 6,000 BC. Flint from the Late Mesolithic has been found all along the mud flats of the Afon Nyfer (Nevern) estuary. Between the estuary, the coast and the mountains, Neolithic mortuary structures occupy the intermediate slopes. Above these slopes, and all along the northern extent of the Mynydd Preseli overlooking Newport, Bronze Age and Iron Age activity is also represented.

Domestic life for Neolithic communities in and around the Nevern valley seems to have been rather favourable. A choice of economic resources would have been available ranging from coastal and riverine fishing and hunting and gathering, to limited animal husbandry and crop cultivation. Samples of wood discovered within the inter-tidal peats of the Nevern estuary (-0.6m OD) have been dated to 6370±150 BP, suggesting that the environment in and around Newport was wooded. Indeed, this and similar samples from Cardigan Bay form part of a now submerged forest. The area within the estuary would, therefore, have been foraged by large mammals such as red and roe deer.

For each of the tombs in this cluster, the primary landscape focus seems to be the rocky outcrop of Mynydd Carningli at the north-eastern extent of the Preseli Mountains. Three of the monuments — Pentre Ifan, Carreg Coetan and Llech-y-Tribedd — all have capstones with a shape that appears to replicate the summit of the outcrop, drawing the landscape within the architecture of the tomb (Children and Nash 1997). It must be stressed, however that what one sees today is only the tomb 'skeleton'. During the Neolithic, this skeleton would have possessed 'flesh' — a covering earthen mound — although the capstone may have been left partly exposed to emphasise the symbolic association with Carningli. Also gone is the façade area and any ritual associated features such as pits and (wooden) platforms.

Apart from the gallery grave of Bedd-yr-Afanc, which probably dates from the latest phase of the Neolithic, the remaining Newport tombs probably embody a process of replication and control which seeks to establish and perpetuate a sense of identity with the landscape. Tombs elsewhere in

South-West Wales reveal a similar pattern of landscape orientation. The chamber at St Elvies Farm (PEM 20), St David's, for example, is angled down towards a small coastal valley, an inlet of the River Solva.

However, given this general association with Carningli, individual monuments of the Newport Group are nevertheless sited within diverse landscape settings, ranging from coastal locations to inland valley floors. Apart from Cerrig-y-Gof and perhaps Carreg Coetan, the tombs appear to ignore

Cupmarks on the destroyed monument of Trefael, (more than 20 cupmarks were noted)

the draw of the sea. Indeed, Llech-y-Tribedd and Trellyffant, although only 0.5km from the coast, appear to be deliberately hidden from the sea, being constructed on south-facing ridges overlooking the Preseli Mountains. This pattern recurs throughout the peninsula.

Due to the diversity of architectural forms, the dating of individual tombs is difficult. One cannot say with certainty that all the tombs in this sub-group were constructed about the same time, although they were probably all in use during the middle and later phases of the Neolithic. It has been suggested that simple Portal Dolmens, such as Carreg Coetan, are the earliest monuments in this area (Barker 1992). This type of monument, incorporating a small chamber, housed a single burial, probably that of an important figure in early Neolithic society. Following burial, the tomb may have continued to function as a significant place within the landscape, changing its symbolic significance through time. Indeed, towards the latter part of the Neolithic and the Early Bronze Age there is evidence for monuments in this area becoming political statements within the landscape — their identity changing, but not their form. For instance, at Trellyffant, the 35 cupmarks on the capstone, possibly Bronze Age in date, indicate a rejection of the old Neolithic order (Children and Nash 1997). A similar defacement is seen on the nearby destroyed monument of Trefael (SN 103 403) where more than 20 cupmarks were present. There is a parallel today, with redundant chapels being reused as workshops and dwellings. Here, the building has changed its meaning, but not its architectural form.

Of the six monuments, Bedd-yr-Afanc stands apart and has been classified as a Late Neolithic gallery grave, its construction, location and orientation suggesting a change in monument ideology. Located inland, and oriented east/west along the valley floor, the tomb ignores Carningli, the sea and other monuments, a similar pattern followed by gallery graves elsewhere. Compared with earlier monuments, they are smaller, less intrusive and sometimes actually hidden. With its covering earthen mound, Bedd-yr-Afanc would have merged with the valley floor. Without specialist ritual knowledge the tomb would have been invisible, with access restricted to select members of the local group.

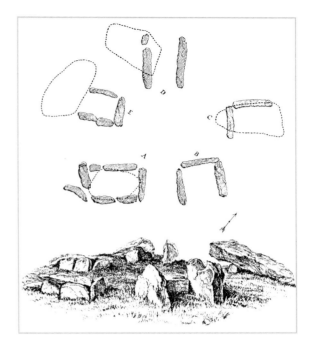

Antiquarian drawing and layout of Cerrig-y-Gof from *Archaeologia Cambrensis*

This monument, (PEM 1; SN 1005 4319) also referred to as the Altar Stone, Llech-y-Drybedd and Samson's Quoit commands one of the most outstanding views of any tomb in the area, and draws in the whole extent of the north Preseli Mountains (Tilley 1994, 105). Legend has it that St Samson originally threw the stones for the monument from the summit of Mynydd Carningli.

This monument, standing around 188m AOD, comprises a single large capstone supported by three uprights and is classified by Lynch as a Portal Dolmen (1972, 77–78). The uprights, derived from locally quarried sandstone, are arranged in a tripod form. Another is located close by suggesting the chamber was once rectangular, indeed, in 1695 it was reported by Lhwyd that this fourth upright was in place and supported the capstone, but was prone by 1950 when reported by Daniel (1950, 198). There is no evidence of any covering mound, but there is some potential cairn material in and around the chamber area. It should also be noted that the surrounding field boundaries are constructed of turf and stone and it is probable that cairn material may have been reused in the boundary fabric.

The massively thick capstone which is triangular in shape and measures 5m x 3m, points towards the mountain, Mynydd Carningli, a focal point for nearly all the tombs in this area. Indeed, the south-eastern point of the capstone appears to replicate its summit. By contrast, Llech-y-Tribedd is completely hidden

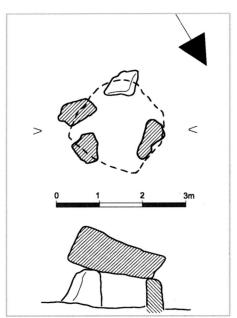

**Plan and elevation of
Llech-y-Tribedd (after Barker 1992)**

Llech-y-Tribedd, looking west towards the coast

from the sea, although located on a south-east facing ridge, only 0.6km from the coast; ignoring any view of the sea appears to be a common trait among monuments within this part of Wales. The monument is also 1.75km north-east of the Trellyffant monument (PEM 2) but not intervisible.

A small pipeline trench, approximately 10m north of the chamber area and aligned east/west, was excavated by Cambria Archaeology (PRN 1121) in October 1977. No prehistoric artifacts were recorded. A site visit in January 2006, revealed that the western upright had cracked and small sections of the crust had started to disintegrate.

Llech-y-Tribedd, looking south-east to the Nevern Valley

Llech-y-Tribedd, looking towards Mynydd Carningli

The much ruined burial monument of Trellyffant (PEM 2; SN 0822 4252), also referred to as Trellyfaint or Trelleffant lies approximately 1.75km south-west of the Llech-y-Tribedd monument at around 137m AOD. Lynch (1969a, 131) describes Trellyffant as a Portal Dolmen. Originally, the chamber seems to have been rectangular, and Daniel, writing in 1950, gave the height of 1.8m with an opening to the south-east. The chamber is constructed of three large uprights with a fourth stone acting as a back-stone. According to Lynch (1972, 78) the voids between the uprights may have been infilled with drystone walling. The small capstone appears to have been oriented north-west/south-east and measures 2.1m x 1.8m.

To the north of the main chamber is a small square feature — possibly another chamber — measuring approximately 1.5m x 1.7m, in which case it would make Trellyffant a double chambered tomb (RCAM 1925, 760).[59] This chamber would have possessed a small capstone, and Lynch (1972, 79) suggests that a cairn or earthen mound would originally have covered both chambers, traces of which are still visible.

There is evidence of later prehistoric ritual defacement on the upper surface of the capstone. The 35 cupmarks identified by the recorder for the RCAM inventory and later illustrated by Lynch (1972, 78–79) and Barker (1992, 19) may be of Bronze Age origin and associated with the appropriation and re-use of the tomb by people seeking to alter its meaning, perhaps transforming what was once principally a mortuary structure into a monument marking the site of exchange transactions or political gatherings. Acts of this kind may be interpreted as attempts to subvert remote and irrelevant beliefs. The authenticity of the Trellyffant cupmarks, however, has been questioned. The RCAM (1925) argued that, owing to the random size and distribution of the marks, they should be regarded as natural. Daniel, however,

The Trellyffant monument

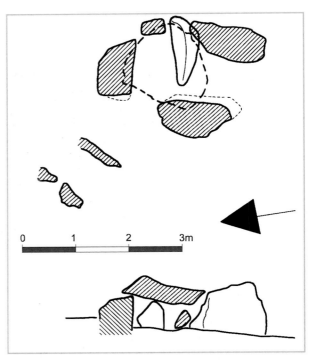

Plan and elevation of Trellyffant (after Barker 1992)

believed these 'pitted' cupmarks to be genuine and some of the finest in southern Britain. The author feels that the cupmarks collectively may delineate some form of semiotic message which is known only to the people that carved them, especially as it is probable that the top of the capstone was exposed when in use.

About 3km to the south-east of Trellyffant burial chamber further cupmarks are visible on a large rock slab,[60] which Daniel believed was the capstone of a destroyed Megalithic chamber. As a footnote, the medieval Welsh historian and geographer Giraldus Cambrensis (Gerald of Wales), believed that Trellyffant ('Toad's Hall') was so-named because a chieftain buried inside the tomb had been devoured by toads.

The Trellyffant monument looking east

This monument (PEM 3; SN 0602 3935), also known as Coetan Arthur (Arthur's Quoit) and Carreg Coetan Arthur, is classified as a small chambered Portal Dolmen, one of a number that are present along the coastal stretches of Pembrokeshire.

One of the earliest accounts of this monument was by Wyndham who in 1775 says of the monument:

> In a small field, between Newport and its harbour, is another monument, still larger, and quite perfect, of the same kind [Cerrig y Gof]; the upper stone is shaped like a mushroom, and is upwards of nine feet in diameter.

This monument did not receive a full appraisal until a plan of the site was published by Frances Lynch in 1972. Prior to this the monument had been briefly commented on and sketched by Gardner Wilkinson in 1871 and engraved by Barnwell in 1872. According to Barker (1992, 19), there has been little or no change to the monument since then.

One of the lowest-lying tombs in Wales, Carreg Coetan stands just 8m AOD close to the Afon Nyfer estuary and 0.5km from the coast. The estuary and Dinas Head lie to the west, while to the south, and rising to a height of 350m, the summit of Carningli provides the obvious topographical focus for the tomb. Legend has it that the stones forming Carreg Coetan were thrown from the summit of the mountain. When aligned with the peak, the capstone appears to replicate its profile, drawing the landscape into the fabric of the tomb.

Carreg Coetan is often described as a 'tripod dolmen', consisting in fact of four uprights, two of which support a massive sloping capstone. Lynch (1972) classifies this monument as a Portal Dolmen whereas Grimes describes it as a simple polygonal chamber (1936a, 132). I see it as a Portal Dolmen with a polygonal chamber. A number of outlying stones belonging to the tomb have been identified, together with traces of a covering mound. Littered within the vicinity and concentrated about 2m in front of the chamber is possible evidence of blocking material or the remains of a mound, oriented roughly east/west.

During the 1979/1980 excavation carried out by Sian Rees (1981), it became evident that a build-up of plough soil, in places over a metre thick,

lay around the uprights. This being so, Carreg Coetan would originally have appeared much taller than it does today.

When excavated, the much disturbed chamber revealed traces of 'powdery, cremated bone' along with two sherds of corded Beaker and three rim-sherds of Grooved Ware. Large amounts of pottery, enough for two pot reconstructions, and more cremated bone lay deeper within the chamber stratigraphy. Charcoal beneath an upright socket was carbon-dated to about 4700±80 BP. Other uncalibrated dates were taken from underneath the mound which have a similar date range. However, the construction method suggests a much earlier monument, possibly Early-to-Middle Neolithic in date.

The fact that both cremated bone and charcoal are present in the chamber suggests that bodies were not deposited in the tomb immediately after death; a more elaborate burial method may have been used. I tend to favour the idea that the dead were exposed to the elements — what is termed as excarnation — possibly on wooden platforms like those used by the north-west American coastal Indians and seen within the archaeological record at Gwernvale monument (BRE 7) and at Wayland's Smithy in Berkshire. Here, the body would decay and the flesh devoured by wild animals, to leave only a skeleton. The tomb would have acted as the final resting place after the body had decayed and lost its flesh and could no longer be recognized as human.

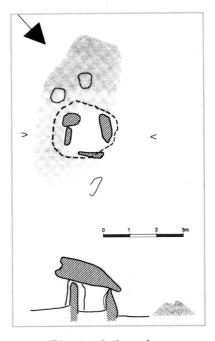

Plan and elevation of Carreg Coetan (after Barker 1992)

Carreg Coetan looking north-west. The Afon Nevern flows some 30m to the north

Also known as Cerrig Atgof (PEM 4; SM 0365 3890), this unusual coastal tomb stands between Dinas Head and the Nevern River, at around 46m AOD. Affinities with tombs in Ireland and Scotland have been noted, and it has been suggested that architectural influences may have been transmitted along Irish Sea trade routes (Castleden, 1992). Daniel (1950) includes the tomb within his Irish Sea cultural province as a late innovation of his local Dyfed Group.

There are many antiquarian accounts of this monument, the earliest by Edward Lhwyd who in 1695 stated:

> In Newport-parish there are five of these Tables or Altars placed near each other, which some conjecture to have been once encompass'd with a circle of stone pillars, for that there are two stones yet standing near them. But these are nothing comparable in bigness to the Gromlech [Pentre Ifan] here described, and not raised above three foot high; nor are they supported with pillars, but stones edgewise ...

A later antiquarian report by Fenton gives a more detailed description of the monument, including details of an excavation that he undertook in 1810. In one of the earliest written accounts in Wales of an excavation, he states that (1810, 554–555):

> ... I come to a singular cluster of Cistvaens, which, having provided myself with labourers, I was prepared to open, permission being politely granted me for that purpose by George Bowen, Esq. of Llwyn gwair, on whose property they were. This group, consisting of five placed in a circle, radiating from a centre once occupied by a denominated Cromlech, long since overturned, stood on a gentle rising in a field to the right of the road, and was almost hid, being overgrown with weeds and briars, and, by several upright stones still to be traced, seemed to have been surrounded by an extensive circle of such, forming a mysterious precinct. Having removed the lid stones of the cists, and digging down about a foot through fine mould, I came to charcoal, and soon after discovered pieces of urns of the rudest pottery, some particles of bone, and a quantity of black sea pebbles. I opened them all, and with a very trifling variation of their contents found them of the same character. In the vacant space between each Cistvaen, as well as in the centre over which the Cromlech had been raised, I likewise dug, but found nothing indicatory of sepulture, furnishing a strong presumption that it was for a very different use. The largest lid stone was thirteen feet three inches in length, nor were the others much less, and the whole group was in circumference forty-two yards.

Fenton believed a central cromlech originally completed the complex, but this hypothesis is disputed because the central area is too small to accommodate a chamber of a size similar to the other five.

The tomb is possibly transitional, suggesting Bronze Age burial practice in its use of multiple cists, or small stone-lined burial chambers, within an oval mound. Close by and to the south of Cerrig-y-Gof is arguably a dense Bronze Age landscape consisting of cairns, hut circles and enclosures. Further Bronze Age evidence is seen in a small rock outcrop some 40m south of the monument. Up to eight large cupmarks are carved into the surface. Furthermore, a possible Bronze Age hillfort, one of only two in

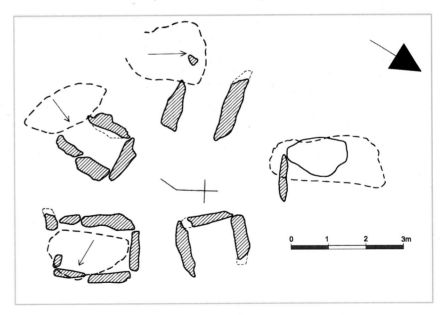

Plan of Cerrig-y-Gof (after Daniel 1950)

The western chamber of Cerrig-y-Gof looking west

Wales, is sited on Carningli. What is undisputed is that the mound measures 9m north/south and 8.2m east/west, and contains five square and rectangular chambers lacking passages.

Lynch suggests (1972) that the chamber settings are 'a haphazard agglomeration which must be the local answer to the need for more burial space within a tradition of single compartment monuments. However, each chamber appears to be deliberately positioned. The north-west chamber encompasses Dinas Head and Newport Bay; the south-west, Mynydd Dinas; the south-east, Mynydd Melyn; and the eastern chamber, Carningli. All of these areas have yielded evidence of intense Bronze Age activity. By indicating significant features, Cerrig-y-Gof is encompassing the whole of the surrounding landscape. It is possible that each chamber may have housed more than one body. Whole families may, over many generations, have been deposited as disarticulated remains or even as cremations.

Pentre Ifan (PEM 5; SN 0993 3707), one of the most impressive chambered tombs in Wales and standing at around 145m AOD, consists of a tilted capstone dipping towards the Nevern valley to the west, perched upon three tall upright megaliths or uprights. The resulting chamber is 3m long, 2m wide and 3m high and was originally cut about 40cms into the ground surface and lined with drystone walling, but has recently been infilled. The blocking stone (doorway) in the forecourt area was packed with small stones around the base. On the outer face of the blocking stone, a single cupmark and ring has been identified (Lynch 1974, 120). Later Morris (1989, 87) noted the cupmark as a spiral, although I failed to recognise any such regular patterning.

The monument is located on the eastern side of Mynydd Carningli and has extensive views of the lower Nevern Valley and the sea. It is also inter-visible with Carreg Coetan (PEM 3) and Llech-y-Tribedd (PEM 1) which lie on the western side of the Nevern Valley.

There are many antiquarian accounts of the site, the earliest dating to 1603 when the site is described as:

> An other thinge worth the noteinge is a stone called Maen y gromlegh upon Pentre Jevan lande: yt is a huge and massie stone mounted on highe and sett on the toppes of iijee other highe stones, pitched standinge upright in the grounde, yt farre passeth for giggnes and height Arthurs stone in the waye between Hereford and the Haye, or Legh yr ast near Blaen Porth in Cardinganshere, or anye other that ever I saw ...
> (George Owen, British Museum Manuscript No. 6250)

The site appears to have changed since Richard Tongue painted it in 1835, for in his painting some of the stones belonging to the chamber are visible. The capstone is dipping towards the west and Carningli can be seen through the chamber.

According to Barker, this monument is an impressive example of a terminally-chambered long cairn with a semicircular forecourt set in the broad southern end of the barrow — a model Closed Portal Tomb (1992, 23). It is possible that the chamber and forecourt were freestanding and any enclosing mound was added later, but this alas remains unproven (Barker: pers. comm.). Daniel compares the forecourt at Pentre Ifan and other chambered tombs in the region with the so-called 'horned cairns' of Carlingford in Ireland, arguing for colonisation by people of the Carlingford culture. He further suggests that the more easterly Cotswold-Severn Tomb Group is derived from the Pentre Ifan type.

Lynch (1972) has suggested that the tomb was built in two phases. Phase one may have consisted only of the chamber, uprights and capstone with a low square cairn. Phase two would have seen the construction of a low mound, perhaps with the capstone left exposed. However, according to the excavation report by Grimes (1960) it is very difficult to find evidence for two phases of construction. Indeed, I would suggest that any phasing of this monument was restricted to ephemeral changes, maybe the replacement of materials that had degraded over periods of time.

Grimes, who excavated the tomb in 1936–1937 (1948, 3–11) and again in 1958–1959 (1960) for the Office of Works, described the forecourt, where ritual feasts may have been held, as consisting of two uprights placed either side of an entrance, itself blocked by a massive upright. Daniel disputes the argument that these blocked chambers, found also at Capel Garmon (DEN 3) and Dyffryn Ardudwy (MER 3), prevented the tomb being fully re-opened after the mound had been piled up (Hemp, 1927).

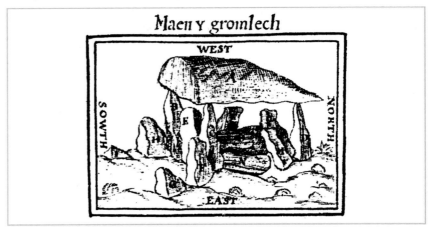

Early 17th-century woodcut of Pentre Ifan

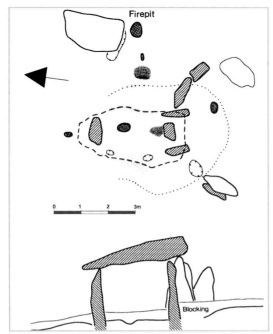

**Plan of Pentre Ifan chamber
(after Grimes 1960)**

tified delineating the long sides of the barrow, but their alignment does not match precisely the orientation of the barrow and they may be linked instead with possible ritual pits found beneath the mound and predating its construction.

Pentre Ifan yielded a small number of flint flakes and fragments of Welsh (Western) pottery. These are similar to artifacts from the excavated chambered monument of Pant-y-Saer (ANG 13), in North Wales. It is more than probable that the pottery from both monuments derived originally from a single source, showing that pottery was traded and replicated within the different Welsh Neolithic core areas. Interestingly, this mundane artifact, used for cooking and storage has become a grave commodity. Grimes (1960) distinguishes between the pottery of the western megalithic groups, with its flattened, expanded hammer-head rims with pottery from the south and east of England. Lynch (1969) has noted similarities of form, but not of fabric, between the neck of an open bowl discovered in the chamber at Pentre Ifan and fragments recovered from the Dyffryn Ardudwy monument in Gwynedd.

Hemp's belief led him to propose the theory that tombs were constructed to house the remains of 'great chieftains', and that the other individuals found in the chambers had, in life, been relatives or attendants who had sacrificed themselves on the death of the great man. The chambers would therefore have been used once only by high-ranking members of a stratified society and would not have been intended for communal use. Daniel, however, argued that 'chamber tombs were for the most part used collectively on a number of occasions' (1950, 146). This is interesting in that the doorway is firmly set into the ground and I would suggest was only opened on special occasions. Rather than fresh bodies being placed into the tomb, collections of bones would be stored up elsewhere before being deposited *en masse* in the chamber. This hypothesis challenges Barker's idea (1992) that the doorway was a permanent feature, otherwise known as a false portal which occurs in hybrid Cotswold-Severn tombs such as Ty Isaf (BRE 5) and Pipton Long Cairn (BRE 8) in the Black Mountains.

The mound itself does not survive, but may originally have measured 40m long and 17m wide. Traces of possible stone kerbing have been iden-

Pentre Ifan chamber

The Pentre Ifan monument

Bedd-yr-Afanc (PEM 27; SN 1089 3459), also known as Bryn Berian, is located at 142m AOD in the centre of a dramatic U-shaped valley, on a slightly raised oval plateau surrounded by a raised bog,, is the only definite example of a gallery grave in Wales. The plateau on which the monument stands, according to the RCAM (1925, 681), measures around 21.3m by 8.2m and is 0.6m in height. Around the monument is a large stone scatter; some are loose, others partially buried and may be associated with possible cairn material which covered the mound. Architecturally, it is quite different from its nearest neighbour, Pentre Ifan (PEM 5), which lies 3.8km to the north-west.

Lacking side chambers and forecourt, the tomb was originally covered by an oval barrow. It consists of 22 small uprights arranged to form a gallery 10.5m long and 2.5m wide, oriented roughly east/west, blocked at its western end. The orientation of the tomb may be governed by the east/west alignment of the rising and setting sun, as well as symbolising the life and death cycle; the west being seen as the termination of life.

The monument was surveyed in 1936 and later excavated in 1938 by W.F. Grimes. He noted traces of two lines of stones or possible kerbing (Grimes 1939b, 258) that may have defined the extent of the mound. Some of the excavation scarring is still visible and shows that little change to this monument has occurred over the past 65 years. There are traces of a slab or flagged stone floor located within the gallery area at the eastern end of the monument. According to the RCAM (1925, 681) the monument is much disturbed which leads to the question of whether or not the gallery was divided into a series of chambers; a number of gallery graves are sub-divided using a portal stone.

Grimes had suggested that the monument represented a 'passage' some 1m in length (30ft) and was slightly wedge-shaped in plan, widening to 1.8m at the western end, similar to those found in Ireland and the Isle of Man (1939b). However, he abandoned this idea after his excavation. According to a conversation between Barker and Grimes in 1986 there were no finds from this site. However, a section of a palaeo-surface, located 5m from the site, revealed several undiagnostic flint chips (Barker 1992, 40).

The tomb is sited on an exposed (raised) ancient land surface. Its axis is oriented along the marshy valley, the location suggesting an intimate

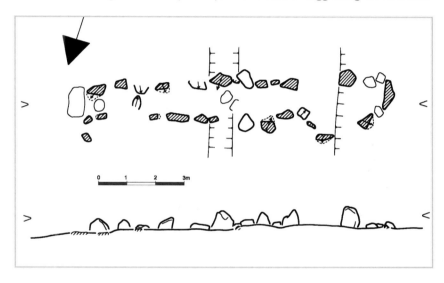

Plan of Bedd-yr-Afanc (after Barker 1992)

affinity with topographic features to either side, especially Cnwc-yr-Hydd, Cerrig Lladron and mountains to the south. During the Neolithic, the tomb may have witnessed seasonal water logging. Like a moat, this would have set up both a physical and mental barrier, maintaining the exclusivity of the site and safely containing the dead within the confines of the tomb and the raised plateau on which it stood. Settlement would probably have been confined to the intermediate slopes, away from the damp valley floor.

Bedd-yr-Afanc looking north-east

The Fishguard Sub-Group

This group consists of ten monuments and eight are discussed here: Garn Wen (PEM 7–9), Carn Wnda (PEM 13), Parc-y-Cromlech (PEM 14), Garn Gilfach (PEM 15), Ffyst Samson (PEM 16), Trewalter Llwyd (PEM 17), Carreg Samson (PEM 18) and Ffynnondruidion (PEM 28). Nearly all appear to conform to the same architectural rules and landscape positioning, embracing the fertile lowlands of Strumble Head, and nearly all are located close to rock outcropping. With the exception of Carreg Samson, all are small, unobtrusive monuments.

At least seven of these tombs may be considered earth-fast: Garn Wen (comprising of three separate monuments), Carn Wnda, Garn Gilfach, Parc-y-Garn and Ffynnondruidion. Tombs of this type have one end of the capstone deliberately placed on the edge of an earth-cut pit, rather than being supported by an upright stone. They are also sited on the intermediate slopes amongst extensive rock outcropping, and it is suggested that they were never totally covered by an earthen mound. Daniel (1950) believes a shallow cairn may have been banked up against the side of the chamber in order to conceal the burial. This being the case, each tomb would have merged with the surrounding rocky landscape, users relying on local ritual knowledge in order to locate it. However, many are in a much ruined state and may in fact have been free-standing monuments. For the sake of continuity I will still regard these as earth-fast

All the earth-fast tombs concentrated to the north of the Fishguard Group take the sea as their main visual focus, even though each is locally oriented. The dramatic landscape of St David's Head to the west is an important focal point for the five southernmost tombs.

The largest tomb in the group is Carreg Samson, which is similar in size to Pentre Ifan (PEM 5) in the Newport Group. Its landscape setting is also comparable, as the monument looks towards the fertile lowlands and sea beyond, while acknowledging the jagged rocky outcropping along Garn Fawr, Garn Gilfach and Garnwnda to the north-east.

The jagged peaks form a natural barrier which divides the coastal plain of Strumble Head with the rest of northern Pembrokeshire, and it is along these ridges that a series of chambered earth-fast monuments are located, all probably dating to the Late Neolithic. Six of these monuments, Carn Wnda, Parc-y-Cromlech and the Garn Wen cemetery, appear to be equally spaced and oriented roughly east/west. Another oriented on the same east/west line, but located on the western side of Strumble Head, is Garn Gilfach. However, this monument, unlike the other sites is located on the southern side of the outcropping, and would have been intervisible with Ffyst Samson, itself standing close to the summit of an exposed rock outcrop. Could it be possible that other equally-spaced monuments once stood between Garn Gilfach and Parc-y-Cromlech? The sites of the Garn Wen cemetery, Carn Wnda and Parc-y-Cromlech are separated by around 700m. The distance between Parc-y-Cromlech and Garn Gilfach is roughly 1,400m suggesting a possible monument may be sited at around SM 921 392, north of Pontiago Farm.

Above Goodwick is a line of at least three chambered tombs (PEM 7–9; SM 9483 3903) that, when constructed and in use, would have commanded views right across Fishguard Bay and Dinas Head. Alas, these are now obscured by several rows of houses that form the northern boundary of the ferry port of Goodwick. Nevertheless, the positioning of the tombs conforms to a pattern that is dominant throughout South-West Wales: that is, the tombs acknowledge only part of the landscape. Blocking views immediately to the west is a large, deep-fissured rock outcrop (known as Carn Wen). This cemetery group lies some 750m east of Garn Gilfach (PEM 15) and possibly forms a linear group of monuments that separates the coastal plain of Strumble Head with the inland landscape of north Pembrokeshire.

The three tombs, standing between 90m and 95m AOD, share a similar construction method. Each is partly rock-cut (sub-megalithic), and according to Daniel (1950, 200), was once incorporated within a round cairn mound. However, Barker has intimated that the present ground surface around each of the monuments does not show evidence of cairn material (1992, 27). Each of the capstones, lying a few centimetres above the present ground level, is supported by low or collapsed uprights.

The northern monument, located 5m north of its central companion, has a dislodged capstone that lies on top of a smaller slab. There appears to be no trace of any uprights, although as the immediate landscape is over-grown and undulating, it is possible that cairn material and dislodged uprights exist underneath the present land surface.

The southernmost tomb, known locally as Carrig Samson, is the best preserved of the three. It comprises five low uprights around a small polygonal chamber (Barker 1992, 27). The capstone appears to be displaced, leaning on two uprights on the north-east side of the chamber. Another two monuments appear to have suffered a similar fate. Fenton (1810, 16–17), who visited the cemetery site in the early 19th century, commented that:

> The most remarkable are three cromlechs in a line, one erect on columnar stones, the other two partly overturned.

It would appear that the cemetery had been 'investigated' some time before Fenton's tour of Pembrokeshire.

I visited the site again in 1993 and in 2003 and noticed a possible fourth tomb, of similar construction (with low supporting uprights) and in line with the other three, lying approximately 5m to the north of the northern monument. Up to nine monuments were reported by members of the Pembrokeshire Archaeological Survey (Laws and Owen 1897–1906), but many slabs considered capstones may in fact be natural outcropping. Making the assumption that more than three monuments existed at this site, it appears that the surviving three monuments would have been sited symmetrically — i.e., each one situated at an equal distance from the others. It is therefore probable that a monument existed between the surviving central and southern monuments. A third visit in 2005 revealed a series of cupmarks carved on rock outcropping close to the monument (Nash forthcoming).

Garn Wen looking north

The inconspicuous monument of Carn Wnda (PEM 13; SM 933 344) standing at around 135m AOD and located on a north-facing rock outcrop, appears to form an alignment with several other monuments: Penrhiw (PEM 14), the Garn Wen cemetery (PEM 7–9) and Garn Gilfach (PEM 15).

The monument is aligned north-west/south-east and is situated on the northern slope of Garnwnda, an exposed rocky outcrop. Fenton eloquently describes both the landscape position and the form of the monument when he says:

> Proceed to the village of Llan Wnda ... where, on the verge of the rocky eminence just above it, stands a Cromlech, resting obliquely on one stone about five feet high from the ground, whose dimensions are fifteen feet by nine, nearly of an equal thickness of two feet (1810, 18).

The capstone (4.6m x 2.8m) of this earth-fast tomb rests on the edge of a rock-cut pit and is supported at the north-west end by a single upright. As such, it is one of a number of 'sub-megalithic' tombs that make use of what Daniel calls a labour-saving 'makeshift device'. Developing the argument, Daniel (1950, 48) follows Grimes in doubting that covering mounds were ever a significant component of these tombs, saying:

> They were probably originally surrounded by a low accumulation of stones sufficient to ensure that the chambers were efficient burial vaults and that they were not disturbed by beasts of prey.

Grimes (1936a, 31) describes in slightly more detail this accumulation of stones, concluding that on the south side of the chamber are four courses of drystone walling. I would add that the drystone walling, seen from a distance, would further hide the monument within the immediate landscape. In addition, the ledge on which the monument stands is too small to have supported a covering mound. This manner of construction would have ensured that the monument would have merged with its surroundings, a trait which is experienced with other monuments on Strumble Head.

An antiquarian excavation inside the chamber revealed evidence of a cremation, indicating a possible Late Neolithic or Early Bronze Age date for the tomb. The burial consisted of a small urn made from a coarse and

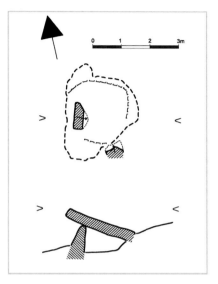

Plan of Carn Wnda (after Barker 1992)

crumbly fabric and containing cremated bone (Fenton 1848, 284). Later, in 1848, Fenton (1848, 284) comments:

> From the quantities of red and black ashes mixed with portions of what seemed to be decomposed burnt bones and small fragments of rude pottery which I found ... in the hollow below, I felt no hesitation in forming the conclusion that it had been a place of interment..

The outlook of the monument takes in all of the northern lowland fertile soils of Strumble Head. There is, however, no intervisibility with any other tomb. It appears to be the only tomb oriented in this way; the rest point towards the east, south and west.

Some 250m to the south of Carn Wnda and located at the north-east foot of Carn Gelli is a standing stone (SM 9336 3915). Whether or not this monument has an association with Carn Wnda is not known. Further standing stones are located to the south-west, lying close to the burial monuments of Ffynnondruidion (PEM 28) and Ffyst Samson (PEM 15).

Carn Wnda looking east

Garn Gilfach, Llanwnda

This burial chamber, also known as Carn Gyllwch (PEM 15; SM 9089 3898), Gillfach Goch (Barnwell 1872), Gilfach, Carn Gyllych (Grimes 1936a and Daniel 1950) and more recently, Garngilfach (Barker 1992), is sited on a small ridge, half way up Garn Gilfach, a large jagged rock outcrop. The monument stands at around 183m AOD. However, it is very difficult to locate — the capstone being only a few centimetres above present ground level. Daniel (1950) suggests the chamber pit was cut and underpinned whilst the capstone lay *in situ*.

Garn Gilfach consists of a large, irregular low capstone (4.6m × 2.5m) supported by four uprights. It is argued that other possible uprights are in fact the collapsed remnants of drystone walling (Barker 1992, 33). The tomb is sub-megalithic, in that the chamber is cut into the underlying bedrock. There is no evidence of a mound — the ridge appears to be too narrow — and is similar in construction and landscape setting to others on the Strumble Head Peninsula. An entrance into the main chamber appears to be located at the eastern end. Barker (1992, 33) remarks correctly that an 'unusually full account' is made by Richard Fenton, in his tour of Pembrokeshire in 1810, who remarks that charcoal and pottery had been found at the site in 1800 (Fenton 1810, 22–23).

He goes on to describe the monument in some detail:

> There is one more remarkable than the rest; a large unshapen mass of serpentine, fifteen feet by eight and a half average thickness; under the edges of it are placed nine or ten small pointed upright stones, embedded in a strong pavement, extending some way round. These small supporters are fixed without any regard to their height as only two or three bear the whole weight of the incumbent stone, one of which is so pressed by it, as to have become almost incorporated with it. On the upper surface of the Cromlech are three considerable excavations near the centre, probably intended to have received the blood of the victim, or waters for purification, if (as is the most general opinion) they were used as altars ... This stone has a small inclination to the north-east. Its height from the ground is very inconsiderable, being scarce one foot high in the lowest side; and on the other only high enough to admit of a person creeping under it, though once entered, the space enlarges from the upper stones having a considerable concavity. The earth below is rich and black ... I have since learned that the blackness I refer to, appears to have been chiefly the effect of fire, as many bits of charcoal and rude pottery have been picked up there.

Barnwell in his account of 1872 (page 137) records that a Mr Blight made an attempt to get underneath the capstone where he found one fragment of flint which in his view had been deliberately placed.

The views from this tomb recall those of nearby Ffyst Samson and Garn Wnda, all three possessing commanding vistas of the dramatic rock outcrops on Strumble Head. Both Garn Gilfach and Ffyst Samson overlook the lowlands to the south and west, as well as St David's Head. It is probable that there was intervisibility between this monument and Ffynnondruidion (PEM 28) and Ffyst Samson (PEM 16), located 2.7km and 4.1km away respectively.

Garn Gilfach looking south

This monument (PEM 16; SM 9059 3492) is sited on the large rock outcrop called Carn Llys. Also known as Trellys Cromlech, Trellysycoed, Ffst Samson and Samson's Quoit, Ffyst Samson is now much damaged. It comprises a single capstone supported by two enormous uprights, each standing to a height of well over a metre above the present ground surface. The original chamber may have been rectangular. Small stones litter the floor, both inside and outside the chamber, indicating either the remnants of a cairn, or a stone-lined chamber. There is evidence around the tomb of a slightly raised, and possibly oval mound (Barker 1992, 33). Indeed, the site was visited by Gardner Wilkinson in 1871 who described the chamber as being incorporated into 'a very slight mound'. This mound, which is aligned roughly east/west, is probably constructed from cairn and appears to be truncated on the south-eastern side by a stone and turf wall.

Unlike other tombs in the locality, Ffyst Samson stands on a high point within the landscape. A few metres to the east stands an exposed rock outcrop which is also visible from the site of the Ffynnondruidion monument (PEM 28). Approximately 500m north-east of the site and located at around 128m AOD is a small tumulus and a standing stone (SM 913 355). It is probable that the standing stone, along

Ffyst Samson looking west

with several others between the site and the Ffynnondruidion chamber, is contemporary.

To the south-west Ffyst Samson is intervisible with the monuments of Cerreg Samson (PEM 18) and Trewalter Llwyd (PEM 17), and is also within full view of the sea and St David's Head to the west. This monument may, therefore, have been an important focal point given its location on such a dramatic rock outcrop. Yet, as the mound would have been constructed of local stone to merge with the exposed rock outcropping close by, the tomb was not so much a visual concept, but one constructed through ritual and symbolic knowledge. A similar idea can be promoted for Garn Gilfach (PEM 15), 4.1km north of Ffyst Samson, another monument that merges within its immediate surroundings.

To the east and beyond the small hill on which Ffyst Samson stands is a large standing stone and cairn, again suggesting possible monument and landscape continuity of use through time. This monument (SM 9135 3550), located 1.1km north-east of Ffyst Samson and standing close to a Bronze Age mound appears to form an alignment with two other standing stones, each standing close to other Late Neolithic chambered monuments.

Trewalter Llwyd, Mathry

The tomb (PEM 17; SM 8682 3176), also known as Parc-y-Garn, comprises a large single capstone measuring 4.1m x 2.5m and up to 1.0m thick which is oriented north-west/south-east, and one visible collapsed upright. Other uprights may well exist beneath the boundary wall structure. The monument stands at around 124m AOD. Now considered much damaged, Trewalter Llwyd would, in earlier times, have looked very much like Llech-y-Tribedd (PEM 1) or the White Horse monument (PEM 47), in other words a tomb of true monumentality. However, this site has previously been considered nothing more than field clearance material by the Ordnance Survey Field Officer; in Barker's words an 'unnecessarily harsh assessment' (1992, 45).

The monument appears to form part of a group that includes nearby Carreg Samson (PEM 18) to the north, and White Horse and Treffynnon (PEM 19) to the west. The four tombs may delineate the inland extent of a territory. It was reported by Fenton in 1810, and by Gardner Wilkinson in 1871, that at least one other tomb may have existed close by, a monument referred to as Glandwr. In the words of Gardner Wilkinson (1871, 232) who sketched and recorded Trewalter Llwyd:

> I looked in vain for two cromlechs to the west of Mathry, and found only one [Trewalter Llwyd], half concealed in a fence [boundary], of which it forms a very efficient part. The capstone is 13ft long by 8ft 8in, and 4ft 5in thick, resting on one of its supporters, which is 5ft 5in high. Another fallen pillar [upright] measures 7ft 6in in length.

Daniel (1950, 201) describes the monument as: '... a collapsed chamber consisting of a capstone ... with a number of uprights lying underneath it.'

Trewalter Llwyd is sited within a slightly undulating landscape and, from the top of the capstone, the sea is visible approximately 4km away to the north. It also shares intervisibility with Carreg Samson, 3km to the north-west. In the far distance, to the west and north-east, are the jagged peaks of St David's and Strumble Head.

Much of the southern section of the monument, including the chamber, is incorporated into a turfed bank field boundary; therefore a sizeable proportion of the monument may be undisturbed and preserved *in situ*. A single partially collapsed upright is the only visual evidence of the northern section of the chamber. Approximately 55m to the south is a standing stone which may be contemporary with the Trewalter Llwyd monument..

Trewalter Llwyd looking east

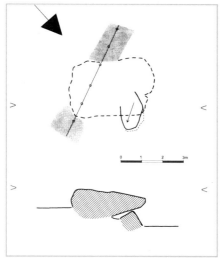

Plan of Trewalter Llwyd

Carreg Samson (PEM 18; SM 8430 3350) is one of South-West Wales' most impressive megalithic tombs, second only to Pentre Ifan (PEM 5). It was once known as the grave of Samson's finger, for it was believed that St Samson was the son of a 6th-century royal courtier who went on to become abbot of the monastery of Piro on Caldey Island, and who lifted the capstone into place with his little finger.

The capstone dips towards the immediate bay and Strumble Head beyond. To the east and north-east the landscape is dominated by the jagged peaks of Garn Fawr, Garn Gilfach and Garnwnda. On all three peaks there is evidence of Neolithic burial. To the south, another two tombs stand close by, Treffynnon (PEM 19) and White Horse (not classified). Hidden from view to the west are the jagged peaks of Carn Llidi, Carnedd-lleithr, Carn-ffald and St David's Head, for the monument, sited on a north-facing slope, is not on the highest point within the immediate landscape. Some 20m to the south-west of the monument are a number of jagged rock sandstone conglomerate outcrops. Further outcropping is visible in the field north-west of the stone boundary wall.

The monument is constructed from an enormous capstone measuring 5.3m x 3.6m and is supported by three of the six large locally quarried sandstone conglomerate uprights to form an oval/polygonal chamber measuring 3.3m x 1.7m.[61] According to Barker (1992, 34) one upright is missing. Both the uprights and chamber have been erected over an irregularly cut pit. The elongated shape of the chamber and capstone suggests that there was once a large rectangular covering mound, possibly comparable in size to that at nearby Pentre Ifan. However, no direct evidence for a mound or cairn survives, although a recent visit to the site in December 2003 has shown that cairn material may lie just below the surface of the field. It is also likely that the cairn has been incorporated into a boundary wall that lies a few metres to the north-west of the monument.

Carreg Samson, also known as Cerreg Samson or The Longhouse, stands around 42m AOD and was excavated by Frances Lynch during August 1968. This revealed that a possible entrance was located within the south-western section of the chamber, from which led an approximately 2m long passage delineated by a number of stone sockets (Lynch 1976,

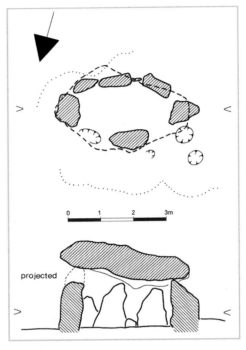

Plan of Carreg Samson (after Barker 19992)

74). Also uncovered was a pit which was located on the northern side of the monument, similar to those found at Pentre Ifan. During the recent past the chamber has been used as a sheep shelter and some investigators have recorded drystone walling or packing between the uprights. I was not able to verify this when visiting the site in 1992, 1996 and 2003, although there was a large number of stones littering the floor of the chamber.

The finds from the eastern side of the chamber were few, but did include fragments of burnt bone. Outside, a hemispherical bowl dating to the Early Neolithic was recovered (Lynch 1976, 75). The chamber was lined with a yellow clay which had been subsequently disturbed by the excavation of three holes, possibly the result of antiquarian investigations.

Carreg Samson looking south

Ffynnondruidion, St Nicholas

The exact location of this monument (PEM 28; SM 9204 3679[?]) is difficult to substantiate as not only do opinions differ but the immediate area has been severely disturbed within the recent past. In addition, according to detailed Ordnance Survey data, the monument is sited within an extensive naturally deposited cairn field; certainly many large stones are haphazardly scattered across a south-facing undulating landscape. A chambered monument certainly stood within view of Ffynnondruidion Farm before 1830 and probabaly stood around 107m AOD. A short reference in *Archaeologia Cambrensis* (1872, 139) notes that the monument was entirely demolished, leaving just one or two stones to mark the site where the chamber once stood. Fifty years earlier Fenton noted that a burial chamber had once existed on the site. In 1950 Daniel noted that only a few stones existed 'which may be the remains of the site' (1950, 203). Yet, the remnants of a possible capstone and uprights are just visible in an overgrown hedge bank.

The landscape position of the monument is similar to others within the area. It has intervisibilty with the sea (Fishguard Bay) as well as the southern extent of the Preseli Mountains. It also is not on the highest point within the immediate landscape, the land sloping upwards to the north, leaving the monument to visually command fertile undulating lands to the south and west. Approximately 1.7km to the south-west is the upland rock outcrop of Carn Llys and the site of Ffyst Samson (PEM 16). However, no intervisiblility exists between the two monuments; Ffyst Samson appears to be deliberately sited on the southern extent of the rock outcropping.

In spite of its poor condition, Ffynnondruidion ('Druid's Spring') does have an interesting early archaeological past. In 1830, whilst levelling the site, labourers discovered two Neolithic flint artifacts: an axe (Celt) and a stone adze. It was believed axes were used for flaying victims, for which, in the opinion of a professional butcher to whom they were shown, they seemed 'admirably calculated' (Fenton 1810, 24).

The polished stone axe (Tenby A8) shown here, made from gabbro, is now in Tenby Museum. If intact, the site together with other finds would have been one of the richest Neolithic discoveries in South-West Wales.

A polished stone axe (Tenby A8), found at Ffynnondruidion

Parc-y-Cromlech (PEM 14; SM 9422 3907) (also known as Penrhiw), now badly damaged, stands 142m AOD in a large south-facing field, away from the coast to the north and east. The site was first recorded by the RCAM in 1925, when the chamber was noted as being filled with 'field gathered stones'. Further, the 'capstone has been overthrown and lies at the feet of its quondam supporters' (*ibid.*, 548). In 1936 Grimes made a plan of the site before re-erecting the capstone (1936a).

This site lies some 750m west of the Garn Wen complex or cemetery. The tomb comprises a large, single, rectangular capstone supported by three uprights. The shape of the capstone and configuration of the three

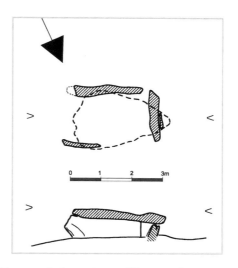

Plan and elevation of Parc-y-Cromlech

Parc-y-Cromlech

uprights suggest the chamber, too, was rectangular. Numerous stones litter the inside of the chamber, and also around the outside edges of the three uprights. These are either cairn material or the result of extensive field clearance. It was noted on a visit to the site that several large stones abutting the monument appeared to be shaped so as to form part of the tomb architecture, although this could be the result of frost shattering. Today there is no evidence of any mound, although Daniel (1950, 201) suggested that there was a slight trace. However, if the chamber arrangement, in particular the uprights, are in their original position, a mound could be suggested to the west of the present monument, with the eastern extent of the chamber exposed to form a forecourt. Unfortunately the ploughing of this field has been rather severe.

Interestingly, this monument, along with the Garn Wen complex and the earth-fast monument of Garn Wnda, appears to be spaced equally at a distance of 750m apart. However, the landscape setting for each of these monuments is very different.

The St David's Sub-Group

The St David's Sub-Group of monuments is sited within two distinct landscapes, one coastal, the other inland. The group comprises five monuments: Coetan Arthur (PEM 3), Carn Llidi (PEM 21 and 22), St Elvies Farm (PEM 20), Treffynnon (PEM 19) and White Horse (not classified). All are locally oriented so as to incorporate a variety of landscape features.

The three coastal sites are all located close to or within exposed rock outcropping, whilst the two inland sites are set within a slightly undulating landscape, usually close to Medieval or Post-Medieval field banks. Not surprisingly, both landscapes appear to have influenced tomb design and construction. The coastal sites usually incorporate large capstones overlying low rectangular chambers, and two of these are classified as double-chambered monuments and occupy similar landscape positions as those on Strumble Head. With the exception of the now much damaged White Horse monument, all possess small chambers. Coetan Arthur and Carn Llidi

are earth-fast monuments and resemble those on Strumble Head. Both are also located in similar rocky landscapes. These earth-fast tombs are probably a later architectural form as they are less monumental than, for example, St Elvies Farm and Treffynnon.

The White Horse site can be classified as a Portal Dolmen and would have been a truly megalithic monument, maybe standing over 2.7m in height.

Sited south of these tombs is Clegyr Boia, a probable contemporary Neolithic settlement. One could imagine the settlers of Clegyr Boia placing the remains of their dead in either of the two St David's Head monuments. The lack of architectural elaboration evident in these tombs should not detract from the idea that towards the later Neolithic the dead were considered special and that, consequently, special places were required in order to honour and bury them.

Antiquarian drawing of Coetan Arthur (PEM 3) (from *Archaeologia Cambrensis*)

Coetan Arthur, St David's

This site (PEM 3; SM 7253 2805) was visited by an antiquarian named Mamby in 1801 who described it as follows (1801, 70):

> At a little distance from St David's Head, upon a plain, is a famous Druidical altar, one of solid stone twelve feet long, eight feet broad, and averaged at 2 feet thick; it formerly was supported by several stones, but now rests on one.

Jones and Freeman made a further description of the site in 1856, when they commented on the missing uprights. The site was also illustrated in several engravings, one by Longueville Jones in 1865 and another by Barnwell in 1872.

This much denuded site, which stands approximately 38m AOD, was first excavated in 1898 by Baring Gould. The results were poor, although the excavators did reveal traces of a drystone lining and a possible revetment associated with the chamber on the south-eastern side of the monument.

Grimes argued that Coetan Arthur never had a prominent mound (1936a), whilst Daniel in 1950 believed that just enough stones were used to ensure 'efficient burial vaults'. He argued for a round barrow as the original tomb covering, and has cautiously identified a passage leading west from the chamber. Probably of Daniel's sub-megalithic earth-fast type, the chamber may have been formed by levering up one end of a stone lying *in situ* and supporting this with a 1.8m upright. Others have suggested the chamber represents a collapsed conventional form, as two further uprights have been identified lying beneath the capstone. Indeed, as a result of my own visit I suggest that Coetan Arthur may have been constructed of four or more uprights. Further, a substantial cairn mound would have surrounded the chamber, the remains of which can be seen to the chamber's north.

The capstone measures about 3.6m long by 2.5m wide and interestingly, resembles the outline of the nearby rocky ridge of Carn Llidi. A few metres to the west of this monument is extensive rock outcropping and from a distance Coetan Arthur appears to blend into the surrounding landscape. However, it is intervisible with the double-chambered monument of Carn Llidi. Between both monuments and hidden away in a small valley oriented north-east/south-west are the remnants of a settlement and field system of unknown date. However, it should be noted that extensive Mesolithic and Bronze Age lithic scatters exist along the coastal fringes of St David's Head. Several hundred metres to the west of Coetan Arthur is a promontory hill enclosure where a single cairn rampart encloses six or seven hut circles. This settlement site, together with the presence of Mesolithic material suggests a near continuous sequence of prehistoric activity within this area for around 6,000–7,000 years.

Coetan Arthur

Treffynnon (PEM 19; SM 8536 2866) stands 125m AOD on a slight south-facing ridge, close to an eroded field bank. The surrounding landscape is slightly undulating, but the tomb does have views of the jagged peaks at St David's Head. Locally, a number of small rocky outcrops are also visible. The River Solva is located south of the monument at the base of the hill on which the monument stands.

This monument consists of a small single capstone that now rests on one of three uprights that stand 1m high, the capstone appearing to be dislodged. The chamber is rectangular (2.2m × 1.5m), and is open on the northern side. According to the RCHM of 1925 (page 435), several flag-stones that may be associated with the monument were uncovered during ploughing. This monument, like many others, has been used as a dump for field debris and stones, possibly cairn material, which litters both the chamber and the area around the monument. However, there is no trace of any mound. Grimes (1939b) had suggested that Treffynnon is a simple chambered monument, one of three in the locality. Both In plan and condition it is similar to the Parc-y-Cromlech monument sited on Strumble Head (PEM 14).

Although much smaller than its neighbour, the White Horse monument, Treffynnon may be considered megalithic in form. Its capstone is similar to a number of earth-fast monuments within the Pembroke Group, including the Devil's Quoit (PEM 25), King's Quoit (PEM 26) and the northern chamber of the Hanging Stone (PEM 24).

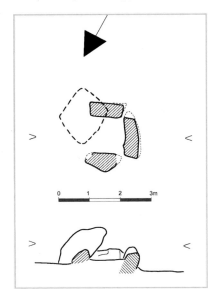

Plan of Treffynnon (after Barker 1992)

Treffynnon looking south

L ocated on a north-west facing slope, around 61m AOD, the tomb (PEM 20; SM 8120 2394) is one of three coastal burial sites in South-West Wales which appear to have been purposely concealed from the sea. The tomb seems to have been intact in 1890 when it was described as a 'double cromlech'. Each capstone, the largest measuring 3.7m × 3.1m, is supported by two uprights. There are traces of a mound between both chambers and on the western side of the west chamber. However, both structures are today badly damaged. It has been suggested that large stones found in nearby walls may have been plundered from the monument. Certainly, during the latter years of the 19th century a tenant farmer from nearby St Elvies Farm was asked to stop 'blasting' bits of the tomb structure away.

Williams, when writing part of the Pembrokeshire Archaeological Survey between 1897 and 1906, remarks on:

> ... two cromlechs, both cap stones thrown down. Twelve years ago the tenant blasted and carried off two legs of the eastern cromlech, but at the request of the writer ceased this work of destruction. The cromlechau stand within two yards of each other. Each has only two legs left.

St Elvies Farm looking south

Although Daniel describes the tomb as 'morphologically indeterminate', the southerly chamber may be of his earth-fast type, with the western end of the capstone resting on the ground and the eastern end supported by uprights and forming the chamber entrance.

There are a few other examples of multiple chambers in South-West Wales. One is the unusual five-chambered tomb of Cerrig-y-Gof (PEM 4), others include The Hanging Stone (PEM 24) near Pembroke and Carn Llidi (PEM 21 and 22) on St David's Head.

Within the recent past, there have been several excavations in and around the monument. The first of these was undertaken in the early years of the 20th century by Felix Oswald. According to Grimes (1936a, 13) and Daniel (1950, 143) these findings were insignificant. Investigations following the recent erection of fencing in order to protect the western side of the monument have revealed traces of a mound (Dyfed Archaeological Trust 1982). Both chambers at St Elvies Farm are aligned north-west/south-east, with capstones dipping towards an inlet of the River Solva. However, due to disturbance it is not known if the capstones have been moved from their original position and, therefore, the plan of the chamber is difficult to discern.

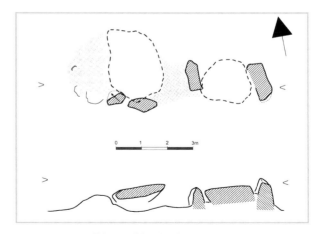

Plan of St Elvies Farm

This monument (PEM 21 and 22; SM 7352 2789), standing at around 122m AOD, commands one of the most dramatic views of all the monuments within South-West Wales. Sited on the rocky western slope of Carn Llidi, the tomb comprises two chambers with views to the north, south and west; the northern section of Ramsey Island and Ramsey Sound are clearly visible. Similar to other monuments of this type, it merges into its immediate surroundings and is not easy to find. There is intervisibility between this monument and nearby Coetan Arthur (PEM 3), located some 1.2km to the west, and between the two is a settlement and an ancient field system, delineated by a series of bleached and weathered drystone walling. According to the Regional SMR, the settlement known as Penlledwen may have its origins within prehistory.[62]

The site appears to have suffered some damage due to the construction of a Second World War gun emplacement; modern brick fragments are incorporated into what is possible cairn material surrounding both chambers. Between 2m and 3m south-west of the western chamber are a series of concrete platforms which are approached by a now much-weathered tarmacadam road. It is more than probable that this gun emplacement may have destroyed any ritual evidence associated with the site.

This double dolmen, similar in architecture to other double dolmen sites in this part of Wales, conforms to a number of rules. Firstly, the monument stands close to rocky outcropping. Secondly, the chamber arrangement consists of one small and one large chamber (similar to The Hanging Stone (PEM 24) and the St Elvies monument (PEM 20)). Finally, a cairn mound is usually present. The larger western chamber consists of a large capstone that is supported by a single upright and is set within an earth-fast rock-cut pit. This capstone, now 'dismounted', is described by Jones (see later), who suggests that the site may have suffered antiquarian investigation prior to

Carn Llidi: eastern chamber

Carn Llidi: western chamber

1863. The northern section of the capstone rests on collapsed cairn or possibly a fragment of shattered capstone. The eastern chamber survives as three uprights that are set within a rock-cut pit, its capstone 'standing' between the cliff-face and the southern upright. Daniel believes the easterly chamber once had its capstone placed horizontally, with one side resting on the ledge of the rock outcrop and supported on the other three sides by uprights inside a rock-cut pit. The smaller eastern chamber is sited at the edge of the rock outcropping. The site was first recorded in the mid-19th century when W.B. Jones (1863) adequately describes the site thus:

> A few days ago, in walking over Carn Llidi, the picturesque rock which towers over Whitesand Bay, to the north-west of St David's. I discovered the remains of a double cromlech on the northern slope of the hill, and near the western extremity of its rocky portion. The two cromlechs, which stood side by side, differ in size: the larger one being on the northern side, and the other standing close under the rock. The capstones of both are dismounted: that of the former is some eight or nine feet in length, and the other considerably smaller. Three of the

supporters of the lesser cromlech are in situ, and stand close together, presenting the appearance of a wall ...

Castlelden (1992) believes that a mound once existed, and possible remnants of a cairn were recorded on visits to the site in 2001 and 2003. Moreover, a plan produced by Barker (1992, 35) shows the remnants of a mound located between the two chambers and to the west of the larger chamber. Grimes (1936, 12), who surveyed the monument in the mid-1930s argues that: '... the mounds [of Carn Llidi and Carn Wnda] must have been small and could never have been elaborate.'

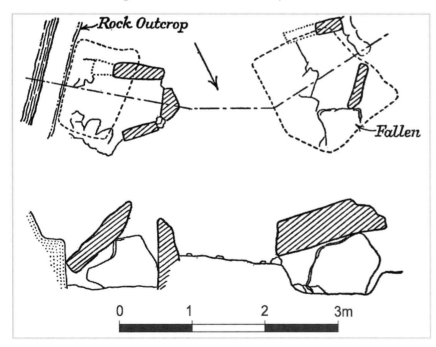

Plan and cross section of Carn Llidi

Carn Llidi looking west

The White Horse monument (Not classified; SM 8258 2839), also referred to as Tresewig is located within a fossilised field bank and stands at around 91m AOD, in a gently undulating terrain with the peaks of St David's Head and localised small rock outcrops clearly visible. The surrounding landscape is very similar to that of the nearby Treffynnon monument (PEM 19).

As far as I am aware the site has never been excavated, but offers considerable research potential — much of the internal chamber appearing intact and undisturbed. Grimes (1960, 11) describes the monument simply as 'a rectangular chamber with portal stones'. A more useful description is provided in Barker[63] (1992, 48):

> ... the remains of this burial chamber are incorporated in a modern hedge bank. They consist of a capstone 2.2 x 1.8 x 1.2m, resting on its side on one supporting stone. The latter is 1.5m high and 2.1m long. On the E side of the chamber opening are two 1.5m high upright stones. In and around the hedge lie several stones ... there is no trace of a barrow.

In the recent past, the tomb has suffered extensive damage through field clearance. Indeed, both Rees (1981) and Barker (1992) noticed field clearance debris piled against the tomb. Furthermore, plough damage is noticeable up to the chamber itself (Barker 1992).

White Horse has five chunky uprights, but no trace of a covering mound. In between the two sets of uprights and within the chamber is the capstone on its edge, which has either been 'placed' or has slipped from its original position. The chamber, probably rectangular in form, now contains a substantial soil and stone deposit, possibly contemporary with the monument's abandonment. The size and original form of the uprights and capstone would have been very similar to The Hanging Stone (PEM 24) near Pembroke. This would have made White Horse a very substantial and

White Horse looking west

highly visible monument, possibly standing over 2.7m in height (based on the length of the uprights and the thickness of the capstone).

In spite of the damage inflicted by Post-Medieval and modern farming practices, the White Horse monument may be classified as a Portal Dolmen. Although there are no traces of a mound, it appears that the surviving chamber forms part of a monument that was once oriented north/south, based on a comparison of the chamber plan with those of Carreg Samson (PEM 18) and Pentre Ifan (PEM 5). There may have been a doorway or entrance to the south that could have led from a sizeable forecourt area.

The Inland St David's Sub-Group

This group consists of at least eight monuments: Gwal-y-Filiast (CRM 1), Carn Besi (CRM 20), Mountain (PEM 6), The Altar at Colston (PEM 10), Garn Turne (PEM 11), Parc-y-Llyn (PEM 12), Llan at Lampeter Velfrey (PEM 30) and the Eithbed complex (PEM 31). They represent several different architectural styles. Gwal-y-Filiast, Mountain and Parc-y-Llyn are possibly Portal Dolmens which would have been placed within a cairn or earthen mound, whilst The Altar and the Eithbed complex are considered short-chambered monuments (i.e. with short uprights supporting a low capstone). Carn Besi may also be placed in this category. The Garn Turne monument, the largest within this group, can be considered an opportunistic design in that it sits within a cairn field where stone would have been easily to hand. This monument, classified as a forecourt tomb, may or may not have possessed a mound.

Although listed by Children and Nash (1997) as one group, this collection of monuments is divided into at least two clusters. The most impressive cluster consists of Garn Turne, Parc-y-Llyn and The Altar, all sited within a 2km square tract of territory; in addition Parc-y-Llyn and The Altar are similar in size and architectural form. Their landscape setting is also similar, but they are dwarfed by the massive capstone and forecourt of Garn Turne.

None of these monuments is intervisible with another, but it is suggested that they were constructed and in use at the same time (Children and Nash 1997, 97). Garn Turne may have been utilised as the main burial place and a focus for non-burial activity by several communities, since it would have required many people and hours of labour to construct and maintain this monument. Small family units were probably using Parc-y-Llyn and The Altar, and it may have been the case that communities outside the immediate sphere of the three monuments also used Garn Turne. Similar nucleated monuments with associated satellite tombs exist elsewhere within South-West Wales.

Farther north, and close to the southern extent of the Mynydd Preseli, is the Eithbed 'complex'. Here, three (or more) tombs are positioned in such a way that they face towards the south and St David's Head. Close by are the monuments of Carn Besi, the Gors Fawr stone circle, the destroyed henge monument of Meini-Gwyr and a number of standing stones. All are located close to, but never on, the Preseli Mountains. They may either be socially controlling the space around the south Preselis or, more importantly, establishing a boundary between familiar social space and the symbolic unknown of the mountains; or both.

**The Cromlech at St David's Head, Pembrokeshire:
an antiquarian drawing from *Archaeologia Cambrensis***

The Gwal-y-Filiast monument (CRM 1; SN 1705 2564) stands on the intermediate slope of a spur that overlooks the Afon Taf at around 100m AOD. The much-ruined chambered monuments of Rhosfach (SN 1490 2555) and Meni-Gwyr (SN 1390 2650) are located 2.2km and 3.3km to the west respectively.[64] These monuments, along with Cefn Brafle (SN 1957 2294), Carn Besi (CRM 20) and the Mountain site (PEM 6), form a small cluster of monuments that occupy the southern hinterlands of the Preseli Mountains.

The earliest account of this monument is made by Lhwyd in 1695 (column 628) when he describes the site thus:

> ... rude stone (capstone) about ten yards in circumference, and above three foot thick, supported by four pillars, which are about two foot and a half in length.

This impressive monument, also known as Bwrdd Arthur and Dolwilym, consists of a large single capstone supported by four uprights that appear to delineate a polygonal chamber. A fifth upright, facing east down the slope, was recorded by Barnwell in 1872, suggesting that this formed an entrance. Also on the eastern side of the chamber area are two uprights that stand 0.3m above the present ground level. Positioned away from the main chamber upright alignment, they appear to form a sill and may in fact be the entrance into the chamber. The position of the sill and possible entrance may suggest that a passage led into the mound.

Surrounding the monument is a series of stones that may form the kerbing of the covering mound. Barnwell claimed that a mound/barrow still covered the chamber and capstone in 1872 and that at least 32 kerb stones were visible which delineated the edge of the mound. This being the case, Gwal-y-Filiast must have suffered either large-scale vandalism or serious deterioration (or both) over the past 120 years. The position of the kerbing suggests Gwal-y-Filiast possessed either an oval or circular mound; traces of possible *in situ* kerb stones are still present within the northern and western areas of the site.

The capstone points towards the Afon Taff (to the west) and the eastern extent of the Preseli Mountains. Views of the mountains are presently obscured by thick woodland, but whether or not the valley was wooded during the Neolithic is unknown. At the point where the Afon Taff flows past Gwal-y-Filiast, the river becomes a violent rapid, a change in the river's character that might have decided the tomb's location upon the ridge (Tilley 1994, 109). Other inland monuments in Wales follow a similar rule: Ty Isaf (BRE 5), Gwernvale (PEM 7), Cwm Fforest (BRE 9) and Garn Goch (BRE 12), all from the Black Mountains Group, and nearby Twlc-y-Filiast (CRM 6).

Plan and cross section of Gwal-y-Filiast (after Barker 1992)

Gwal-y-Filiast looking north west

This monument (PEM 6; SN 1657 3286), also referred to as Llech-y-Gwyddon[65] consists of a massive capstone (3.7m × 3.3m) incorporated within a field boundary. According to antiquarian accounts in Barker (1992, 26), by 1885 much of the monument had slipped into a modern ditch. When standing, The Mountain would have been an impressive tomb, similar to that of The Hanging Stone (PEM 24) in south Pembrokeshire and probably standing over 3.5m in height.

Standing at around 236m AOD, The Mountain lies within the northwest corner of a waterlogged field. It is probable that the waterlogged area extended to the east of the monument when it was built, thus surrounding the site with water and creating an 'island for the dead'. Lying prostrate around and underneath the capstone are five large stones, probably collapsed uprights. Other smaller stones are also present, including one visible support for the capstone. Located within the fabric of the boundary

Mountain looking west

is a probable chamber upright, oriented east/west. Lynch (1972, 81–82), who was the first to record this monument, suggests that The Mountain is a Portal Dolmen that may have been centred within a round mound. The size of the recumbent uprights (one of which is over 3m in length) and the position of the capstone certainly indicate this, but Barker (1992, 26) suggests that the site is too damaged to make any valued assessment.

Although The Mountain is very much damaged on its eastern side, the majority of the central and western chamber area is incorporated into the large, earthen field boundary, oriented north/south.

Recorded by the author in 1997 was an extensive quantity of possible cairn debris now either incorporated into the field boundary or spread across the western corner of the field. It is probable that the chamber and uprights would have been covered by an extensive rubble mound that was oriented roughly north/south, with an entrance to the east. Rees (1981) on visiting the site remarks that there were traces of a 7m diameter circular mound that rose to a height of around 0.6m. However, a recent visit to the site suggests that the mound was probably oval, measuring approximately 25m × 7m.

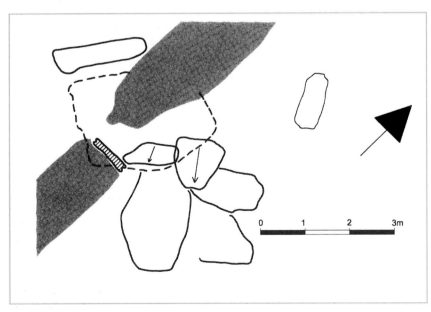

Plan of Mountain (after Barker 1992)

The Altar (also referred to as Colston) at Colston is the smallest monument (PEM 10; SM 9828 2812) in this sub-group. Standing at around 102m AOD, this monument is located a few metres south of the Afon Anghol. Although The Altar is sited in a small valley, the southern extent of the Preseli Mountains is visible from the monument. Several kilometres to the east is Mynydd Castle which stands at 347m AOD. However, due to its location within the landscape, little of the dramatic topography can be seen from this monument.

The RCHM inventory of 1925 (page 396) claims that:

> About half a mile south-east of Little Newcastle village, on the farm of Ffynnonau, is a small but perfect cromlech, and on its south side the ruined remains of a second [The Altar ?]. The first cromlech is separated from the road to Beulah bridge by a fence which is carried over the mound on which the stones are placed.

This account is significant for it suggests that a further megalithic monument existed during the early part of the 20th century. Unfortunately, no other reference to the missing monument has been made, not even within Barker's extensive inventory. One can only assume that the missing monument is Parc-y-Llyn (PEM 12) or that The Altar once possessed a second chamber that was located within the road, on the southern side of the field bank or within the southern field bank on the opposite side of the road.

The tomb has suffered much cattle damage, especially on its northern side. However, the southern section of the monument forms part of a hedge boundary and probably remains intact. The monument consists of a small, rectangular capstone supported by two or more uprights, the two that are visible supporting the western section of the capstone. The capstone, measuring 2.1m × 1.9m and 0.97m in thickness, is encased within the field bank. It has been suggested in Barker (1992, 28) that the shape of the mound has been much disturbed by the hedge and the road.[66] Several uprights located to the north-east of the chamber area may represent the remains of a forecourt area or even kerbing. These uprights are within an extensive spread of cairn material that must be the result of recent disturbance to the monument. Two of the slabs in the forecourt area, over a metre in length, may have once formed part of the kerbing.

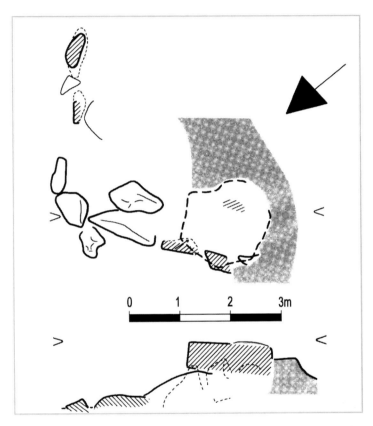

Plan and cross-section of The Altar (after Barker 1992)

Based on early Ordnance Survey evidence, Barber and Williams (1989, 111) have commented that another possible chambered monument exists 40m due south of this monument. I have yet to locate this. Further, a single pointed stone stands 1m above ground level, but is hidden within the boundary hedge. I would suggest that this stone shares a landscape affinity with nearby Parc-y-Llyn (PEM 12) and a group association with nearby Garn Turne (PEM 11), maybe as a marker between the monuments.

The Altar looking south

Garn Turne (PEM 11; SM 9793 2725), also known as Carn Turne, Garne Tarne and Old Coldstone, the largest of all the inland monuments in Wales, is one of three megaliths clustered around the hamlet of Colston some 10.5km from the nearest coastline. This monument, standing at around 137m AOD, consists of a chamber constructed of a series of uprights that support a capstone. Immediately east of the chamber is a large forecourt area. One of the earliest accounts of this monument is by Fenton (1810, 337–338) who states:

> Repassing below Little Newcastle [a nearby village] I turn to the right, and enter a field covered with detached fragments of broken rock, called Garn Twrne ... it appears to have been a great resort of the Druids, if to them are to be ascribed those monuments called cromlechs, of a dimension exceeding that of Pentre Evan [Pentre Ifan, PEM 5], for it measured in length about sixteen feet and a half by thirteen and half in breadth, and from four to five feet five inches in thickness, and its circumference sixty-three feet eight inches. This immense incumbent stone and its three columnar props stood in a circle of upright stones, some of them yet standing.

Early Bronze Age cup-and-ring art recently found on the top of the capstone

The massive volcanic capstone (5m × 4.1m), arguably one of the largest in Britain, weighs more than 60 tons and is now collapsed, resting on a series of dislodged uprights. Recent research undertaken by the author and a team from the University of Bristol have discovered rock-art on the top of the capstone in the form of a cup-and-ring carving. This art, probably Early Bronze Age in date, may represent a form of

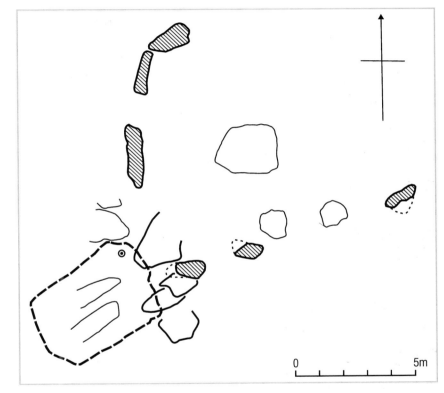

Plan of Garn Turne (after Barker 1992)

ancestral marking and suggests that this monument was in use after the Neolithic. The cup-and-ring carving is considered to be the only one of its type found so far in South Wales associated with a megalithic monument (Nash *et al* forthcoming). An unusual V-shaped forecourt is similar to that of Pentre Ifan and the Irish Court Tombs of southern Ireland, an architectural trait which was endorsed by Grimes as the 'Pentre Ifan type' (Grimes 1932, 92; 1948, 13). Here, Grimes refers to the forecourt area as an 'asymmetric funnel-shaped upright forecourt'. However, both Castleden (1992) and Houlder (1978) suggest the forecourt arrangement is 'familiar with the general western family of long cairns'. This forecourt and entrance area, constructed of at least six uprights, faces north-east towards a large rock outcrop. This may be replicated within the forecourt itself, as a large, pointed block is located within its centre, although it is not certain that this boulder was in place (and therefore in use) when the monument was being utilised. The northern forecourt arrangement, consisting of three uprights, appears to form an arc, thus enclosing the central and northern section of the forecourt area. However, on the southern side three uprights are set in a straight line. The two lines of uprights are not symmetrical and it is more than probable that a southern inward sweeping arc was present. The two uprights located within the southern section of the forecourt area may have been re-erected at a later date.

Sited as it is close to localised substantial rock outcropping, the tomb merges into its immediate surroundings. Indeed, so well is it 'hidden' within the landscape that, despite the monument's size, it is difficult to locate. Apart from the nearby rock outcrop, the surrounding landscape is gently undulating. Nevertheless, the southern extent of the Preseli Mountains is in full view. The question remains: how much of the stone construction of Garn Turne would have been visible — was this megalithic structure once entirely concealed beneath an earthen mound?

Barker (1992, 29) does not entirely agree that this monument is a portal tomb, rather, that it may be an earth-fast type. However, many of the earth-fast monuments within this region are located and constructed differently and are small and unimposing. Others have suggested that the southern part of the monument, which incorporates the chamber and capstone, may have been part of a long cairn. However, I have found no evidence of this.

Grimes (1932, 92) has claimed that a peristalith (or kerbing) existed around the monument. My own observations have shown that outside the forecourt area, and 150m beyond the monument, is a ridge outcropping that may have provided construction material for the tomb itself. On either side of this rock outcropping are marshy areas.

Garn Turne looking south west

Approximately 50m to the west of the monument and obscured by natural cairn field debris is a large monolith standing at around 1.2m in height, possibly contemporary with the Garn Turne monument. If this is the case, Garn Turne and its surroundings represents an important and complex Neolithic landscape. Indeed, despite Grimes surveying this monument in 1932, there has been little interest in the area located beyond the monument and it is more than probable that further sites exist. Rees, for example, on an inspection of the site in 1981 for CADW has noted that a possible long cairn may exist among the natural rock outcropping.

Parc-y-Llyn, Ambleston

Standing in the corner of a banked field, Parc-y-Llyn (PEM 12; SM 9823 2659) appears to be hidden away within a small narrow valley. Although this monument appears to be small in comparison with nearby Garn Tune (PEM 11), it is nonetheless an important site as part of it is hidden within a nearby field bank and therefore archaeologically undisturbed.

The monument, standing at around 128m AOD, is sited on the north facing rise within the valley of the Western Cleddau. Constructed of a small single capstone (2.5m x 1.8m) supported by four uprights, the monument has suffered much cattle damage in recent years. Many large stones, possibly belonging to a covering mound, are scattered nearby.

One of the earliest accounts of this monument was made by Gardner Wilkinson (1871, 224) who stated that:

> At Ffynnonnau ('The Wells') two miles west of the Roman Station, and a little beyond Carn Tarn, is a low cromlech, supported on three stones, having a capstone 8ft long by 6ft broad, and 1ft 6in thick; with many small stones lying about it.

Plan of Parc-y-Llyn (after Barker 1992)

Within the field boundary to the east is a possible second chamber with one supporting upright. Other large stones, which may be uprights, are located north of the monument. Other double dolmens of this size and form exist elsewhere in South-West Wales including Carn Llidi (PEM 21–22), the Hanging Stone (PEM 24) and Trellyffaint (PEM 2). The RCHM inventory of 1925 adds that:

> In the hedge to the east, and largely concealed by it, is what may have been the capstone of a second cromlech ... both remains stand on a slightly elevated platform of 180ft circumference.

According to Barker's plan (1992, 31) the entrance faces north-west, in which case it appears not to be oriented to any particular nearby feature. However, 1km in the same direction is the Garn Turne monument. Very little of the regional landscape is visible. Similar landscape positioning is evident at The Altar, Colston, approximately 1.6km north of Parc-y-Llyn. The chamber and the remains of the other possible chamber are aligned east/west and Barker (*ibid.*, 32) suggests that both chambers were enclosed within a north-west/south-east elongated cairn perhaps up to 15m in length. If this is the case, the entrance would, in fact, have probably been west-facing.

Parc-y-Llyn looking east

Carn Besi, Llandyssilio East

The denuded Carn Besi (CRM 20; SN 1560 2768) monument, also known as the Dolwilim Dolmen, stands a few metres north-west of the A487 at around 236m AOD. Carn Besi, easily the most unimpressive of all the monuments listed in this book, does, nevertheless, occupy a site with outstanding views over the northern and western extents of the Preseli Mountains. It stands 1.5km north of, and may be incorporated into a Late Neolithic landscape that includes a burial chamber (SN 145 255), several standing stones (SN 137 255, SN 154 258 and SN 137 254) and a cairn circle (SN 142 267) at Meni-Gwyr. The site has been classified by Barker as a 'large capstone' (1992, 59),[67] whilst the RCAHM inventory (1917, 321) describes the monument as a 'cromlech'.

The monument consists of a small single capstone, measuring 2.5m × 2.1m × 0.35m in thickness, supported by a number of short or collapsed uprights that do not rise above the surrounding ground level. The chamber area is therefore partially submerged, cutting into the drift geology. The capstone, oriented east/west, appears to point towards the general area of the Gors Fawr stone circle, 2.7km to the west. To the south, west and south-east there is much evidence of a Bronze Age landscape, Carn Besi possibly marking the northern boundary of this symbolic landscape. Despite the fact that it is undoubtedly Neolithic, the monument would have played an important role in organizing and controlling later landscapes. I would add that monuments such as this would have been known only to people who used the site, as they merge so completely into the surrounding landscape (Children and Nash 1997, 99). Yet its appearance suggests that Carn Besi, along with examples at the nearby Eithbed complex, should be described as a single slab rather than as an earth-fast monument.

Carn Besi looking west

The Llan group of monuments (PEM 30; NGR 147 140), standing at around 60m AOD and located close to the village of Lampeter Velfrey is one of two inland cemetery groups within South-West Wales. This denuded group is sited on a small north-facing spur overlooking a small valley. A series of springs are located on either side of the group and flow into the Afon Marlais. Although listed under 'doubtful sites', Daniel's note on Llan (1950, 203) recognises three 'groups of megaliths' within the vicinity of Pen-lan Farm which he considers 'collapsed chambers'. Although grouped within the Inland St David's Group, this monument is very much isolated from other monuments. Indeed, the nearest are the Morfa Bychan cemetery group which are located some 10km to the south-east.

The Llan complex appears today as three groups of stone with little to suggest that they were once burial monuments. The earliest reference is made within the Pembrokeshire Archaeological Survey (Laws and Owen 1897–1906) where a Mr A. Lascelles remembered several complete cromlechs standing 30 years previously, i.e. in the mid-19th century. According to the same account, all that remained even then were clusters of three and six stones. The RCAHM (1925, 405) states further that:

> What is now visible are the remains of a group of certainly three structures. That to the north consists of four stones, one, 6ft in length, prostate, and recently broken at one end; a second stone, about 2ft above the ground, and two stones of similar height in close proximity to each other. About 180ft to the south-west are portions of another cromlech comprising one erect stone 3ft high, 5ft in length, and 1ft thick; one other erect stone 3ft above ground and 18in thick, and by their side, a prostate boulder, probably a capstone, 9ft 6in long by 3ft 6in broad. Distant 25ft from the last cromlech is a third consisting of four stones all prostate, and partially buried in the soil.

When visiting the site in 1992, I noticed that all three structures were roughly in the same condition as reported by Barker in 1986 (1992, 46). The western structure, comprising four stones, has no clear architectural form except perhaps for the group of three possible uprights located within the northern part of the site. These stones may represent the remains of a chamber; further aligned stones may exist underneath the present ground

surface. The site of the eastern structure comprises of up to three slabs which appear only partially submerged into the ground and may represent the result of monument destruction rather than the remains of in situ uprights. The north-eastern structure, which is comprised of only three stones, has no architectural form.

Although the three areas of stone bear no resemblance to chambered monuments within this part of Wales, I acknowledge and accept the antiquarian accounts of this site. It is probable that the monuments may have been simple in form, consisting of a small chamber, delineated by low uprights and covered by a capstone; possibly surrounded by a low cairn.

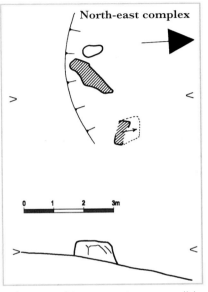

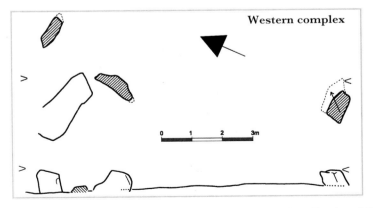

Plans and cross-sections of the Llan Complex (after Barker 1992)

The Llan monument looking east

The much disturbed Eithbed Group of monuments (PEM 31; SM 080286 080280) are one of four megalithic cemeteries in South-West Wales, the others being the Garn Wen Complex (PEM 7–9), the Llan Complex (PEM 30) and the Morfa Bychan Group (CRM 2–5). Both Barker (1992, 51) and the original excavator Done Bushell (1911) record up to four monuments within this complex; all aligned roughly north/south.

The remains of the Eithbed monuments are located close to a series of natural springs that feed into the Afon Syfynwy and once formed a complex multi-phased monument group which includes a possible stone circle and enclosure.[68] Approximately 3km to the north of this monument group is Cerrig Lladron, which stands at 468m AOD. Immediately to the north-east the land forms a spur which rises to 427m AOD. This dramatic setting forms a typical backdrop to this and other inland monuments within this part of Wales.

Standing between 240 and 250m AOD, the Eithbed cemetery consists of a North, Central and South monument located on the edge of a south-facing field, and is a victim of recent clearance that is believed took place between 1905 and 1909 (Done Bushell 1911, 303). The presence of irregular placed large stone slabs makes the actual identification of the monuments very difficult.

Gardner Wilkinson (1871, 227) provides the clearest account (along with engravings) of the precise location of two of the sites:

> A little to the north [of Maenclochog] are two fallen cromlechs, or 'Coetan', the capstone of the first being 8ft 4in by 5ft 3in, 6ft thick and one of the stones on which it stood 6ft high by 3ft 6in. Fifty feet north by east of this is a large fallen stone; and nine feet beyond it an upright slab, 5ft in height by the same in breadth; twenty-nine feet from which is another fallen cromlech, with a capstone 11ft 6in long by 6ft 6in, amidst some fallen stones. Thirty-three feet from it to the west is a small stone circle, 21 feet in diameter; and about eighty yards to the north-east, is a circular enclosure within a mound composed of earth, and once encircled by large stones, most of which have been taken away for

fences [walling]. It is on the slope of the hill, its smallest diameter being about 170ft, and within the area on the south side is a spring of water.

Debate over whether three or four monuments exist at the site has continued for well over 120 years. Gardner Wilkinson (1871, 227) remarked that two (of the three) cromlechs were 'fallen'. Later, Done Bushell (1911, 300–301) recognized three capstones. Today, all are low-lying (almost at ground level), with little or no evidence of uprights or covering mound. They may all be similar in architecture to the Carn Besi (CRM 20) and Garn Wen (PEM 7–9) monuments.

The largest tomb of the 'complex' recorded by Done Bushell and his son in 1911 was The Gorse Grave, enclosed within the north-east section of a possible stone circle. However, Done Bushell (1911, 305) had doubts as to whether or not this was a burial chamber:

> The Gorse Grave, if it be a grave, is 20ft by 7ft. It was opened by my son, Mr Warin Foster Bushell, on April 26th … He found within it, on the level of the external surface of the ground, a pavement of flat stone of no great thickness roughly fitted together, and underneath the pavement, in the centre of the barrow, a small amount of black ashes. The stones had been roughly shaped and were of considerable size, some of them being nearly two square feet in area.

A visit in 1915 by officers compiling the RCAHM confirmed that the remnants of a cairn did exist, in particular the survival of three 'pillars', probably representing chamber uprights, plus two large slabs, possibly capstones, which were lying against a nearby hedge bank.

The monuments, plus the remains of burial chambers at Glandy Cross (Meini-Gwyr),[69] Carn Besi (CRM 20), Gwal-y-Filiast (CRM 1), and Mountain (PEM 6) appear to be deliberately placed around the southern hinterland of the Preseli Mountains. All of them could either delineate and encompass a social/political territory, including the mountains, or mark a symbolic frontier between what is known, and what is unknown and dangerous (i.e. the Preseli Mountains); no monuments appear to be sited on the mountains.

Eithbed Cemetery Group

The Pembroke Sub-Group

The Pembroke sub-group is located along the southern coastline of the county (with the exception of the Morfa Bychan cemetery which is in Carmarthenshire) and occupies quite different landscape locations to monuments on St David's and Strumble Head. Based on monument distribution and different styles of monument building, it is probable that a continuous Neolithic influence stretched from Angle in the west to the Gower Peninsula in the east.

The seven monuments within this group — the Devil's Quoit (PEM 25), The King's Quoit (PEM 26), Morfa Bychan A, B, C and D (CRM 2-5) and The Hanging Stone (PEM 24) — are constructed and located according to a number of different architectural and spatial rules. They involve different chamber and capstone designs; The Hanging Stone, for example uses a large rounded block for a capstone, whilst Morfa Bychan D uses an angular slab. This choice of stone is restricted to local availability. Many other differences include chamber size, shape and mound construction.

Despite these differences, there are several monuments that seem to share some common rules, both in form and landscape setting. For example, The King's Quoit and The Devil's Quoit, although located in different landscapes, are similar architecturally. Both are earth-fast, their capstones supported by a series of uprights at one end. Furthermore, the capstones of each monument are similarly shaped and are made from red sandstone. The four tombs on Ragwen Point — the Morfa Bychan Group — are all constructed, located and oriented in the same way. Although close to the sea, all seem to ignore it, their chambers and possible passage alignments pointing inland, a pattern repeated in many of the coastal monuments of south-west Wales. The most obvious example is The King's Quoit at Manorbier. Here, the monument is just a few metres from the edge of the sea, but the capstone has been deliberately placed so as to point inland, towards the beach and headland. Other monuments such as The Devil's Quoit and The Hanging Stone are positioned in a more subtle way. Even so, although close to the coast, they share no orientation, no relationship with the sea.

Three, perhaps four, architectural styles are used throughout this group, which may suggest either a localised building tradition incorporating a symbolism unique to each monument, or, equally plausibly, different construction dates. Within the Neolithic core areas of western Britain, new trends affected a monument's identity through time and space. Thus, small polygonal chambers supporting large boulder-like capstones were succeeded by tombs having flat, wedge-shaped capstones overlying square or rectangular chambers of the earth-fast type. Each monument is probably constructed so as to organize a social (public) and symbolic (private) space.

An antiquarian drawing of King's Quoit (PEM 26) (from Barnwell 1872, *Archaeologia Cambrensis*)

The Hanging Stone (PEM 24; SM 9722 0822) forms part of the boundary between a field and garden and is located just south of the village of Hill Mountain, at around 75m AOD. The surrounding landscape is gently undulating with open fields to the north and east. Milford Haven Sound, approximately 3km to the south, is clearly visible from the top of the capstone. This monument can be considered as being in a reasonable state of repair, no doubt partially due to its location within the bounds of a garden.[70]

An anonymous account made in 1864 (1864, 346–347) stated that the structure:

> ... at present consists of the remains of its supporters and a covering stone. A huge mass of rock lies touching part of it, which looks as if it had at one time formed a portion of the gallery or chamber. There is also the remains of original small, dry masonry, by which the gaps between the larger stones were always carefully filled up. Few traces of its former covering, or tumulus, could be made out.

Barnwell illustrated the monument in 1872, and it was described by Grimes (1936a), Daniel (1950) and Lynch (1976). Grimes (1936a, 131) suggested that The Hanging Stone is a possible passage grave and may be more complex than previously considered. Lynch prefers the term 'chamber and passage' monument (1976, 26), a term that conveniently fits with the Western seaways tradition. There are a number of similarities between this monument and Irish court monuments, but I consider that there is little in the way to distinguish it from other passage graves in Wales as no passage and little of the mound's form remains.

Today, the tomb consists of two large and substantial capstones, one measuring 3.1m x 2.6m. This capstone is supported by three uprights and forms the southern chamber, rectangular in shape. In a nearby hedge there is a possible second capstone and two uprights which both Grimes (1939) and Lynch (1975) suggest may represent 'the vestiges of a short passage'.[71] Revised plans by Barker suggest that the capstone has been dislodged. There is, immediately to the north of the boundary, a build-up of soil which may represent disturbed cairn or mound material, thus suggesting that the covering mound was oriented north-east/south-west (in line with the chamber and suggested passage).

The southern chamber appears to be polygonal and, until 1864, it was reported that drystone walling was visible in between the uprights (Anon 1864, 346–347). Also present was a substantial amount of possible cairn material. The drystone walling and remains of the covering mound have long since gone.

I am of the opinion that The Hanging Stone and the nearby displaced second capstone and dislodged uprights are in fact two chambers forming a double dolmen with the remains of a passage located at the north-eastern end of the monument. The northern chamber is possibly smaller than its southern neighbour, with the top of the capstone reaching the height of the base of the southern capstone. A similar architectural trait is seen within the double-chambered monument at Trellyffant (PEM 2). Other examples of multi-chambered tombs exist elsewhere in South-West Wales, for example, St Elvies Farm (PEM 20) and Twlc-y-Filiast (CRM 6).

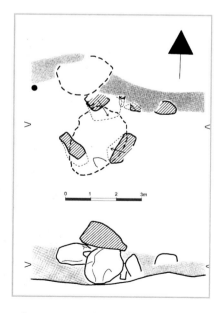

Plan and cross-section of The Hanging Stone

The Hanging Stone looking north-west

This monument, (PEM 25; SM 8865 0084) also known as Broomhill Burrows is constructed of a large rounded capstone supported at the western end by three uprights. At the opposite end, the capstone is set firmly into the earth. Daniel (1950) refers to this construction as earth-fast, a form found throughout the region. However, in his notes on this site he refers to it as a collapsed chamber to be compared with the Cors-y-Gedol monument in Merionethshire (MER 4) (1950, 203). I would agree with his initial interpretation of the site as being earth-fast, although Barker (1992, 38) suggests that, in this particular case, the term is misleading because the capstone sits on an earthen surface that may not be contemporary with the construction of the tomb.

The first account of this site was made by Richard Fenton (1810, 405) who eloquently describes the site and its surroundings:

> A little further on, across an extensive tract of sandy burrows, in the centre of which stands a Cromlech resting on two upright stones, the third overturned. There seems to have been a low circular agger of earth raised around it, of no inconsiderable area. This is the only druidical relic of the kind I have observed in Castle Martin, such monuments being much less frequent in the lower part of the country than they appear to be near the mountains.

Interesting comments derive from Fenton's observations. Firstly, the depression and 'low circular agger' suggests that some type of antiquarian investigation was undertaken prior to 1810. Secondly and more important, Fenton has started to understand the concept of deliberate landscape positioning of monuments. He notices that the Devil's Quoit is in an unusual place and should be 'near the mountains'; by mountains, he is probably referring to the jagged rock outcropping on, say, St David's Head and along Strumble Head.

The site was later recorded by Longueville Jones in 1865 (page 281) where he notices 'traces of a carnedd of stones' further suggesting some subsequent damage to this monument. An engraving by Barnwell in 1872 (page 142) and published in *Archaeologia Cambrensis* claims to be a more accurate representation than the Longueville Jones engraving of 1865. Barker (1992, 38) records on a visit in 1986 that a slab 'protrudes through the turf some 3m north-east of the chamber'.

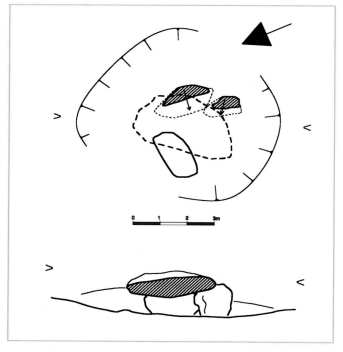

Plan of Devil's Quoit (after Barker 1992)

The capstone, made from local sandstone, is similar in shape to the King's Quoit at Manorbier. There appears to be no trace of a mound, but the chamber is set within a shallow depression (Barker 1992), suggesting that the chamber area may be sub-megalithic. However, the depression, measuring roughly 8m by 7m, may also be the result of continuous cattle or sheep trampling.

Although located on a small ridge and standing around 37m AOD, the tomb does not look out towards the open sea but rather takes in a visual sweep of Milford Haven Sound, 5km to the north. Other burial monuments which similarly ignore the sea are Llech-y-Tribedd (PEM 1) and nearby St Elvies Farm (PEM 20).

Devil's Quoit looking north

Broomhill Burrows lies adjacent to Freshwater West, an extensive beach system where Mesolithic and Neolithic lithic activity has been recorded. The remains of a submerged forest dating to the Early Post-Glacial period (c.10–14,000 BC) can be seen at low tide from this beach.

Approximately 150m to the east of the Devil's Quoit is an extensive sand dune system, possibly representing an ancient sea inlet (known as Kilpaison Burrows), whilst approximately 300m south-east is a probable Bronze Age mound (SM 8899 0060).

The King's Quoit (PEM 26; SM 0593 9728) has one of the most dramatic landscape settings in South-West Wales and is one of only a few monuments located on the coast. Others include Carreg Samson (PEM 18), Garn Wnda (PEM 13), Coetan Arthur (PEM 23), Carn Llidi (PEM 21-22) and the four rock-cut monuments of Morfa Bychan A, B, C, and D (CRM 2–5).

The monument, standing at 18m AOD is located on a small bank above a cliff face and comprises a huge single capstone supported by two uprights — although there is a third stone located at the south-eastern end which is probably a recumbent upright. The three uprights form a rectangular chamber. In 1865 Longueville Jones noted (1865, 282) its unusual landscape position by stating that:

> On the south-eastern side of the little cove at Manorbeer ... is to be seen a cromlech ... it is curious from its position, because, instead of lying on an elevated or bare patch of ground, it is just under a ridge of rocks ... in this respect it resembles the cromlech near Llanwnda [Carn Wnda?] ... the cause in each of these cases has, no doubt, been the convenience of using large slabs from adjoining, or rather overhanging cliffs.

The monument may be regarded as earth-fast (Daniel 1950). The capstone, made from local sandstone, points inland towards Manorbier Bay, suggesting that the King's Quoit is in some way ignoring the sea.

The King's Quoit was once regarded as a natural 'accidental formation' of stone (Anon. 1851, 315). Recently, Barker (1992, 38) has supported Daniel's earth-fast classification and I believe no covering mound would have existed during the Neolithic because the ledge on which the monument stands is far too narrow. This being so, the King's Quoit is similarly constructed to, and shares a comparable landscape setting with, both Garn

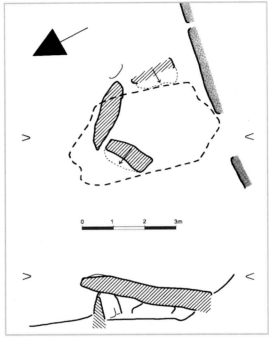

Plan and cross-section of King's Quoit (after Barker 1992)

Gilfach (PEM 15) and nearby Devil's Quoit (PEM 25). However, there is a possibility that the capstone was not earth-fast as a probable upright exists at the rear southern end.

King's Quoit perched above the sea

The Morfa Bychan (CRM 2–5; SM 22 07) cemetery group consists of four monuments that stand between 75m and 120m AOD.[72] Situated among rock debris, they merge into the surrounding landscape to the extent that during the Neolithic, only those with special ritual knowledge may have known the precise whereabouts of each monument. Similar monument locations are evident within other coastal headlands of this part of Wales.

The landscape seen from these monuments is extremely dramatic. All four tombs are aligned north/south, and all appear to face Gilman Point rather than the sea (like the capstone of the King's Quoit, Manorbier). Pendine Sands and the surrounding headland are clearly visible beyond Gilman Point.

In addition to the four monuments mentioned below, a possible long mound is located further west, above the extensive rock outcropping between Morfa Bychan B and C (SN 2213 0751). This site, described as a wedged-shaped long cairn, measures roughly 20m in length by 10m in width and is aligned north-east/south-west. The mound was first recorded by Treherne in 1926 and later by Murphy in 1985. If it is a long mound, its size and, more importantly, its shape would make this the earliest monument within the cemetery group and could be compared with monuments constructed within the Cotswold-Severn tradition, such as Parc-le-Breos-Cwm (GLA 4) and the Nicholaston monument (GLA 11), both on the Gower Peninsula.

Barker quite rightly refers to this series of monuments as the Morfa Bychan cemetery (1992, 10). Morfa Bychan A, B and C are intervisible with each other and all are similar in construction. Morfa Bychan D, a submerged monument set within the loose rock debris, is closest to the rock outcropping above the tombs.

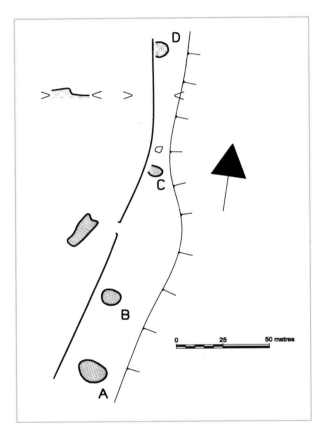

Morfa Bychan: plan showing the location of all the monuments

226

Morfa Bychan A (CRM 2; SM 2213 0743) is the farthest south of the group and stands at around 75m AOD. It comprises a single capstone, now dislodged, which was originally supported by nine uprights. The stone material is local, possibly frost-shattered debris from the nearby cliff face. The chamber is rectangular (2m × 1.5m) with evidence of a passage (Castleden 1992). This, plus remnants of an oval cairn, place Morfa Bychan A in the passage grave tradition. Its landscape setting suggests the tomb could be compared with the Anglesey passage grave of Barclodiad-y-Gawres (ANG 4), albeit on a much smaller scale. Castleden (1992) suggests the other three Morfa Bychan monuments may also be passage graves. In the case of Morfa Bychan D, there is evidence of a single passage upright, but this is by no means conclusive evidence that it is a passage grave. However, it may be that these monuments are possibly the only group within this part of Wales that conform to the passage grave tradition.

When visiting this monument in 1993, I saw little or no evidence of either a passage or cairn material. The whole area in front of the cliff face was littered with weather-shattered rock debris. I suggest the tomb's morphology represents very much a localised tradition, utilising local materials, with the uprights and capstones either cut or conveniently shaped by nature, rather than by design.

The four monuments were excavated and restored during 1910–1911 and a few artifacts were found within a stratified sequence within the chamber of Morfa Bychan A. In the southern part of the chamber a small lithic assemblage was recovered, including scrapers and waste flake material. Also found were charcoal and a few fragments of human bone (Ward 1910), probably reflecting cremation burial deposition. The artifacts, according to Ward (1918, 69–70), overlay a 'rude pavement'.

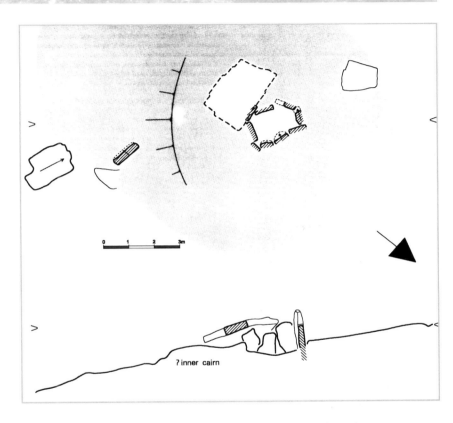

Plan and cross-section of Morfa Bychan A
(after Barker 1992)

Morfa Bychan A, looking north over the sea and Pendine Sands

Morfa Bychan B (CRM 3; SM 2214 0748) stands on a natural ledge about 50m north of Morfa Bychan A, at around 100m AOD. Here, there is clear evidence for a small cairn on the southern extent, but certainly no passage. Barker (1992, 12) questions whether or not this monument had a proper entrance. However, I suggest that a possible entrance may be located to the south, facing the open sea. A similar 'opening' exists with Morfa Bychan A.

According to Gardner Wilkinson (1870, 42–43), the pear-shaped cairn was surrounded by kerbing. However, rock debris now covers any traces. In the vicinity of the cairn are two large flat slabs, one of them a possible displaced capstone. The chamber, now much disturbed, is pentagonal and consists of six or seven (confused) uprights that open out to the north-west. Some of the uprights have slumped into the centre of the chamber; probably the result of dislodgement from antiquarian excavation. Further disturbance is found with a shallow depression extending around the chamber. To the west of the chamber are three uprights that may represent an east/west aligned passage, although one of them is oriented north/south in contradiction to such a theory.

Treherne, Gibbins, Clarke and Ward excavated the site on a single day — 17th May 1910. Apart from discovering previous excavation disturbance, three flint flakes were found (Ward 1918).

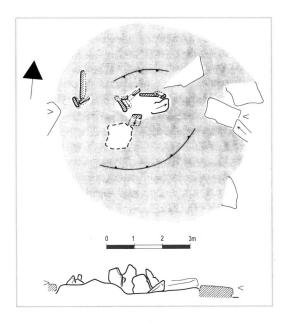

Plan and cross-section of Morfa Bychan B

Morfa Bychan B, looking south

Approximately 90m north of Morfa Bychan A is the third tomb (CRM 4; SM 2216 0754), standing at around 110m AOD. Gardner Wilkinson first recorded the site in 1870 and described it as 'an irregular enclosure of uncertain time' (1870, 43). However, Treherne (1911), Ward (1918), Daniel (1950) and Barker (1992) have all speculated that this site is a megalithic burial chamber.[73] I would add that the morphology of this monument and its landscape setting is very similar to others within this group. According to Castleden (1992), this tomb, now much damaged, consists merely of a 'collection' of stones.

The author notes that the chamber area is Y-shaped (in plan), delineated by a series of uprights and a possible sill-stone. These uprights, along with a number of recumbent stones, form the eastern corner of a large chamber and a possible passage approximately 2.5m long. In total there are 12 uprights. There is no trace of any entrance. However, the east/west alignment of six stones appears to terminate at the eastern edge of the cairn mound. The construction of passages elsewhere tends to favour this orientation. If this is so, one of the large uprights that form the eastern section of the chamber may act as a doorway that was periodically removed in order to gain access to the chamber. It is also probable that the two recumbent stones within the chamber area are in fact dislodged chamber uprights. I have also noted a small section of what may be a capstone.

An upright stone, located along the north-eastern edge of the mound may be the remains of kerbing. It is probable that further kerbing underlies loose cairn material.

This monument marks the axis point whereby intervisibility exists between Morfa Bychan A and B, but not with D. Morfa Bychan A, B and C have definite landscape affinities that are seaward. However, Morfa Bychan D, although having intervisibility with the sea, is oriented inland. The three seaward monuments are similarly constructed.

Plan and cross-section of Morfa Bychan C (after Barker 1992)

The fourth monument (CRM 5; SM 2216 0762) within this group is possibly the most interesting. Again located on a natural ledge, just below the cliff face, Morfa Bychan D has a chamber submerged within the rocky soil. The position of this monument, constructed up against a rock face, is similar to sites such as Carn Llidi (PEM 21–22) on St David's Head and Garn Gilfach (PEM 15) on Dinas Head. Along with the other monuments within the Morfa Bychan Group there appears to be a deliberate attempt to conceal its precise location. Indeed, the position of Morfa Bychan D is by far the most concealed of all the Morfa Bychan monuments and cannot be seen from any position east of Ragwen Point.

The large capstone (almost at ground level) covers a rectangular chamber and is supported by at least 11 uprights, with irregular drystone walling between. Outside, there is a possible small, low earthen mound. The size of the mound is difficult to calculate but certainly extends some 2.3m around the chamber area. Cut into the mound and, unusually, at the side of the chamber, is an entrance with a doubtful passage. Two uprights are positioned on the north-western cut. Immediately to the west of this cut is a

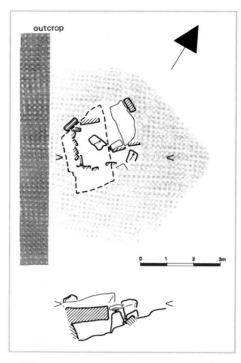

Plan and cross-section of Morfa Bychan D (after Barker 1992)

large slab which may be a passage roofing stone. The entrance looks out towards Gilman Point and Pendine Sands beyond.

The chamber appears to have been constructed by underpinning the large capstone initially with natural slabs, which appear to have then been replaced with purposefully cut and placed uprights. The chamber is partially cut into the surrounding geology.

The tomb was discovered by Treherne and Evans on 11th June 1910 and excavated a few days later (1911). The massive capstone (4.1m × 2.3m) and passage were partially covered by loose cairn rubble, whilst a thin slab blocked the chamber entrance. Inside the chamber was 'a considerable accumulation of brownish soil, on the surface of which lay bones of recent animals' (Ward 1918, 72–73). The excavation, conducted over two days, was halted when it was discovered that the capstone had become unsafe and the chamber uprights had started to slip inwards. The excavators found the original chamber floor but no artifacts. Since Ward's excavation three uprights within the northern corner of the chamber have been removed and the southern section of the probable passage has partially collapsed inwards.

Morfa Bychan D with surrounding cairn, looking west

98 Twlc-y-Filiast

99 Bedd Taliesin

100 Cerrig Llwydion

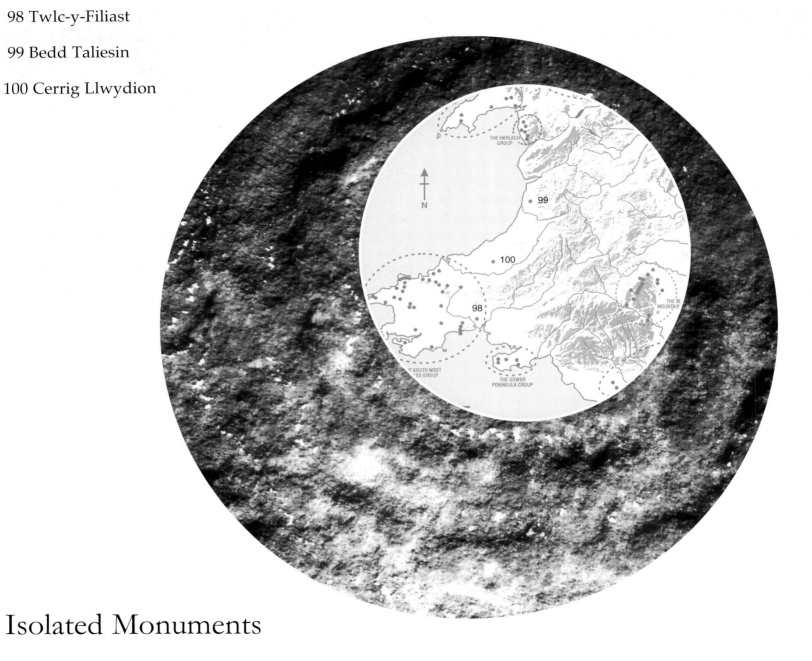

Isolated Monuments

Most of the monuments discussed have fitted comfortably within a series of groups, but scattered throughout Wales, in particular in the central and southern central regions, are a number of sites that can be considered isolated monuments. In the past this may not have been the case, for there are other, enigmatic, sites that are either damaged, lost or unidentified. Barker (1992), for example, identified an additional 85 such sites although several of these, including the Eithbed Complex are listed in this volume.

The Cerrig Llwydion (double) dolmen may be designated as an isolated monument to the extent that its nearest definite neighbour is situated well over 20 kilometres away to the south (Twlc-y-Filiast), although Barker (1992) recognizes a possible chambered monument of Yr Len Llech 8km to the north-east. Analysis reveals that the mean distance between tombs in Carmarthenshire is between 2 and 3km, and it is most probable, therefore, that Cerrig Llwydion, and for that matter, Bedd Taliesin, some 70km north, near Aberystwyth, would have been part of a more concentrated distribution.

The Twlc-y-Filiast monument, isolated from the main megalithic clustering in South-West Wales, is a substantial monument. The nearest group of monuments with clear megalithic morphology is the Morfa Bychan cemetery, located some 13km to the south-west. The rectangular chamber and large capstone resembles that of The Hanging Stone (PEM 24) but the latter is sited within a completely different landscape. Twlc-y-Filiast is hidden within a narrow secluded steep-sided valley with rock outcropping.

The Bedd Taliesin monument, located in the parish of Llanfihangel Genau-y-Glyn, in central west Wales, is rather an enigma in that very little is known about it. It is not catalogued in any of the popular volumes of Welsh megaliths except by Barber and Williams (1989, 118–119). References are made, however, albeit fragmentary, in 19th-century accounts of the site in *Archaeologia Cambrensis*. Unlike other isolated monuments in Wales, Bedd Taliesin is sited within a typical monument location; that is not on the highest point within the immediate landscape but at the same time possessing commanding views, in this instance to the north and west towards the Dovey estuary.

Twlc-y-Filiast (CRM 6; SN 3383 1608), also known as Ebenezer and Arthur's Table, is one of a handful of Megalithic monuments in total isolation from the main megalith clusters within South-West Wales, but does have a similar landscape setting. The monument, standing at around 124m AOD, lacks visibility with the sea despite standing only 5.5km from the coast and around 4km from the Afon Taf and Tywi Estuaries. Its excavator, Hubert Savory, remarked that the site is hidden, lying in a steep-sided valley with a small stream running by.

This much denuded monument has similar architecture to a number of monuments within South-West Wales, in particular Treffynnon, Llandeloy (PEM 19), Gwal-y-Filiast (CRM 1) and The Hanging Stone at Burton (PEM 24). But it is only the Gwal-y-Filiast monument that has both similar architecture and an identical landscape position, standing on the eastern banks of the Afon Taf.

The tomb comprises a small chamber delineated by three uprights that stand in shallow sockets packed with small stones. A displaced capstone located outside the chamber is supported by two of the three chamber uprights. At the southern end of the chamber is evidence of a sill, delineated by the setting of five small upturned slabs. Houlder (1978) argues that the chamber is trapezoidal. However, I would suggest that the shape is actually rectangular.

Early investigations found no trace of a covering mound (Daniel 1950). However, an excavation carried out in 1953 by H.N. Savory discovered the remnants of an elongated mound, measuring 18m by 9m, a possible ante-chamber and a series of ritual pits. Three shallow stone settings and a fallen slab delineated the ante-chamber, which lies to the the south of the main chamber. The mound is oriented north-north-east/south-south-west, following the axis of the valley, and one side of the mound has been eroded by the brook. Savory (1953, 225–228) suggests that this possible Portal Dolmen had an extensively damaged entrance area.

The 1953 excavation yielded very few artifacts. Nothing at all was found in the chamber except for a dark brown earth deposit that contained fragments of charcoal. This deposit was cut into the clay floor suggesting recent antiquarian disturbance. However, a small flint scraper, a stone pendant and

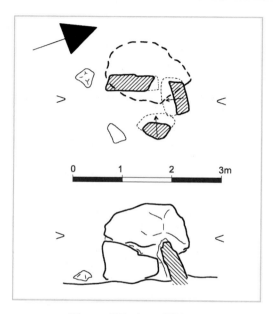

Plan of Twlc-y-Filiast

a few fragments of unidentifiable pottery were recovered close by within the cairn. The stone pendant is said to represent a metal axe, suggesting that this particular artifact is either Late Neolithic or Early Bronze Age in date. Uncovered below the cairn was a charcoal-flecked clay surface that may represent pre-cairn activity or the preparation phase prior to the construction of the monument. Within the area of stone settings flecks of charcoal were found and also burnt bone.

In 1999 and 2003, I noted that seven or so stones appeared to delineate a possible narrow passage and forecourt area. Indeed, Savory records a curved line of stones south-west of the ante-chamber which may delineate the remains of a revetted forecourt area. If this is so, then the supposed ante-chamber could be actually the remains of a passage. These additions could establish Twlc-y-Filiast as an important site, especially as it is located away from the main South-West Wales Group.

Twlc-y-Filiast looking west

Bedd Taliesin (CRM 6; SN 6724 9126), one of the most enigmatic and isolated monuments in central Wales, stands on the west-facing slopes of Moel-y-Garn, north-west of the settlement of Tal-y-bont and the Dovey estuary, at around 220m AOD. Thomas Evans noted in 1781 (page 107):

> The spurious sepulchre of the Bard Taliesin, who flourished in the 6th century and one which stood near the highway, has, within these five years, been entirely plundered and the broken stones are now converted into gateposts.

The monument has a central passage or long chamber with a displaced capstone that is set within an oval or long mound. Located around the capstone and the chamber are a number of loose sub-angular and angular stone blocks which either form part of the cairn or may be fragments of another capstone. It seems likely that the capstone is not *in situ*. Surprisingly, there has been very little archaeological investigation of this site. It is certainly outside the major Neolithic core areas, but is close to important Mesolithic environmental sites along the Dovey estuary and within the marshlands of Cors Fochno, near Borth. Approximately 4km to the south-east of the site are the remnants of a Bronze Age landscape, including a standing stone (SN 689 877). A large number of cairns are also located 2km to the north and east of the monument on Foel Goch.

According to the RCAHM this monument dates to the Bronze Age. However, its sheer megalithic appearance suggests a Neolithic date and is in some ways similar to the sub-megalithic monument of Capel Garmon (DEN 3). If so, it may have a trapezoidal mound with a horned forecourt and false portal along with the chamber and passage alignment located within the centre of the monument.

Bedd Taliesin:
showing a possible spare passage and dislodged capstone

Cerrig Llwydion (CRM 10; SN 3738 3258) is a substantial tomb incorporating at least two chambers within a possible long mound, perhaps having similar dimensions to that of Pentre Ifan (PEM 5) near Newport. If this is the case, then other smaller tombs may have been located close by. There is certainly evidence of megalithic structures in woodland at Nant-y-ffin (SN 5527 3060) and the site of Yr Hen Llech (SN 4128 3602), located 17.5km and 4km to the east of Cerrig Llwydion respectively.[74] The presence of Bronze Age barrows and cairns in the vicinity indicates ritual and symbolic continuity within the landscape. It could be suggested that the Cerrig Llwydion dolmen housed at least two members of a ranked society, with one burial per chamber. The erection of single burial barrows and cairns

during the subsequent Bronze Age would have carried on the 'tradition' of high-status single burials. On this basis I suggest the monument was constructed and in use during the Late Neolithic, and was possibly contemporary with the smaller earth-fast tombs farther south.

The denuded monument of Cerrig Llwydion, also referred to as Conwil Elvet, is one of a handful of monuments benefiting from the protection afforded by being incorporated into a stone and turf boundary wall. There appears to be little evidence of a covering mound. However, disturbance in the field to the east of the monument may represent mound material. Large stone blocking may be cairn material or even part of the chamber fabric.

This isolated monument, standing at 291m AOD, was first commented on as far back as 1811 when Carlisle describes the site as being located:

> On the side-land summit of a high mountain, facing the south, is a centre stone of a huge magnitude, from 10 to 15 tons, horizontal, oblong, two feet thick, supported by four uprights, one of which has declined from its original position, and sunk deeper into the ground. For other similar, but smaller stones, of about four to five tons, surround it: but these have all slipped from their respective fulcra, and now lie in a shelving position. Scattered about, at various and irregular distances around, are several smaller stones, distributed and broken up by the masons building the house at Nant y clawdd ucha.

The description by Carlisle infers that the site had suffered similar fates to other stone monuments in Western Britain, in that it has served to support the late Post-Medieval building industry. Barnwell's description of 1877 shows that little had changed since the early 19th century, but claimed that there were traces of an oval mound measuring roughly 21.5m by 15.2m (1877, 82–86).[75] Later, Jones notes that the capstone had fractured by 1907 (Jones 1907, 141).

The large, irregular elongated capstone is supported at the northern end by three uprights forming a small rectangular chamber. The capstone (and therefore the chamber) is, unusually, oriented north/south. Directly behind the main capstone is a smaller slab and what appears to be an extension of the main chamber. Separately, approximately 3m behind the main chamber

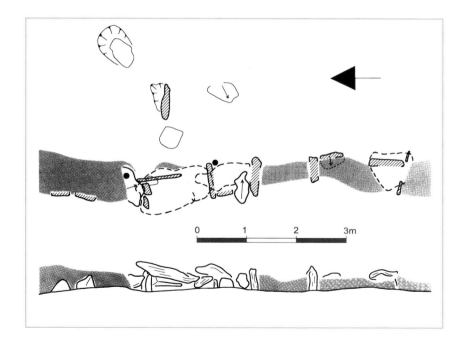

Plan and cross section of Cerrig Llwydion (after Barker 1992)

is a second chambered structure, comprising a capstone and five uprights (Barker 1992). Daniel (1950) classifies this monument as a large cist, whereas Houlder (1978, 175) has suggested that this monument is a segmented cist that is unique to Wales. Barker (1992, 17) tends to agree with this comment, but adds that probably more internal architecture existed. Although the architecture suggests a gallery-grave type monument (of which a small version would equate to a large cist), I firmly believe that Cerrig Llwydion is a double dolmen of massive proportions.

Although isolated from other similar monuments, Cerrig Llwydion lies within a dense concentration of Bronze Age barrows. The landscape is bare, almost moor-like, the barrows dominating all of the high ground. However, the tomb's location is typical of other megalithic monuments, in that it is sited on a ridge rather than the highest point in the landscape. It overlooks a river valley — the Afon Bele — and has dominant views to the south, towards the upper reaches of the Afon Duad valley and the eastern section of the ridge on which it stands.

The northern chamber at Cerrig Llwydion looking south-east

Concluding Remarks

The introduction to this book has given some insight to how and why these monuments were constructed, used and later abandoned. However, there are still many questions that remain unanswered. Scholars such as Tilley (1994), Thomas (1999), Whittle (2003) and Cummings and Whittle (2004) have attempted to incorporate a number of socio-political mechanisms using philosophical discourse. Despite the complete lack of physical evidence, the detail of drama, emotion and religious experience has been boldly proposed by Deveraux (2001), Dronfield (1996), Lewis-Williams and Pearce (2005), Chippindale and Nash (forthcoming), each of whom have looked at such thought-provoking topics as acoustics, shamanism and sublime experiences inside and outside chambered monuments.

I have drawn together one hundred monuments from nine distinct Neolithic core areas of Wales as well as several monuments within the central Marches. It is more than probable that as many as three or four times that number existed during Neolithic times. The antiquarian accounts on Anglesey, for example, give testimony to the number of monuments that were either damaged or destroyed between the 17th and 19th centuries and what we see today may be only a fraction of what was being constructed and used during the Neolithic. Antiquarian accounts in other Welsh core areas suggest similar scenarios. Given this, I think one has to be careful when making general assumptions on, say, the trends in site location or deposition of material culture (Flemming 1999).

The monuments discussed in this volume represent a two-thousand year social-religious movement where the dead were as important as the living. Whilst there appears to be many variations in style, all the monuments are constructed of stone, all possess a chamber, some have a passage, some a façade and most have (or had) a covering mound or cairn. They have been chronologically classified into four main architectural groups: Portal Dolmens, long mounds, passage graves and earth-fast monuments, starting with the earliest and ending with the latest. The Irish Sea Province identified and discussed at length by Lynch (1972) and more recently by Cummings and Whittle (2004) and Lynch et al (2000) appears to be a melting pot where many different types of architecture are being experimented with, resulting in multi-phased construction activity.

We can never know what people in our recent past must have thought of these enigmatic monuments. The fact that little or no destruction occurred up until the early Post-Medieval period suggests that they were tolerated, even revered. The Breconshire monument of Ty Illtyd (BRE 6) was used as a hermitage by St Illtyd during the Medieval period. Here, in great contemplation, St Illtyd may have carved a series of Christian symbols on the uprights of the chamber, establishing his mark on a monument that had been known for many generations.

Old ways, New Ways

The transition from a hunting/fishing and gathering way of life to sedentism, agriculture and burying the dead in a certain way would have been no overnight affair. The spread of agriculture from the Fertile Crescent of the Middle East to north-western Europe took around 6,000 years. Was this, what I call Neolithicisation, an invasion of ideas or an invasion of people? Certainly, researchers such as Humphry Case (1969) have advocated that grain, pottery, cattle and, more importantly, new ideas came over with colonising groups. However, many of the old ways of doing things — food production, gender roles and the celebration of the stages of life — must have been maintained, at least in part, during the early part of the Neolithic. If this were the case, the transition between the Mesolithic and Neolithic becomes more difficult to define and, arguably, the transition period may have extended over some 1,000 years, and it is within this transition that Britain witnesses the construction of the first burial monuments.

Dealing with death

In the past, archaeologists have tended to draw a dramatic line between the Neolithic and the preceding Mesolithic, essentially seeing the Mesolithic as a period based on a hunter/gatherer economy and the Neolithic as one focussed on death and burial. This unbalanced approach is based on the surviving archaeological evidence and it is obvious that other things were going on in the Neolithic other than the treatment of the dead. Similarly, during the Mesolithic, and based on southern Scandinavian burial evidence, hunter/gatherers were in any event symbolically burying their dead. The treatment of the dead appears to be a most important process in both societies. Certainly, during the Neolithic in Britain, it is not just the monument and how it is constructed that is important but also the way the body was prepared and positioned within his or her final physical resting place. In the case of the chambered monuments in western Britain, the dead or their remains are usually placed within chambers and sometimes in the passage area. From the sometimes fragmentary evidence three clear burial processes are in operation: disarticulation, excarnation and cremation. These burial processes appear to be very different to the cemetery burials from the late Mesolithic sites of Skateholm and Vedbaek in southern Scandinavia. Here, male, female and child extended burials are accompanied with ornate grave goods. More interestingly, some burials appear to represent family groups and all burials have been garnished with a light scattering of red ochre. The grave goods and the red ochre probably represent items which were to be taken with the deceased to the next life. Of course, parallels exist with the way the dead were treated during the Neolithic. It appears that the monument itself was an extension of the body; the chambers, façade, passage and the mound all have an intimate association with the way the dead were presented, treated and garnished before interment (Chippindale and Nash, forthcoming).

Despite the archaeological evidence, it is now becoming clearer that chambered monuments were more than just repositories for the dead. They also appear to embrace many social and political attributes that are inextricably intertwined with the day-to-day life of the social elite. This volume has highlighted a number of traits which display ostentatiousness of architectural design, an essential prerequisite for any social elite.

ANON. 1851. Account of the Fifth Annual Meeting of the Cambrian Archaeological, held at Tenby. *Arch. Camb,* Series 2, 315.

ANON. 1864. Account of the Eighteenth Annual Meeting of the Cambrian Archaeological, held at Haverfordwest. *Arch. Camb.,* 346–347.

ASHBEE, P. 1978. *The Ancient British, Norwich.* Geo Abstracts.

ATKINSON, R.J.C. 1961. Parc le Breos Cwm. *Archaeology in Wales,* 1, 5.

ATKINSON, R..J.C. 1968, Old Mortality: some aspects of Burial and Population in Neolithic England. In *Studies in Ancient Europe (Essays presented to Stuart Piggott,* Leicester, Leicester University Press, 83–93.

AUBREY, J. 1695. *Monumenta Britannica,* Parts 1and 2 edition. J. Fowles ed. Reprinted by Dorset Publishing Company.

BAGNALL-OAKELEY, M.E. 1889. *An account of some of the Rude Stone Monuments and Ancient Burial Mounds in Monmouthshire.* Monmouthshire and Caerleon Antiquarian Association. Newport.

BARBER, C. and WILLIAMS, G.W. 1989. *The Ancient Stones of Wales.* Abergavenny. Blorenge Books.

BARING GOULD, S., BURNARD, R. and ENYS, J.D. 1899. Exploration of the Stone Camp on St David's Head (in 1898). *Arch. Camb.,* Series 5, 16, 105–131.

BARING GOULD, S. 1902. The Exploration of Clegyr Voya. *Arch. Camb.,* Series 6, 3, 1–11.

BARKER, C.T. 1992. *The Chambered Tombs of South-West Wales: a re-assessment of the Neolithic burial monuments of Carmarthenshire and Pembrokeshire.* Oxford: Oxbow Monograph 14.

BARNWELL, E.L. 1868. Alignments in Wales. *Arch. Camb.,* Series 3, 14, 169–179.

BARNWELL, E.L. 1869. Cromlechs in North Wales. *Arch. Camb.,* Series 3, 15, 118–47.

BARNWELL, E.L. 1872. Notes on some South Wales Cromlechs. *Arch. Camb.,* Series 4, 3, 81–143.

BARNWELL, E.L. 1875. On Pillar Stones in Wales. *Arch. Camb.,* Series 4, 6, 299–306.

BARNWELL, E.L. 1877. Early remains in Carmarthenshire. *Arch. Camb.,* Series 5, 1.

BARNWELL, E.L. 1884. On some South Wales Cromlechs. *Arch. Camb.,* Series 5, 1, 129–144.

BAYNES, E.N. 1908. The Excavations at Din Lligwy. *Arch. Camb.,* Series 6, 8, 183–210.

BAYNES, E.N. 1909. The Excavation of Lligwy Cromlech in the County of Anglesey. *Arch. Camb.,* Series 7, 9, 217–231.

BAYNES, E.N. 1910–1911. The Megalithic remains of Anglesey. *Trans. Hon. Soc. Cymmrod,* 3–91.

BENDER, B. 1978. Gatherer-hunter to farmer: a social perspective. *World Archaeology,* 10, No. 2, 204–222.

BEZANT LOWE, S. 1912. *The Heart of Northern Wales.* Vol. 1.

BOWEN, E.G. and GRESHAM, C.A. 1967. *History of Merioneth.* Vol. 1, Dolgellau.

BOYD DAWKINS, W. 1901. The Cairn and Sepulchal Cave at Gop, near Prestatyn. *Antiquaries Journal,* 1, VIII, 322–341.

BOYD DAWKINS, W. 1902. On the cairn and sepulchral cave at Gop, near Prestatyn. *Arch. Camb.,* 2, 161–185.

BRADLEY, R. 1993. *Altering the earth.* Edinburgh, Society of Antiquaries of Scotland. Monograph, Series 8.

BRADLEY, R. 1998. *The Significance of Monuments.* London, Routledge.

BRADLEY, R. 2000. *The Archaeology of Natural Places.* London, Routledge.

BRADLEY, R. 2002. *The Past in Prehistoric Societies.* London, Routledge.

BRITNELL, W. 1979. The Gwernvale Long Cairn. *Antiquity,* 53, 132–134.

BRITNELL, W. 1984. The Gwernvale Long Cairn, Crickhowell, Brecknock. In W. Britnell and H. Savory, *Gwernvale and Penywyrlod: Two Neolithic Long Cairns in the Black Mountains of Breconshire.* Cambrian Archaeological Monographs, No. 2, Cardiff, 43–93.

BRITNELL, W. 1991. The Neolithic. In Manley, J., Ganter, S. and Gale, F. (eds.), *The Archaeology of Clwyd.* Clwyd Archaeology Service.

BRITNELL, W. and SAVORY, H. 1984. *Gwernvale and Penywyrlod: Two Neolithic Long Cairns in the Black Mountains of Breconshire.* Cambrian Archaeological Monographs No. 2, Cardiff.

BROWN, A.E. 1963. Records of surface finds made in Herefordshire, 1951–1960. *Trans. Woolhope Natur. Field. Club,* XXXVII, 76–91.

BURGESS, C. 1980. *The Age of Stonehenge.* London, Dent.

BURL, A. 1976. *The Stone Circles of the British Isles.* London, Yale University Press.

BURL, A. 1985. *Prehistoric Stone Circles.* Shire Archaeology.

BURNHAM, H. 1995. *A guide to ancient and historic Wales: Clwyd and Powys.* CADW, Cardiff.

CARLISLE, N. 1811. *A Topographic Dictionary of the Dominion of Wales.*

CASE, H.J. 1969. Neolithic explanations. *Antiquity* 43, 176–86.

CASELDINE, A. 1990. *Environmental Archaeology in Wales.* Cadw Welsh Historical Monuments and Dept. of Archaeology, St David's University

College, Lampeter.

CASTLEDEN, R. 1992. *Neolithic Britain: New Stone Age Sites of England, Scotland and Wales*. London, Routledge.

CHAPMAN, R., KINNES, I. and RANDSBORG, K. (eds.) 1981. *The Archaeology of Death*. Cambridge, Cambridge University Press.

CHILDREN, G. and NASH, G.H. 1994. *Monuments in the Landscape: The Prehistory of Herefordshire*. Vol. I, Logaston Press, Hereford.

CHILDREN, G. and NASH, G.H. 1996. *Monuments in the Landscape: The Prehistory of Monmouthshire*. Vol. IV, Logaston Press, Hereford.

CHILDREN, G. and NASH, G.H. 1997. *The Neolithic Sites of Cardiganshire, Carmarthenshire and Pembrokeshire*. Vol. V. Reprinted and revised 2002. Logaston Press, Hereford.

CHILDREN, G. and NASH, G.H. 2001. *Monuments in the Landscape: The Prehistory of Breconshire*. Vol. IX, Logaston Press, Hereford.

CHIPPINDALE, C. and NASH, G.H. (forthcoming). *Edmund Burke's the Sublime and Neolithic Life*.

CLOUGH, T.H. McK., and CUMMINS, W.A. 1988. *Stone Axe Trade: The petrology of prehistoric stone implements from the British Isles*. Vol. 2, CBA Research Report, No. 67.

CLOUTMAN, E. 1983. *Studies of the vegetational history of the Black Mountain Range, South Wales*. Ph.D. thesis (unpublished), University of Wales.

COONEY, G. 2000. *Landscapes of Neolithic Ireland*. London, Routledge.

CORCORAN, J.X.W.P. 1969. The Cotswold-Severn Group. In Powell, T. G.E., Corcoran, J.X.W.P., Lynch, F. and Scott, J.G. (eds.), *Megalithic Enquiries in the West of Britain*. Liverpool University Press, Liverpool.

CRAMPTON, C.B. and WEBLEY, D.P. 1968. A section through Mynydd Troed long barrow, Brecknock. *Bull. Board Celtic Studies*, 22, 71–77.

CRAWFORD, O.G.S. 1920. Account of the Excavations at Hengwm, Merionethshire, August and September 1919. *Arch. Camb.* (1921), 99–133.

CRAWFORD, O.G.S. 1925. *The Long Barrows of the Cotswolds*. Gloucester.

CUMMINGS, V. 2002. All cultural things: Actual and conceptual monuments in the Neolithic of western Britain. In *Monuments and Landscape in Atlantic Europe*, C. Scarre (ed.). London, Routledge, 107–121.

Cummings, V. & Whittle, A. 2004. *Places of Special Virtue: Megaliths in the Neolithic Landscapes of Wales. Oxbow Books.

DANIEL, G.E. 1937. The Chambered Barrow in Parc le Breos Cwm, South Wales. *Proceedings of the Prehistoric Society*, III, 1937, 71–86.

DANIEL, G.E. 1950. *The Prehistoric Chambered Tombs of England and Wales*. Cambridge, Cambridge University Press.

DANIEL, G. 1958. *The Megalithic builders of Western Europe*. London, Hutchenson.

DANIEL, G. 1972. *Megaliths in History*. London, Thames and Hudson.

DARVILL, T.C. 1982. *The Megalithic Chambered Tombs of the Cotswold-Severn Region*. Vorda Research Series No. 5.

DARVILL, T.C. 1989. The Circulation of Neolithic Stone and Flint Axes: a case study from Wales and the mid-west of England. *Procs. of the Prehistoric Society*, 55, 27–43.

DAVID, A. 1990. Some aspects of the human presence in west Wales during the Mesolithic. In C. Bonsall (ed.), *The Mesolithic in Europe*, 241-253. Edinburgh: John Donald.

DAVID, A. and WILLIAMS, G. 1995. Stone axe-head manufacture in the Preseli Hills, Wales. *Procs of the Prehistoric Society*, 61, 433–460.

DAVIS, M. 1945. Types of Megalithic Monument of the Irish Sea and North Channel Coastlands: A Study of Distributions. *Antiquity*, 25, 125–144.

DEVARAUX, P. 2001. *Stone Age Soundtracks, The Acoustic Archaeology of Ancient Sites*, Vega.

DIMBLEBY, G. 1973. Report on two soil samples from Dyffyn Ardudwy. *Archaeologia*, 104, 4–5.

DONE BUSHELL, W. 1911. Among the Prescelly circles. *Arch. Camb.*, Series 6, 11, 287–333.

DRONFIELD, J. 1996. Entering alternative realities: Cognition, art and architecture in Irish passage-tombs. Cambridge Archaeological Journal 6: 37–72.

EVANS, J.G. 1975. *The Environment of Early Man in the British Isles*.

FARRINGTON, R. 1769. *Snowdonia Druidica*.

FENTON, R. 1804–1813. *Tour in Wales*. Cambrian Archaeological Association, published 1917.

FENTON, R. 1811. *An historical tour through Pembrokeshire*. London.

FENTON, J. 1848. *Cromlechs of Llanwnda, Pembrokeshire*. London.

FIGGIS, N.P. 2001. *Prehistoric Preseli*. Atelier Productions.

FLEMMING, A. 1999. Phenomenology and the megaliths of Wales: a dreaming too far? *Oxford J of Archaeology*, 18, 119–125.

FORDE-JOHNSON, J.L. 1956. The Calderstone, Liverpool. In T.G. Powell, T. and G.E. Daniel, *Barclodiad y Gawres: The excavation of a Megalithic Chambered Tomb in Anglesey*. Liverpool, Liverpool University Press.

FOWLER, P. 1983. *Prehistoric Farming*. Cambridge, Cambridge University Press.

FRISS JOHANSON, K. 1919. Une station du plus ancien age du la pierre dans la Tourbiere do Svaerdborg. *Men. d. Antiqu. du. Nord.*, 241–359.

AVIN ROBINSON, R.S. 1934. Flint workers and flint users of the Golden Valley. *Trans Woolhope Natur. Field Club*, 54–63.

GIBSON, A. 1990. A cropmark enclosure and a sherd of later Neolithic pottery from Bryn Derwen, Llandysul, Powys. *Montgomeryshire Collections,* No. 78, 13.

GIBSON, A. 1999. *The Walton Basin Project: Excavation and survey in a prehistoric landscape 1993–1997.* CBA research report, 118, CBA, York.

GIBSON, A. 2002. *Prehistoric Pottery in Britain and Ireland.* Tempus.

GREENWELL, W. and ROLLESTON, G. 1877. *British Barrows.* Oxford.

GRIFFITHS, W.E. 1956. The Cors y Gedol Cromlech. *Journal of the Merioneth Historical and Record Society,* 1956, II, 293–296.

GRIMES, W.F. 1932. Prehistoric Archaeology in Wales since 1925. The Neolithic Period. *Procs of the Prehistoric Society of East Anglia,* 7, 85–92.

GRIMES, W.F. 1936a. The Megalithic Monuments of Wales. *Procs of the Prehistoric Society,* Vol. 2, 106–139.

GRIMES, W.F. 1936b. The Long Cairns of Breconshire Black Mountains. *Arch. Camb.,* XCI, 259–282.

GRIMES, W.F. 1936c. Map of South Wales showing the distribution of Long Barrows and Megaliths. Ordnance Survey, Southampton.

GRIMES, W.F. 1938. Excavations at Meini Gwyr, Carmarthen. *Procs of the Prehistoric Society,* 4, 324–325.

GRIMES, W.F. 1939a. The excavation of Ty Isaf Long Cairn, Breconshire. *Procs of the Prehistoric Society,* V, 119–142.

GRIMES, W.F. 1939b. Bedd y Afanc. *Procs of the Prehistoric Society,* 5, 258.

GRIMES, W.F. 1945. Early Man and the Soils of Anglesey. *Antiquity,* XIX, 1945, 169–174.

GRIMES, W.F. 1948. Pentre Ifan Burial Chamber, Pembrokeshire. *Arch. Camb.,* 100, 3–23.

GRIMES, W.F. 1951. *The Prehistory of Wales.* The National Museum of Wales, Cardiff.

GRIMES, W.F. 1960. *Excavations of Defence Sites 1939–1945, I: Mainly Neolithic and Bronze Age.* Ministry of Works Archaeological Reports No. 3, London, 1960.

GRINSELL, L.V. 1981. The later History of Ty Illtud. *Arch. Camb.,* 131–139.

GRINSELL, L.V. 1984. *Barrows in England and Wales.* Shire Publications.

GRØNNOW, B. 1987. Meiendorf and Stellmoor Revisited: An analysis of late Palaeolithic Reindeer exploration. *Acta Archaeologica,* 131–166.

HAWKES, J. 1936. *The Archaeology of the Channel Islands,* Vol. 2. St. Helier, The Baliwick of Jersey.

HEALEY, E, and GREEN, S. 1984. The Lithic Industries. In W. Britnell and H. Savory, *Gwernvale and Penywyrlod: two Neolithic Long Cairns in the Black Mountains of Breconshire.* Cambrian Archaeological Monographs, No. 2, Cardiff, 113–134.

HEMP, W.J. 1926. The Bachwen Cromlech. *Arch. Camb.,* 1926, 429–431.

HEMP, W.J. 1927 The Capel Garmon Chambered Long Cairn. *Arch. Camb.,* 82, 1–43.

HEMP, W.J. 1930. The Chambered Cairn of Bryn Celli Ddu. *Archaeologia,* IXXX, 1930, 179–214.

HEMP, W.J. 1935a. Arthur's Stone, Dorstone, Herefordshire. *Arch. Camb.,* XC, 288–292.

HEMP, W.J. 1935b. A Possible Pedigree of Long Barrows and Chambered Cairns. *Procs. of the Prehistoric Society,* 1, 1935, 108–114.

HEMP, W.J. 1938. Cup Markings at Treflys. *Caernarvonshire,* XCIII, 1938, 140–141.

HODDER, I. 1990. *The Domestication of Europe.* Oxford, Blackwell Press.

HOULDER, C.H. 1978. *Wales: An Archaeological Guide.* London, Faber and Faber.

HOULDER, C.H. 1988. The Petrological Identification of Stone Implements from Wales In T.H. Clough and W.A. Cummins (eds.), *Stone Axe Studies.* Vol. 2, 133–136 and 246–260.

HUGHES, W. 1999. *The Prehistoric Sites of the Gower.* Logaston Press, Hereford.

HUNTLEY, B. 1990. European vegetation history: Palaeovegetation maps from pollen data — 13,000 years, BP to present. *Journal of Quaternary Science,* Vol. 5, No. 2, 183–222, Willey.

HWCC. 1981. *Countryside Treasures of Herefordshire.* Hereford and Worcester County Council.

JACOBI, R. 1980. The Upper Palaeolithic in Britain, with special reference to Wales. In J.A. Taylor (ed.), *Culture, Environment in Prehistoric Wales,* BAR 76, Oxford, 15–99.

JARMAN, M.R., BAILEY, G.N. and JARMAN, H.N. 1982. *Early European Agriculture.* Cambridge, Cambridge University Press.

JONES, T. 1809. *History of the County of Brecknock.* Vol. 2.

JONES, W.B. 1863. Double Cromlech on Carn Llidi, in the Parish of St David's, Pembrokeshire. *Arch. Camb.,* Series 3, 9, 73.

JONES, W.B. and FREEMAN, E.A. 1856. *The History and Antiquities of St David's.* London and Tenby.

JOUSSAUME, R. 1985. *Dolmens for the Dead: Megalithic Building throughout the World.* London, Batsford.

KINNES, I. 1992. Non-Megalithic Long Barrows and Allied Structures in the British Neolithic. *British Museum Occasional Paper,* No. 52.

LAWS, E. and OWEN, H. 1897–1906. *Pembrokeshire Archaeological Survey.*

LEWIS, E.T. 1969. *Mynachlog-ddu — an historical survey of the past thousand years.* Jones, Cardigan.

LEWIS-WILLIAMS, D. and PEARCE, D.G. 2005. *The Mind in the Tomb:*

Neolithic consciousness, religion and monuments. London: Thames & Hudson.

LHWYD, E. 1695. Additions to the entries for Carmarthenshire and Pembrokeshire. In Camden's *Britannia*, Gibson edition.

LHWYD, E. 1699. *Parochalia*.

LONGUEVILLE JONES, H. 1865. Pembrokeshire Antiquities. *Arch. Camb.*, 3rd series, 11, 281–285.

LOWE W.B. 1912. *The Heart of Northern Wales*. i, Llanfairfechan.

LUBBOCK, J. 1872. *Prehistoric Times*. London, Williams and Norgate.

LUKIS, J.W. 1875. On the St Lythan's and St Nicholas' Cromlechs and Other Remains near Cardiff. *Arch. Camb.*, Series 4, 6, 171–185.

LYNCH, F. 2000a. The Early Neolithic. In. F. Lynch, S. Aldhouse-Green and J. Davis (eds.), Prehistoric Wales, 42–78. Stroud: Sutton.

LYNCH, F. 2000b. The Later Neolithic and earlier Bronze Age. In. F. Lynch, S. Aldhouse-Green and J. Davis (eds.), Prehistoric Wales, 79–138. Stroud: Sutton.

LYNCH, F.M. 1967. Barclodiad y Gawres: Comparative Notes on the Decorated Stones. *Arch. Camb.*, Vol. CXVI. 1–22.

LYNCH, F.M. 1969a. The Megalithic Tombs of North Wales. In T.G.E. Powell, J.X.W.P. Corcoran, F. Lynch and J.G. Scott (eds.), *Megalithic Enquiries in the West of Britain*. Liverpool, Liverpool University Press, 107–148.

LYNCH, F.M. 1969b. The Contents of Excavated Tombs in North Wales. In T.G.E. Powell, J. X.W.P. Corcoran, F. Lynch and J.G. Scott (eds.), *Megalithic Enquiries in the West of Britain*. Liverpool, Liverpool University Press, 148–74.

LYNCH, F.M. 1970. *Prehistoric Anglesey*. Anglesey Antiquarian Society.

LYNCH, F.M. 1972. *Prehistoric Man in Wales and the West*. Lynch, F. and Burgess, C. (eds.), 1972. Adams and Dart, Bath, 81–82.

LYNCH, F.M. 1976. Towards a chronology of megalithic tombs in Wales. In G.C. Boon and J.M. Lewis (eds.), *Welsh Antiquity (Essays mainly on Prehistoric Topics. Presented to H.N. Savory upon his retirement as Keeper of Archaeology*. Cardiff, National Museum of Wales, 63–79.

LYNCH, F.M. 1991. *Prehistoric Anglesey: the archaeology of the island to the Roman conquest.*. Llangefni, Anglesey Antiquarian Society.

LYNCH, F.M., ALDHOUSE-GREEN, S. and DAVIES, J. 2000. *Prehistoric Wales*. Stroud, Sutton.

LYNCH, F.M. and BURGESS, C. (eds.), 1972. *Prehistoric Man in Wales and the West*. Bath, Adams and Dart, Manchester.

MANLEY, J., GANTER, S. and GALE, F. (eds.), 1991. *The Archaeology of Clwyd*. Clwyd Archaeology Service.

MASTERS, L. 1981. Chambered Tombs and Non-Megalithic Barrows in Britain. In C. Renfrew (ed.), *The Megalithic Monuments of Western Europe*. London, Thames and Hudson, 97–112.

MATHIASSEN, T. 1943. 1937. Gudenne-Kulturen. En mesolitisk inlandsbe byggelse i jyland. *Aarboger*, 1–186.

MATHIASSEN, T. 1943. *Stenalderbopladser i Aamosen*. Copenhagen.

MAZEL, A., NASH, G.H., WADINGTON, C. (eds.) (forthcoming). *Prehistoric Narratives in British Rock-art.*, Oxford Archaeology Press.

MEGAW, J.V.S. 1984. The Bone ?Flute. In W. BRITNELL and H. SAVORY, *Gwernvale and Penywyrlod: Two Neolithic Long Cairns in the Black Mountains of Breconshire*. Cambrian Archaeological Monographs, No. 2, Cardiff, 27–28.

MORGAN, W.E.T. and MARSHALL, G. 1921. Excavation of a long barrow at Llanigon, Breconshire. *Archaeologia Cambrensis* 79, 296–299.

MORRIS, R.W.B. 1989. The Prehistoric Rock Art of Great Britain: a survey of all sites bearing motifs more complex than simple cup-marks. *Procs of the Prehistoric Society*, 55, 48–88.

MURPHY, K. 1985. Marros Mountain, Eglwys Cummin. *Archaeology in Wales*, 25, 36.

NASH, G.H. 1997. Monumentality and the Landscape: The Possible Symbolic and Political Distribution of Long Chambered Tombs around the Black Mountains, Central Wales. In G.H. Nash (ed.), *Semiotics of Landscape: Archaeology of Mind*. Oxford, BAR International Series, 661, 17–30.

NASH, G.H. 1998. *Exchange, Status and Mobility: Mesolithic Portable Art of Southern Scandinavia*. Oxford, BAR International Series, 640.

NASH, G.H. 2000. Re-evaluating monumentality: Arthur's Stone, Dorstone, Herefordshire. *Trans Woolhope Natur. Field Club*, Vol. L, Part 1, 37–50.

NASH, G.H. (forthcoming). Non-megalithic rock-art near Neolithic Chambered Burial Monuments in Wales, in A. Mazel, G.H. Nash, C. Waddington (eds.). *Prehistoric Narratives in British Rock-art*. Oxford Archaeology Press.

NASH, G.H., GEORGE, A., STANFORD, A., SWANN, J., WAITE, L. (forthcoming). Cupmarks and ritual landscape at Bryn Celli Ddu, Anglesey.

NASH, G.H., BROOK, C., GEORGE A., HUDSON, D., PARKER, C., SMITH, STANFORD, A., SWANN, J., WAITE, L. (forthcoming). Cup-and-ring marks on the Neolithic Chambered Burial Monument of Garn Turne, Pembrokeshire, SW Wales. *Antiquity*.

O'CONNOR, T.P. 1987. Report on the cremated bone from Din Dryfol, Anglesey. In CA. Smithy and F.M. Lynch, *Trefignath and Din Dryfol: The Excavation of Two Megalithic Chambered Tombs in Anglesey*. Cambrian Archaeological Monographs, No. 3, 129–130.

OLDING, F. 2000. *The Prehistoric Landscape of the Black Mountains.* Oxford, BAR 271.

OWEN, G.1603/1892. *The Description of Pembrokeshire*, Parts 1–4 (1603). Ed. H Owen with notes and appendix.

OWEN, N. 1775. *A History of the Island of Anglesey.*

PARKER-PEARSON, M. 1993. *Bronze Age Britain.* London, English Heritage.

PATTON, M. 1995. New light on Atlantic seaboard passage-grave chronology. *Antiquity*, Vol. 69, No. 264, 582–586.

PENNANT, T. 1783. *Tours in Wales.* Reproduced by J. Rhys (ed.). Caernarvon, 1883.

PETERSON, R. 2003. *Neolithic Pottery from Wales: Traditions and Constructions of Use.* Oxford: BAR British Series 344.

PHILLIPS, C.W. 1936. An Examination of the Ty Newydd Chambered Tomb, Llanfaelog, Anglesey. *Arch. Camb.*, XCI, 1936, 93–99.

PIGGOTT, S. 1954. *Neolithic Cultures of the British Isles.* Cambridge, Cambridge University Press.

PIGGOTT, S. 1962. *The West Kennet Long Barrow*, H.M.S.O.

PITTS, M. 1980. *Later Stone Implements.* Shire Archaeology Series.

POWELL, T.G.E. and DANIEL, G.E. 1956. *Barclodiad y Gawres: The exacavtion of a Megalithic Chambered Tomb in Anglesey.* Liverpool, Liverpool University Press.

POWELL, T.G.E. 1973. Excavation of the Megalithic Chambered Cairn of Dyffryn Ardudwy, Merioneth, Wales. *Archaeologia*, 104, 1–49.

POWELL, T.G.E., CORCORAN, J.X.W.P., LYNCH, F. and SCOTT, J.G. 1969. *Megalithic Enquiries in the West of Britain.* Liverpool, Liverpool University Press.

POWELL, T.G.E. and DANIEL, G.E. 1956. *Barclodiad y Gawres.* Liverpool, Liverpool University Press.

PRINGLE, J. and NEVILLE GEORGE, T. 1970. *British Regional Geology: South Wales.* 2nd edition, HMSO.

PRITCHARD, H. 1871. Mona Antiqua: Tyn Trefoel or Dindryfol. *Arch. Camb.*, Series 3, 2, 300–312.

PRITCHARD, H. 1873. Cromlech at Ty Mawr. *Arch. Camb.*, Series 5, 1, 22–30.

RCAHMW. 1976. *An Inventory of the Ancient Monuments in Glamorgan.* vol. 1, Part 1. Stone and Bronze Age, London, HMSO.

RCAHM(W) 1986. *An Inventory of the Ancient Monuments in Breconshire (Brycheiniog): Later Prehistoric Monuments and Unenclosed Settlements to 1000 AD.* Part I, London, HMSO.

RCAHM(W) 1997. *An Inventory of the Ancient Monuments in Breconshire (Brycheiniog): The Prehistoric and Roman Monuments.* Part II, London, HMSO.

RCAM (Wales) 1912. *An Inventory of the Ancient Monuments in the County of Flintshire.* London, HMSO.

RCAM (Wales) 1914. *An Inventory of the Ancient Monuments in the County of Denbigh.* London, HMSO.

RCAM (Wales) 1917. *An Inventory of the Ancient Monuments in the County of Carmarthenshire.* London, HMSO.

RCAM (Wales) 1925. *An Inventory of the Ancient Monuments in the County of Pembrokeshire.* London, HMSO.

RCAM (Wales) 1937. *An Inventory of the Ancient Monuments in the County of Anglesey.* London, HMSO.

RCAM (Wales) 1956. *An Inventory of the Ancient Monuments in the County of Caernarvonshire.* Part I, London, HMSO.

REES, T. 1815. *A Topographical and Historical Description of South Wales.* Sherwood, Neely and Jones, London.

REES, S. 1992. *A guide to ancient and historic Wales, Dyfed.* CADW, Cardiff.

RENFREW, C. 1976. Megaliths, territories and populations. In S. de Laet (ed.), *Acculturation and continuity in Atlantic Europe.* Bruges, de Tempel, 98–220.

RENFREW, C. 1979. *Investigations in Orkney.* London, Society of Antiqaries.

ROBERTS, C. and MANCHESTER, K. 1995. *The Archaeology of Disease.* New York: Cornell University Press.

ROWLEY-CONWY, P. 1981. Mesolithic Danish Bacon: Permanent and temporary sites in the Danish Mesolithic. In A. Sheridan and G. Bailey (eds.), *Economic Archaeology: Towards an Integration of Ecological and Social Approaches.* BAR International Series, No. 96, 51–65.

RUTTER, J.G. 1949. *Prehistoric Gower: An early archaeology of West Glamorgan.* Swansea, Welsh Guides.

SALMON, N. 1728–1729. *A New Survey of England, wherein the defects of Camden are supplied and the errors of his followers remarked.*

SANT, J. 2000. *Stone Spotting in Herefordshire.* Moondial.

SAVORY, H.N. 1953. The Excavation of Twlc y Filiast Cromlech, Llangynog, Carm. *Bull. Board Celtic Studies*, XV, 1953, 225–228.

SAVORY, H.N. 1956 The Excavation of the Pipton Long Cairn, Brecknockshire. *Arch. Camb.* 105, 7–48.

SAVORY, H.N. 1973. Pen-y-wyrlod: a New Welsh Long Cairn. *Antiquity*, 47, 187–192.

SAVORY, H.N. 1980. The Neolithic in Wales. In J.A. Taylor (ed.), *Culture and Environment in Prehistoric Wales.* British Archaeological Report, No. 76, Oxford, 207–232.

SAVORY, H.N. 1984. The Penywyrlod Long Cairn, Talgarth, Brecknock. In W. Britnell and H. Savory. *Gwernvale and Penywyrlod: Two Neolithic Long Cairns in the Black Mountains of Breconshire.* Cambrian Archaeological

Monographs, No. 2, Cardiff, 13–36.

SCOTT, W. 1933. The chambered tomb of Pant y Saer, Anglesey. Archaeologia Cambrensis 38, 185–228.

SHEE-TWOHIG, E. 1981. *The Megalithic Art of North-Western Europe*. Oxford, Oxford University Press.

SHERRATT, A. 1981.Plough and pastoralism: Aspects of the Secondary Products Revolution. In I. Hodder, G. Issac and N. Hammond (eds.), *Pattern of the Past*. Cambridge: Cambridge University Press. p. 261–305.

SKINNER, J. Reverend. 1802. *Ten Days Tour through the Island of Anglesey*. Reprinted with an introduction by T. Williams, 2004.

SMITH, A.G. and CLOUTMAN, E. 1988. Reconstruction of Holocene vegetation history in three dimensions at Waun-Fignen-Felen, an upland site in South Wales. *Phil. Transactions. of Royal Society*, London, B322, 159–219.

SMITH, C. 1992. *Late Stone Age Hunters of the British Isles*. London, Routledge.

SMITH, C.A. 1981. Trefignath Burial Chambers, Anglesey. *Antiquity* 55, 134–136.

SMITH, C.A. and LYNCH, F.M. 1987. *Trefignath and Din Dryfol: The Excavation of Two Megalithic Tombs in Anglesey*. Cambrian Archaeological Monographs,No. 3, Cardiff.

SMITH, I.F. 1974. The Neolithic. In C. Renfrew (ed.), *British Prehistory: A New Outline*. London, Duckworth, 100–136.

SOIL SURVEY OF ENGLAND and WALES 1983. Silsoe.

STANFORD, S.C. 1990. *The Archaeology of The Welsh Marches*. 2nd edition, S.C. Stanford, 2–73.

STANLEY, W.O. 1870. On the tumulus in Plas Newydd Park, Anglesey, *Archaeologia Cambrensis* (4th Series), I, 51–58.

STARTIN, B. and BRADLEY, R. 1981. Some notes on work organisation and society in prehistoric Wessex. In C.N.L. Ruggles and A.W.R. Whittle (eds.) *Astronomy and Society in Britain during the period 4000–1500 BC*. Oxford BAR Series 88, p. 289–296.

STUIVER, M., REIMER, P.J., BARD, E., BECK, J.W., BURR, G.S., HUGHEN, K.A., KROMER, B., McCORMAC, F.G., v. d. PLICHT, J. and SPURK, M. 1998. *Marine delta 14C and radiocarbon ages. Radiocarbon*. University of Edinburgh Press.

STUKELEY, W. 1778. *Itinerarium Curiosum*. Centuria II, London.

TAYLOR, J.A. ed., 1980. The Culture and Environment in Prehistoric Wales. *British Archaeological Report*, British Series 76.

THOMAS, D. 1799. *Cambrian Register*.

THOMAS, J.S. 1988. The Social Significance of Cotswold-Severn burial practices. *Man* 23, 540–559.

THOMAS, J.S. 1993. The politics of vision and the archaeologies of landscape.

In B. Bender (ed.), *Landscape, Politics and Perspectives*. Berg.

THOMAS, J.S. 1988. *Rethinking the Neolithic*. Cambridge, Cambridge University Press.

THOMAS, J.S. 1999. *Understanding the Neolithic*. London, Routledge.

TILLEY, C. 1993. Art, architecture and the landscape in Neolithic Sweden. In B. Bender (ed.), *Landscape, Politics and Perspectives*. Berg.

TILLEY, C. 1994. *A Phenomenology of Landscape: Places, Paths and Monuments*. Oxford, Berg.

TILLEY, C. and BENNETT, W. 2001. An archaeology of supernatural places: the case of West Penrith. *Journal of the Royal Anthrological Institute*, 7, 335–362.

TREHERNE, G.G.T. 1910. Brief note on my work in Laugharneshire. *Transactions of the Carmarthenshire Antiquarian Society*, 6, 58–60.

VULLIAMY, C.E. 1921. The Excavation of a Megalithic Tomb in Breconshire. *Arch. Camb.*, Series 7, IXXVI, 300–305.

VULLIAMY, C.E. 1923. Further excavations in the Long Barrows at Ffostyll. *Arch. Camb.*, Series 7, 3, 320–324.

VULLIAMY, C.E. 1929. Excavation of an unrecorded Long Barrow in Wales. *Man*, XXIX, No. 29, 34–36.

WAINWRIGHT, G.J. 1967. *Coygan Camp: A Prehistoric Romano-British and Dark Age Settlement in Carmarthenshire*. The Cambrian Archaeological Association.

WARD, J. 1915. The St Nicholas chambered tumulus, Glamorgan. *Arch. Camb.*, Series 15, 253–320.

WARD, J. 1916. The St Nicholas Chambered Tumulus, Glamorgan. *Arch. Camb.*, Series 16, 239–267.

WARD, J. 1918. Some prehistoric sepulchral remains near Pendine, Carmarthenshire. *Arch. Camb.*, 18, Series 6, 35–79.

WARD, A.H. 1976. The Cairns on Mynydd Llangyndeyrn: A Focal point of the Early Bronze Age in South-East Dyfed. *The Carmarthenshire Antiquary*, 12, 3–21.

WARD, P.A., WILLIAMS, G.H., MARSHALL, E.C. and DRAKE, I.M. 1987. The Glandy Cross Complex. *Archaeology in Wales*, 27, 9–13.

WARRILOW, G. 1986. The Pollen. In W. Warrilow, G. Owen, and W.J. Britnell, *Eight ring-ditches at Four Crosses. Llandysilio*, I, 1981–1985. *Procs of the Prehistoric Society*, 52, 53–88.

WATKINS, A. 1928. Arthur's Stone. *Trans. Woolhope Natur. Field. Club*, XIV, 149–151.

WESTERBY, E. 1927. *Stenalderbopladser ved Klampenenborg*. Copenhagen.

WEBLEY, D. 1959. The Neolithic Colonization of the Breconshire Black Mountains. *Bull. Board Celtic Studies*, XVIII, 1958–1960, 290–294.

WEBLEY, D. 1961. Y Garn Llwyd, Newchurch West, Monmouthshire: A Reassessment.. *Bull. Board Celtic Studies*, XIX, 1960–1962, 255–258.

WHITTLE, A. 1985. *Neolithic Europe: A Survey*. Cambridge, Cambridge University Press.

WHITTLE, A. 1988. *Problems in Neolithic Archaeology*. Cambridge, Cambridge University Press.

K WHITTLE, A. 2003. *The archaeology of people: dimensions of Neolithic life*. London: Routledge.

WHITTLE, A. and WYSOCKI, M. 1998. Parc le Breos Cwm transepted long cairn, Gower, West Glamorgan: date, contents and context. *Proceedings of the Prehistoric Society* 64, 139–182.

WILKINSON, J.G. 1870. Avenue and Cairns about Arthur's Stone in Gower. *Arch. Camb.*, Series 4, 1, 23–45.

WILKINSON, J.G. 1871. Cromlechs and other remains in Pembrokeshire. *Collectanea Archaeologia*, Vol. 2, Part 2, 219–240.

WILLIAMS, W.W. 1875. Excavations at Pant y Saer Cromlech, Anglesey. *Arch. Camb.*, 341–348.

WILLIAMS, A. 1953. Clegyr Boia, St David's, Pembrokeshire: Excavations in 1943. *Arch. Camb.*, 102, 20–47.

WILLIAMS, G. 1984. A Henge Monument at Ffynnon Newydd, Nantgaredig. *Bull. Board of Celtic Studies*, 31, 177–190.

WYMER, J.J. 1977. *Gazetteer of Mesolithic sites in England and Wales*, CBA (Council for British Archaeology), Research Report, No. 22.

WYNDHAM, H.P. 1775. *A Gentleman's Tour through Monmouthshire and Wales in the Months of June and July 1774*. London.

YATES, M.J. and JONES, M. 1991 Excavation and Conservation at Capel Garmon Chambered Tomb, Betws-y-coed, Gwynedd, 1989. *Archaeology in Wales*, 31, 1–5.

1. Early Bronze Age 2,500–1,600 BC.
2. For example, from the mid-18th century onwards the corporate approaches to death had far reaching effects on the communal burial practices and the allied trades that supported it.
3. One fine example where both Neolithic and Bronze Age activity co-exist within the same monument can be seen at the Neolithic passage grave of La Hougue Bie, Jersey. Here, within the massive chamber area is evidence of a rectangular cist that has been cut into the floor. Although no bone material was recovered, possibly as a result of later disturbance, it does suggest that this monument, which was used as a corporate burial monument, became a single status monument some time between the Late Neolithic and early Bronze Age.
   Other evidence includes a series of cup-marks both within the chamber and along the 9m passage, and most conclusive of all, is the extensive blocking of the monument and destruction of the entrance which has been clearly dated to this transition period (Hawkes 1937; Patton 1995; Nash 1998).
4. See also Shee-Twohig (1981, 229).
5. Within the bounds of Graig Lwyd Farm.
6. Lynch (1970, 46) mentions that nine full term foetuses were found at Pant-y-Saer, Anglesey (see also Scott 1933, 224–227).
7. I would recommend the rather eclectic volume The Ancient Stones of Wales by Barber and Williams (1989) where they discuss in some detail the antiquarian history and literature of some of the Welsh monuments.
8. Not to be confused with Penywyrlod (BRE 14), Talgarth.
9. An important review of this group of monuments has been produced by Britnell (1984, 3–9).
10. The chamber originally measured 0.7m by 1.7m (RCAHMW 1997, 60).
11. It is believed that the two sherds formed part of a pot that would have been 0.16m in basal diameter (RCAHMW 1997, 61).
12. The RCAHMW inventory suggests that the coin may have been deliberately 'planted' in order to confuse the excavators (1997, 62).
13. Found within the spoil were 27 teeth.
14. As a result of 19th-century quarrying and excavation followed by ploughing close to the edge of the mound, the classification of this monument is difficult to assess. The RCAHMW (1997, 43) suggests the possibility that there may have been a further chamber located at either terminal end.
15. RCAHMW notes the bones that were deposited at the Royal College of Surgeons by Sir Arthur Keith were lost during the Second World War. However, some survive at the British Museum, including a mandible (RCS 4901), and the National Museum of Wales. The latter have not been officially located.
16. It should be noted that very little of the mound fabric is present. All that is visible is a single pointed upright stone, standing about 1.2m high.
17. Grimes states that there had been much reduction to this woodland between 1905 and 1936. Evidence to support this is seen with the presence of stools, a product of coppicing of hazel (corylus) and alder (alnus).
18. Referred to as Chamber 1 (Britnell 1984, 5).
19. This structure is referred to as the Main Chamber. The eastern uprights to this chamber were partially exposed during quarrying.
20. This early Neolithic four post-hole structure was dated to 3230 bc (4,100 BC) and was in use prior to the construction of the monument.
21. Bach Neolithic Long Barrow (SO 2773 4294) is badly damaged at the northern end. Drystone walling can be clearly seen on the woodland side of the mound. The mound is oval-shaped, approximately 13m × 10m and 2m high. This tomb is the most north-westerly of the Golden Valley Group. Interestingly, Bach Long Barrow is sited on a north-facing slope, overlooking the upper Wye Valley towards the Clyro Court Farm monument.
22. A rather simplified and incorrect plan of this monument is published in Darvill (1982, 99).
23. On re-examination in 1975, only one red deer upper molar (M1) was recorded.
24. These are now considered lost.
25. According to footnotes within the RCAHMW (1979, 53), Vulliamy presented the bone material to the Royal College of Surgeons in 1934. The assemblage was re-catalogued in 1955, registered as RCS 4.901–4.9015. Some of this assemblage was re-examined by Powers and Briggs in 1975.
26. Ruth Richardson personal communication.
27. An information board present at the site shows the monument being utilised for burial during the Neolithic.
28. During the late 1920s and early 1930s the Golden Valley was extensively walked by Gavin-Robinson (1934).
29. According to Olding (2000) there are two further sites that have been recently discovered. However, their form has not been fully verified. Garway Long Barrow is located at SO 4395 2550, close to a television mast on Garway Hill, and stands around 335m AOD. According to Olding, Garway Long Barrow is well preserved. The oval mound is aligned east/west and measures 30m × 16m × 2m. A further possible long barrow may be present at SO 3440 4140 on Woodbury Hill, Peterchurch. This monument is located at around 287m AOD, and is approximately 1.8m in height. The barrow was discovered by Gavin-Robinson in 1936 and was later classified by Leslie Grinsell (referred to as Peterchurch 1). When visiting the site in the late 1990s, Olding was informed that the site had been ploughed-out. There were a number of Neolithic diagnostic flint tools recovered within the vicinity of the monument.
30. The author has labeled the Thornwell Farm monument as MON 4, continuing on from Daniel's referencing system.
31. A port-hole is usually constructed of one or two pieces of rectangular shaped stone from which a hole is cut. If two pieces of stone are used, a semi-circular shape is cut out of each piece.
32. Crawford (1925, 151) suggests the length of the mound to be around 45m in length.

33. See also Crawford 1925.
34. It is also referred to in the same volume as a long cairn with a lateral chamber (Corcocran 1969, 20–21).
35. According to Crawford (1925, 157) a pencil drawing of the site was made by Sarah Ormerod dated 9th August 1837 and is located within the Library of the Wiltshire Archaeology Society in Devizes.
36. See Inquisitions Post Mortem of Roger, Earl of Norfolk, March, 1306–1307.
37. James Scource (School of Ocean Sciences, University of Wales, Bangor) has suggested, based on radiocarbon dating of marine deposits, that sea-level rise inundated the present shore-line during the late Mesolithic (personal communication).
38. David Thomas's Cambrian Register of 1796 lists 30 monuments.
39. A full transcription is in Smith (1987, 3).
40. It should be noted that the Reverend Nicholas Owen's account should be treated as false. He is regarded as a notorious charlatan who appears to have plagiarized an original manuscript produced by the Reverend John Thomas in the early 1760s.
41. I should stress that this monument has been poorly recorded.
42. Skinner's *Ten days Tours through the Isle of Anglesea* (1802).
43. Perthi Duon is now a collapsed and consists of a capstone partially supported by two fallen uprights. Skinner's sketch made in 1802 shows the monument to have three uprights, two lying away from the capstone. No evidence of any cairn or mound.
44. Daniel (1950, 9) recognizes eight classifications of burial monument. B-Dolmens are monuments that possess a polygonal chamber.
45. Lynch (1969a, 116) refers to the chamber as roughly polygonal.
46. A similar type pin has been found at Ty Isaf (BRE 5) in Breconshire (Grimes 1939, 131).
47. Skinner appears to only mention the larger of the two chambers and refers to the larger chamber as a separate cromlech.
48. Lynch (1969a, 121) suggests that the Glyn monument (ANG 12) is sub-megalithic in form. The monument consists of a single capstone that has been propped up against a natural limestone rock outcrop forming a cavity. This monument was excavated but nothing was found.
49. See Lynch (1991).
50. SAM No. A094.
51. The axe factory at Penmaenmawr, sitting within an extensive Bronze Age landscape, is formed from the augite granophyre scree that runs down the mountainside. Excavations took place in 1920, when a series of rough-outs were found which formed part of an extensive trading network over Britain. A Graig Lwyd mace-head was found at Windmill Hill causewayed enclosure. Modern quarry waste dumping has destroyed much of the Neolithic activity around this part of the mountain.
52. Powell *et al.* (1969, 307) classifies this site as a structure with a possible Bronze Age

53. cist rather than as a chambered tomb.
54. The RCHM (Merioneth) states that the site consists of a 'capstone of a demolished cromlech'. However, Daniel (1950, 197) has doubts that this site is a Neolithic chambered tomb.
55. A similar relationship can be argued with that of the Bronze Age monuments located to the north of Gwern Einion (MER 1).
56. Originally noted in *Archaeologia Cambrensis* (1869, 134).
57. This site was described by Pennant as having 'three chambers' (see Barnwell 1868, 481).
58. Daniel (1950, 117) suggests there are 70 cupmarks.
59. Barker (1992) identifies 31 recognised monuments along with 16 sites that are listed as probable burial chambers.
60. This additional chamber is not present on two 19th-century illustrations made by Gardner Wilkinson (1871) and Barnwell (1884).
61. This site, known as Trefael (SN 1030 4030) comprises a single slab with at least 28 cup-marks, 17 of which are shallow depressions that, according to Barker (1992, 52) have been obscured by lichen. Lynch (1972, 79–80) agrees with Daniel that this stone may well be a capstone from a now destroyed monument.
62. Fenton states four uprights supported the monument rather than three (1810, 31).
63. The field systems appear to be multi-phased, dating to the prehistoric, Roman and Medieval periods (PRN 2631 and SAM 14689 – Prehistoric, Roman and Medieval field systems).
64. An account was also written by an OS Field Officer in 1966.
65. Both monuments are listed in Barker (1992).
66. Noted by Lewis (1969, 137).
67. Personal communication between Barker and Lynch.
68. Grimes (1936c) and Daniel (1950) classify this monument as a burial chamber.
69. Not listed in Burl (1976).
70. Ward *et al.* 1987, 9–13.
71. However, Barker (1992, 37) notes that certain stones incorporated into the bank which was recorded by Frances Lynch in 1976 are no longer there.
72. First recorded by Grimes in 1936.
73. Ignore the recent Ordnance Survey 'Pathfinder' map for this area. The map clearly shows the tombs to be located about 100–200m west of their present position (inland, behind Ragwen Point).
74. I have previously suggested that this monument may house two chambers. In light of reinterpretation, I now consider the site to only have one chamber. Part of this reinterpretation is based on revisiting the site in December 2002.
75. Both sites visited in August 1994.
76. Within the same paper, Barnwell has published three illustrations of the site from various locations.

Site No.	Daniel's Class	Site Name	Grid Ref.[80]	Metres AOD	Distance from open water (Km)[81]
1	BRE 1	Pen yr Wyrlod	SO 2248 3986	251	54
2	BRE 3	Ffostyll North	SO 1788 3487	312	52
3	BRE 4	Ffostyll South	SO 1788 3487	312	52
4	BRE 8	Pipton	SO 1603 3728	145	55
5	BRE 5	Ty Isaf	SO 1819 2905	211	50.5
6	BRE 9	Cwmfforest	SO 1833 2844	274	51.
7	BRE 14	Pen y Wyrlod	SO 1505 3156	253	48.
8	BRE 6	Ty Illtyd	SO 0984 2638	215	53
9	BRE 10	Mynydd Troed	SO 1614 2843	258	51
10	BRE 7	Gwernvale	SO 2110 1920	69	46
11	BRE 12	Garn Goch	SO 2123 1771	84	45
12	RAD 1	Clyro Court Farm	SO 2123 4313	90	56
13	BRE 2	Little Lodge Barrow	SO 1822 3806	137	54
14	HRF 1	Arthur's Stone	SO 3180 4313	280	52
15	HRF 4	Cross Lodge Barrow	SO 3325 4168	180	50.5
16	HRF 6	Dunseal	SO 3913 3382	175	51
17	GLA 4	Parc-le-Breos-Cwm	SO 5372 8983	31	1.5
18	GLA 3	Maen Ceti	SS 4913 9055	147	2.2
19	GLA 1	Sweyne's Howes North	SS 4211 8991	140	0.8
20	GLA 2	Sweyne's Howes South	SS 4209 8981	136	0.8
21	GLA 5	Penmaen Burrows	SS 5315 8813	46	0.3
22	GLA 9	Tinkinswood	ST 0921 7331	75	6.6
23	GLA 10	Maes y Felin	ST 1010 7230	70	5.6
24	MON 1	Cleppa Park	ST 2740 8571	43	4.3
25	MON 2	Y Gaer Llwyd	ST 4476 9678	209	10.7
26	MON 3	Heston Brake	ST 5052 8865	35	1.5
27	ANG 1	Trefignath	SH 2590 8051	19	1.2
28	ANG 2	Presaddfed	SH 3486 8091	20	5.2
29	ANG 3	Ty Newydd	SH 3442 7386	37	2.7
30	ANG 4	Barclodiad y Gawres	SH 3290 7072	19	0.1
31	ANG 5	Din Dryfol	SH 3963 7254	18	6.0
32	ANG 6	Bodowyr	SH 4632 6825	38	3.2
33	ANG 7	Bryn Celli Ddu	SH 5086 7023	33	1.6
34	ANG 8	Bryn yr Hen Bobl	SH 5190 6900	33	0.3
35	ANG 9	Plas Newydd	SH 5203 6972	30	0.2
36	ANG 10	Ty Mawr	SH 5390 7224	73	0.8
37	ANG 11	Hen Drefor	SH 5512 7731	112	5.5
38	ANG 13	Pant y Saer	SH 5097 8241	99	1.3
39	ANG 14	Lligwy	SH 5014 8604	63	1.1
40	CRN 1	Llety'r Filiast	SH 7722 8295	165	0.8
41	CRN 2	Maen y Bardd	SH 7416 7188	305	5.3

Appendix I Summary of Site Data

Site No.	Daniel's Class	Site Name	Grid Ref.[80]	Metres AOD	Distance from open water (Km)[81]
42	CRN 4	Porth Llwyd	SH 7703 6777	8	14.1
43	CRN5	Sling	SH 6055 6696	210	3.5
44	DEN 1	Hendre Waelod	SH 7931 7487	21	5
45	DEN 2	Tydden Bleiddyn		122	11.5
46	DEN 3	Capel Garmon	SJ 0104 7203	264	26
47	FLT 1	Gop Cairn	SH 8182 5441	250	4.3
48	FLT 2	Gop Cave	SJ 0862 8024	215	4.4
49	MER 7	Tyn y Coed		154	37
50	MER 1	Gwern Einion	SJ 0862 8005	106	1.9
51	MER 2	Bron y Foel Isaf West	SJ 0485 3963	214	4.2
52	MER 3	Dyffryn Ardudwy		50	1.8
53	MER 4	Cors y Gedol	SH 5873 2861	191	2.9
54	MER 5	Carneddau Hengwm North	SH 6088 2472	283	2.4
55	MER 6	Carneddau Hengwm South	SH 5887 2294	283	2.4
56	CRN 6	Penarth	SH 6033 2281	26	0.7
57	CRN 7	Bachwen		24	0.2
58	CRN 8	Ystum Cegid Isaf	SH 6143 2058	99	3.2
59	CRN 9	Cefn Isaf	SH 6141 2052	90	3.6
60	CRN 10	Cist Cerrig	SH 4300 5117	73	1.9
61	CRN 11	Four Crosses	SH 4076 4957	66	2.6
62	CRN 12	Mynydd Cefn Amlwch	SH 5000 4132	99	2
63	CRN 13	Tan y Muriau		132	0.5
64	PEM 1	Llech y Tribedd	SH 4846 4090	188	1.4
65	PEM 2	Trellyffant	SH 5436 3845	137	1.1
66	PEM 3	Carreg Coetan		8	0.5
67	PEM 4	Cerrig y Gof	SH 3981 3858	46	0.8
68	PEM 5	Pentre Ifan	SH 2301 3465	145	4.2
69	PEM 27	Bedd yr Afanc	SH 2381 2886	142	7.9
70	PEM 7-9	Garn Wen Cemetery		90-95	0.3
71	PEM 13	Carn Wnda	SN 1005 4319	135	1
72	PEM 15	Garn Gilfach	SN 0822 4252	183	1.9
73	PEM 16	Ffyst Samson	SN 0602 3935	128	2.3
74	PEM 17	Trewalter Llwyd	SM 0365 3890	124	2
75	PEM 18	Carreg Samson		42	0.3
76	PEM 28	Ffynondruidion	SN 0993 3707	107	3.4
77	PEM 14	Parc y Cromlech	SN 1089 3459	142	1
78	PEM 3	Coetan Arthur	SM 9483 3903	38	0.3
79	PEM 19	Treffynnon		125	4.4
80	PEM 20	St Elvies Farm	SM 9335 3444	61	0.4
81	PEM 21-22	Carn Llidi	SM 9089 3898	122	0.9
82	N/A	White Horse	SM 9059 3492	91	4.1

Appendix I: Summary of Site Data

Site No.	Daniel's Class	Site Name	Grid Ref.[80]	Metres AOD	Distance from open water (Km)[81]
83	CRM 1	Gwal y Filiast	SN 1705 2564	100	18
84	PEM 6	Mountain	SN 1657 3286	236	13
85	PEM 10	The Altar	SM 9828 2812	347	10.1
86	PEM 11	Garn Turne	SM 9793 2725	137	10.2
87	PEM 12	Parc y llyn	SM 9823 2659	128	11.1
88	CRM 20	Carn Besi	SN 1560 2768	236	15
89	PEM 30	Llan	SS 1475 1402	60	7.1
90	PEM 31	Eithbed Cemetry Group	SM 0800 2860	240-250	11.9
91	PEM 24	The hanging Stone	SM 9722 0822	75	2.9
92	PEM 25	Devil's Quoit	SM 8865 0084	37	1
93	PEM 26	King's Quoit	SM 0593 9728	18	0,1
94	CRM 2	Morfa Bychan A	SM 2213 0743	75	0.2
95	CRM 3	Morfa Bychan B	SM 2214 0748	100	0.2
96	CRM 4	Morfa Bychan C	SM 2216 0754	110	0.2
97	CRM 5	Morfa Bychan D	SM 2216 0762	120	0.2
98	CRM 6	Twlc y Filiast	SN 3383 1608	124	6.1
99	N/A	Bedd Taliesin	SN 6724 9126	220	6.7
100	CRM 10	Cerrig Llwydion	SN 3738 3258	291	12.4

Appendix II: Radiocarbon Dates for Neolithic Chambered Monuments

Trefignath (ANG 1), Anglesey

HAR 3932	5,050±70 bp	Palaeosol from underneath cairn
HAR 3933	2,210±70 bp	Deposit within eastern chamber

Gwernvale (BRE 7), Breconshire

CAR - 113	5,050±75 BP	Pit F68 (pit below cairn)
CAR - 114	4,390±70 BP	Pit F58 (pit outside cairn)
CAR - 115	4,590±75 BP	Pit F47 (pit outside cairn)
CAR - 118	6,895±80 BP	Charcoal from Mesolithic pit

Penywyrlod (BRE 14), Breconshire

HAR 674	4,970±80 BP	sample of human bone from Chamber NE II

Parc le Breos Cwm (GLA 4), Glamorgan

OxA-6487	4,685±65 bp	adult male, SE chamber
OxA-6496	4,850±65 bp	adult, SE chamber
OxA-6641	4,690±55 bp	adult, SE chamber
OxA-6488	4,780±60 bp	adult ?male, SW chamber
OxA-6489	4,445±60 bp	adult ?female, SW chamber
OxA-6493	4,875±55 bp	adult, NE chamber
OxA-6494	4,645±60 bp	adult, NE chamber
OxA-6490	4,660±60 bp	adult ?male, NW chamber
OxA-6491	4,805±55 bp	adult, NW chamber
OxA-6492	4,805±55 bp	adult ?male, NW chamber
OxA-6495	3,705±55 bp	sub-adult, passage
OxA-6497	3,750±55 bp	adult female, passage
OxA-6499	7,665±65 bp	badger, passage
OxA-6500	10,625±80 bp	large undulate, passage

Lower Luggy Long Barrow (MNT 3), Montgomeryshire

BM-2954	4,830±45 bp	Charcoal from post hole in east ditch
BM-2955	4,710±40 bp	Charcoal from post hole at end of east ditch

Carreg Coetan (PEM 3), Pembrokeshire

CAR-392	4,830±80 bp	Charcoal sealed by stone kerb
CAR-394	4,700±80 bp	Charcoal from socket hole of chamber
CAR-391	4,560±80 bp	Old ground surface sealed by mound
CAR-393	4,470±80 bp	Charcoal from within mound